THE FUTURE OF COUNSELLING
AND PSYCHOTHERAPY

THE FUTURE OF COUNSELLING AND PSYCHOTHERAPY

Edited by

STEPHEN PALMER AND VED VARMA

SAGE Publications
London • Thousand Oaks • New Delhi

Editorial selection and matter © Stephen Palmer and Ved Varma
Chapter 1 © Albert Ellis
Chapter 2 © Jeremy Holmes
Chapter 3 © Douglas Hooper
Chapter 4 © Pat Milner
Chapter 5 © Greg J. Neimeyer and John C. Norcross
Chapter 6 © Stephen Palmer
Chapter 7 © John Rowan
Chapter 8 © Andrew Samuels
Chapter 9 © Brian Thorne
Chapter 10 © Richard L. Wessler and Sheenah Hankin Wessler

First Published 1997

SAGE Publications Ltd
6 Bonhill Street
London EC2A 4PU

SAGE Publications Inc
2455 Teller Road
Thousand Oaks, California 91320

SAGE Publications India Pvt Ltd
32, M-Block Market
Greater Kailash – I
New Delhi 110 048

British Library Cataloguing in Publication data

A catalogue record for this book is available
from the British Library

ISBN 0 7619 5106 7
ISBN 0 7619 5107 5 (pbk)

Library of Congress catalog record available

Typeset by Mayhew Typesetting, Rhayader, Powys
Printed in Great Britain by Redwood Books, Trowbridge, Wiltshire

Contents

This edited book consists of ten chapters written by well known contributors from Britain and the United States of America in honour of Professor Windy Dryden's unique contribution to the field of counselling and psychotherapy. In addition to his special contribution to rational emotive behaviour therapy, in the past ten years Windy Dryden has been responsible for encouraging British therapists to write books for the home market. In fact, by 1996 he had authored or edited over 100 books himself. This has helped the development of psychotherapy and counselling in Britain by providing many useful and learned books for both beginner and experienced psychotherapists and counsellors.

His contribution has also been recognized by the British Psychological Society and the British Association for Counselling as both professional bodies have elected him a Fellow. To honour Windy Dryden's contribution to counselling, in 1996 the first 'Dryden Lecture' was held at The Royal Society of Medicine, and the paper (see Chapter 9) was given by Professor Brian Thorne.

Notes on contributors

Albert Ellis is the President of the Albert Ellis Institute for Rational Emotive Behavior Therapy in New York. He is the founder of Rational Emotive Behavior Therapy (REBT) and the 'grandfather' of Cognitive Behavior Therapy. He has published over 60 books and 700 articles on psychotherapy and counselling.

Jeremy Holmes is a Consultant Psychiatrist/Psychotherapist in north Devon and a member of the Severnside Institute for Psychotherapy. He is a member of the Royal College of Psychiatrists psychotherapy executive, and college representative on UKCP. His recent publications include: *Introduction to Psychoanalysis* (1995 with A. Bateman) and *Attachment, Intimacy, Autonomy: Using Attachment Theory in Adult Psychotherapy* (1996).

Douglas Hooper is a Consultant Chartered Clinical Psychologist and a Fellow of the British Psychological Society. As Emeritus Professor at the University of Hull, he has taught, practised and researched in counselling and psychotherapy in the UK, USA, India and Australia. He has a particular interest in counselling in primary medical care and also in cooperation between the caring professions. His recent publications include *Couple Therapy: A Handbook* (with Windy Dryden, Sage 1991)

Pat Milner has been a counsellor, supervisor and trainer for 30 years. She is currently a consultant to the Centre for Stress Management in London and the centre's honorary adviser in counselling and education. Her experience as a tutor to counselling courses is diverse; from the self-directed learning of South West London College to the original master's degree in the psychology department at University of London Goldsmiths College. Her most recent publication is *Counselling: The BAC Counselling Reader* (with Dainow and Palmer, Sage 1996).

Greg J. Neimeyer is Professor and Director of Training in the Department of Psychology at the University of Florida. The author of more than 100 books and articles, Dr Neimeyer specializes in the constructivist approaches to psychotherapy, including co-editing (with R. Neimeyer) the *Journal of Constructivist Psychology*. He is the 1996 recipient of the American Psychological Association's John Holland Award and is the past-Chair of the Council of Counseling Psychology Training Programs in the United States.

John C. Norcross is Professor and former Chair of Psychology at the University of Scranton and a clinical psychologist in part-time practice. His most recent books include *Changing for Good* (with Prochaska and DiClemente), *Handbook of Psychotherapy Integration* (with Goldfried), and *Systems of Psychotherapy: A Transtheoretical Analysis* (third edition, with Prochaska).

Stephen Palmer is Director of the Centre for Stress Management in London. He is a Fellow of the British Association for Counselling (BAC). His most recent books are *Counselling: The BAC Counselling Reader* (with Dainow and Milner, Sage 1996), *Dealing with People Problems at Work* (with Burton, 1996), *Stress Management and Counselling: Theory, Practice, Research and Methodology* (with Dryden, 1996), *Stress Counselling: A Rational Emotive Behaviour Approach* (with Ellis, Gordon and Neenan, 1997) and *Client Assessment* (with McMahon, Sage 1997). He is also co-editor of *The Rational Emotive Behaviour Therapist* and former editor of *Counselling*. He is on the editorial boards of 7 professional journals.

John Rowan is a qualified psychotherapist (AHPP) and an accredited counsellor (BAC). He practises Primal Integration and also teaches, supervises and leads groups at the Minster Centre in London. He is a founder member and on the Board of the Association of Humanistic Psychology Practitioners and a Fellow of the British Psychological Society. He is the author of a number of books including *Healing the Male Psyche: Therapy as Tuition* (1996) and is on the editorial board of *The Journal of Humanistic Psychology*.

Andrew Samuels is Professor of Analytical Psychology at the University of Essex and a Training Analyst of the Society of Analytical Psychology in London. His books include *Jung and the Post-Jungians*, *The Father*, *A Critical Dictionary of Jungian Analysis*, *Psychopathology*, *The Plural Psyche*, and *The Political Psyche*.

Brian Thorne is Director and Professor of Counselling at the University of East Anglia, Norwich. He was a founder member of the Norwich Centre, Britain's first person-centred agency for counselling and training, established in 1980. His books include *Person-Centred Counselling in Action* (with David Mearns, Sage 1988), *Carl Rogers* (Sage, 1992) and *Behold the Man* (1991).

Richard L. Wessler is a clinical psychologist and psychotherapist at Cognitive Psychotherapy Services in New York, and Professor of Psychology at Pace University, Pleasantville, New York.

Sheenah Hankin Wessler is a psychotherapist practicing in New York city who specializes in the treatment of personality disorders. She has published many articles in professional journals and books on Cognitive Appraisal Therapy. She also appears regularly on national television and contributes to articles in leading women's magazines in the USA.

Preface

This book has been written by distinguished psychotherapists and coun-sellors, all well known for their contribution to the therapeutic field. For this book the contributors were asked to write about the future of counselling and psychotherapy with regard to the following: professional issues; developing and moribund approaches; and practical and philo-sophical issues. Each contributor focused on different aspects of the evolution of therapy with predictions about the future.

The book starts with Albert Ellis, looking at the future of cognitive-behaviour and rational emotive behaviour therapy. He predicts that if we have a high frustration tolerance and scientific flexibility, our future as counsellors and therapists looks bright. In the next chapter Jeremy Holmes suggests that there will be an increasing convergence between the psycho-dynamic therapy and the cognitive-behavioural therapy camps. Douglas Hooper believes that it is most unlikely that there will be a grand meta-theory which will emerge, although he is confident that practitioners will learn from researchers the core elements of competent practice. In the next chapter Pat Milner focuses on 'hard heads, tough minds and tender hearts'. She suggests that tender-heartedness alone will not survive in the world outside counselling and she asks counsellors to reflect on this thought. In the following chapter Greg Neimeyer and John Norcross focus on the future of psychotherapy and counselling psychology in the USA. They rely on Delphi polls to determine the future. The Delphic method uses the consensus of observers representing diverse orientations on what will occur in psychotherapy, in contrast to what they personally would like to happen.

Stephen Palmer concentrates on the past, present and future of stress counselling and management. He hopes that eventually theories of stress will have a greater impact upon the practice of stress counselling and management. He predicts that therapies that do not adapt to brief or time-limited settings will become obsolete or relegated to private practice. John Rowan writes about the future of primal integration. He believes that 'we in humanistic psychology just have to keep on fighting our corner and not letting go of what we believe'. Andrew Samuels considers 'pluralism' and suggests that psychotherapy can learn from political theory. He asks us, 'what is the moral function of psychological pluralism'?

Brian Thorne looks at the sickness and the prognosis of counselling and psychotherapy. In his more cynical moments he sees the current obsession with registration of therapists and counsellors as little more than the neurosis of a profession which is desperate for approval and terrified of the dole queue. Finally, Richard and Sheenah Wessler reflect upon counselling and society. They believe that the overall success of counselling in the twenty-first century depends upon well trained and creative counsellors. Therein lies the problem! They conclude the chapter by reminding us of Windy Dryden's significant contributions to the field of counselling.

Both American and British spellings have been retained to reflect the individual author's preference.

This book is suitable for both beginner and experienced practitioners interested in the development of psychotherapy and counselling within the social and political context, looking both backwards and forwards in time. The predictions are not always optimistic yet they may be realistic. The reader is offered a useful and possibly challenging foresight into the different hypothetical future paths counselling and psychotherapy may follow. A step into the unknown.

Stephen Palmer
Ved Varma

1

The Future of Cognitive-Behavior and Rational Emotive Behavior Therapy

Albert Ellis

In writing about the future of counseling and psychotherapy, I shall naturally take a biased view and hold that its future will largely be eclectic and integrative, as that is the way therapy is developing. At the core of this eclecticism and integrationism, however, will be cognitive-behavior therapy (CBT) in general and my own form of CBT, now called rational emotive behavior therapy (REBT).

Cognitive-behavior therapy (CBT) is one of the youngest of today's popular psychotherapies, and I think I can immodestly say that I seem to have originated it in January 1955, under the names of rational therapy (RT) and rational emotive therapy (RET) (Ellis, 1957, 1958, 1962). Psychoanalysis had previously existed for over a half century, and client-centered, existential-humanistic, and behavior therapy were about a decade old at that time. Cognitive therapy, without the emotive and behavioral aspects included in REBT, originally became popular in the latter part of the twentieth century (Dubois, 1907; Ellenberger, 1970) and was particularly developed by Alfred Adler (1927, 1931). Eclectic and integrative therapy also was becoming fairly well known in the 1950s (Thorne, 1950) but grew enormously in the 1980s (Beutler, 1983; Goldfried, 1980).

Cognitive-behavior therapy, in general, and rational emotive behavior therapy in particular significantly overlap with early cognitive therapy as well as with existential-humanistic and behavior therapy; and REBT is exceptionally eclectic and integrative, as is Arnold Lazarus's multimodal therapy (Ellis, 1980, 1988, 1994, 1996; Ellis and Dryden, 1987, 1991; Ellis and Grieger, 1977, 1986; Ellis and Harper, 1975; Lazarus, 1989; Yankura and Dryden, 1994). Together CBT and REBT have been tested in over 500 outcome studies, the great majority of which have shown them to be more effective than other forms of therapy or of waiting list groups (Beck, 1991; Ellis, 1979c; Hajzler and Bernard, 1991; Hollon and Beck, 1994; Lyons and Woods, 1991; McGovern and Silverman, 1984; Meichenbaum, 1977; Silverman et al., 1992; Smith and Glass, 1977).

Because of their clinical effectiveness, CBT and REBT have recently become very popular forms of therapy and even therapists who ostensibly practice other forms of psychological treatment, such as psychoanalysis, transactional analysis, and existential-humanistic therapy include, and one might say, sneak in CBT methods. Therapy that is called eclectic or integrative also often mainly consists of cognitive-behavioral practice.

I predict that the future of cognitive-behavior therapy will be exceptionally promising and that it will consciously or unconsciously, overtly or covertly, continue to influence and be used by most therapists in individual psychotherapy, and is already becoming the rule. In group therapy it is still not the main modality employed by most therapists but, once again, many of its best procedures, such as cognitive homework assignments, are creeping into experiential and analytic therapies (Ellis, 1992). In marital and family therapy it is also becoming much more popular and will, I prognosticate, continue to grow (Baucom and Epstein, 1990; Beck, 1988; Ellis, 1986b, 1993b; Ellis et al., 1988; Huber and Baruth, 1989).

In the field of sex therapy, CBT has practically taken over and is easily the most popular form of treatment (Ellis, 1976, 1979; Kaplan, 1974; LoPiccolo and LoPiccolo, 1978; Leiblum and Rosen, 1989; Masters and Johnson, 1970). It certainly looks as though its preeminence in this important area of psychological treatment will continue and will expand.

So the future of CBT in regular fields of therapy seems quite bright. But in several related fields it appears to be even brighter. For unlike several other forms of therapy that insist on an intimate intense relationship between the clients and their therapists – especially psychoanalysis and humanistic existentialist psychotherapy – CBT can be effectively taught in a number of psychoeducational and mass media ways. Let me mention a few important areas in which it is already quite popular and seems well on its way to becoming even more influential.

Self-help materials

Both REBT and CBT include many psychoeducational approaches that can easily be explained in written and audio-visual materials and thereby set up to teach literally millions of readers, listeners, and viewers. The last two decades have spawned a myriad of self-help, best-selling books – such as *Your Erroneous Zones* (Dyer, 1976), *A New Guide to Rational Living* (Ellis and Harper, 1975), and *The Road Less Traveled* (Peck, 1978) – that are heavily cognitive behavioral. Millions of CBT oriented audio and video tapes have also been sold and used. An increasing number of self-help materials by reputable CBT therapists have also been widely employed (Barlow and Craske, 1989; Ellis, 1988; Foa and Reid, 1991; Lewinsohn et al., 1984).

The future of CBT oriented self-help materials looks bright; it is probable that they will be increasingly used by themselves and as adjuncts to individual, family, and group therapy in the next decade and beyond. At our psychological clinic at the Albert Ellis Institute in New York, we have found that clients who use the self-help materials that we recommend often improve quicker and more intensively than those who make little use of these materials; and several studies have shown that cognitive-behavioral writings and cassettes are effective when used by themselves (Barlow and Craske, 1989; Craighead et al., 1984; Foa and Wilson, 1991; Goleman, 1989; Forest, 1987; Pardeck and Pardeck, 1984; Scoggin et al., 1989). Other studies have shown that nearly 90% of psychologists use bibliotherapy in their practice and that only 4% found this unhelpful. Considerable evidence for the widespread use of self-help materials by different kinds of therapists has also been found (Atwater and Smith, 1982; Pardeck and Pardeck, 1984). It would be most surprising if the present-day effective use of cognitive-behavioral materials by therapists and by users who are not undergoing therapy does not continue and expand.

Self-help groups

Ever since Alcoholics Anonymous and Recovery groups started in the 1930s, self-help groups have become very popular and have literally millions of active members today. Most of the groups, like AA, Recovery Inc., Over-eaters Anonymous, and Gamblers Anonymous, have a clearcut cognitive-behavioral orientation; and one of the newer groups, Self-Management and Recovery Training (SMART), specifically follows and teaches REBT and CBT in its regular weekly meetings (Knaus, 1995). Virtually all the other self-help groups, too, use rational coping statements, behavioral procedures, CBT-oriented self-help literature, and other cognitive-behavioral materials. The anti-addiction pamphlets, books, and audio-visual cassettes now used in this large-scale movement sell millions of copies every year and seem to be growing in popularity. The future of cognitive-behavioral self-help groups and paraphernalia appears to be quite assured.

Stress management training

Stress management training today is actually a very popular form of psychotherapy but one that is mostly done by trainers, educators, employment assistance personnel, and other non-therapists. It reaches great numbers of people, many of whom reduce their stress and anxiety with no other forms of treatment; and it mainly consists of cognitive-behavioral techniques and includes the kind of self-help materials mentioned above. More and more organizations – such as business, educational, non-profit, political, professional, athletic, and religious organizations – are teaching their employees and members stress management procedures and are using REBT and CBT materials and methods. At the Albert Ellis Institute in New York, for example, we have a very active Corporate Services Division, directed by Dr Dominic DiMattia, that works with business and other organizations to teach their members rational effectiveness training, which is done through workshops, courses, written and audio-visual materials, and other cognitive-behavioral methods (Abrams and Ellis, 1994; DiMattia, 1987; DiMattia and Long, 1990; Ellis, 1972a, 1988; Ellis et al., 1997; Gschwander and DiMattia, 1991; Klarreich, 1990; Wolfe, 1974; Wolfe and Brand et al., 1977).

Applications of REBT and CBT in the workplace or in other organizations are very likely to have an increasingly active and popular future.

School programs

Both REBT and CBT are ideally, and perhaps most importantly, suited for school programs – from nursery school through graduate school. They are, of course, one of the most didactic forms of therapy and many studies and reports have shown that their main methods can be taught in large and small groups in the form of classes, lectures, workshops, and audio-visual presentations (Bernard and Joyce, 1984; Ellis and Bernard, 1983, 1985; Gerald and Eyman, 1981; Knaus, 1974; Seligman, 1995; Vernon, 1989; Wolfe and Brand et al., 1974).

Considering that the vast majority of children, adolescents, and adults all over the world receive schooling of some sort, and that relatively few of them receive any amount of emotional education, and considering that cognitive-behavioral methods of enhancing emotional health are unusually didactic and homework-assigning, the potential use of REBT and CBT in the school system is enormous. Significant beginnings in this direction have already been made and numerous regular education and continuing education programs on personal growth and development are now being offered, almost all of which are heavily cognitive-behavioral. My conviction is that these programs will continue to expand greatly, so that within the next decade or two few high school and college graduates will fail to acquire considerable emotional education along with their academic and vocational learning.

Brief therapy

Brief therapy has been pushed into unusual prominence in the 1990s, largely because of the insistence of health maintenance organizations (HMOs) and other insurance agencies. However, REBT and CBT have always been intrinsically brief procedures and most of the studies showing their effectiveness have been with subjects who have had from ten to twenty sessions (Hollon and Beck, 1994; Lyons and Woods, 1991; McGovern and Silverman, 1984; Silverman et al., 1992).

This is hardly surprising; I originated REBT in 1955, after I had previously practiced psychoanalysis, because I found psychoanalytic, person-centered, and most other therapies to be too long-winded and inefficient.

One of the main theories of REBT is that disturbed people usually have an underlying and core belief system that includes powerful absolutistic musts and demands. They not only get influenced and affected by negative life events but also create and maintain dysfunctional philosophies that are integrated with their self-defeating feelings and behaviors; and they also have innate and acquired constructivist thoughts, feelings, and behaviors that help them change themselves and become more functional (Ellis, 1991a, 1994, 1996; Kelly, 1955; Mahoney, 1991).

In particular, REBT is a highly active-directive, philosophical form of therapy that shows clients how they specifically upset themselves and how to use a number of cognitive, emotive, and behavioral methods to reduce their disturbances and help themselves be happier, more self-actualized individuals. It assumes that effective REBT can often be done in relatively few sessions – though hardly with all clients all of the time (Broder, 1995a, b; Dryden, 1994, 1995a, b; Ellis, 1991d, 1992, 1996; Warren and Zgourides, 1991). Cognitive-behavior therapy also specializes in relatively brief therapy and has shown some remarkable successes in this regard (Barlow, 1989; Beck et al., 1979; Foa and Wilson, 1991; Shapiro, 1995).

Because REBT and CBT are experimental procedures that stress efficiency as well as philosophical depth (Ellis, 1985; Ellis and Dryden, 1991, 1997) they are likely to remain in the vanguard of brief therapies well into the twenty-first century.

Elegant therapy to help clients feel better and get better

Since the early 1970s I have stressed the fact that while most therapies try to help people *feel* better, REBT emphasizes helping them *get* better as well (Ellis, 1972b, 1979d). I have become even more convinced about this in recent years and have contended that even brief therapy, when it is philosophically done can be better, deeper, and more enduring than some of the longer therapies, such as classical psychoanalysis (Ellis, 1985, 1991a, 1994, 1996).

Elegant therapy that is designed to help people get better in addition to feeling better includes several goals: (1) reducing their presenting symptoms, such as performance anxiety or depression over a serious loss; (2) discovering and reducing their related and more general symptoms, such as anxiety and/or depression in other aspects of their lives; (3) helping them reach a point where they rarely disturb themselves about unfortunate life situations and therefore make themselves less disturb*able*; (4) showing them how, if and when they do fall back to emotional and behavioral upsetness, they can use their previously learned therapy methods to quickly undisturb themselves again and make themselves even less disturbable.

Although several methods of therapy vaguely try to achieve this elegant goal, REBT is especially oriented in this direction. It hypothesizes that a prime factor in disturbance is cognitive-emotional musturbation – the dogmatic, rigid, and forceful holding of absolutistic shoulds, oughts, and demands on oneself, on others, and on external conditions; and it focuses on showing people how to become aware of and change their core dysfunctional philosophies, including their innate tendencies to overgeneralize, reify, and absolutize, which Korzybski (1933) and others have pointed out (Piatelli-Palmarini, 1994; Ellis, 1994, 1996).

Some other cognitive-behavior therapists have followed REBT in this respect (A. Beck, 1995; J. Beck, 1995; Mahoney, 1991; Meichenbaum, 1992), while many solution-focused and social constructionist therapists have not (deShazer, 1985; Guterman, 1994). My prediction is that the future of effective psychotherapy lies in this direction and will be much more concerned than it now is with helping clients feel better *and* get better, and thereby make themselves significantly less disturb*able*.

Helping clients achieve unconditional self-acceptance (USA)

Existentialist thinkers, such as Paul Tillich (1953), emphasized helping people achieve unconditional self-acceptance (USA) – that is, to accept themselves as 'worthy' persons just because they are alive and human (Bordin, 1979; Ellis and Harper, 1961; Rogers, 1961). Many other therapists have endorsed this philosophy, as opposed to that of conditional self-esteem, as advocated by Branden (1970) and others.

Rational emotive behavior therapy especially teaches clients how to achieve USA, first by the therapist's accepting them (Beck, 1976; J. Beck, 1995; Bordin, 1979; Ellis, 1972a; Meichenbaum, 1992; Rogers, 1961); but also by actively–directively teaching them how to give it to themselves and achieve it *whether or not* their therapist or anyone else gives it (Ellis, 1972a, 1973, 1985, 1988, 1994, 1996; Ellis and Harper, 1975; Hauck, 1991; Mills, 1993). Like Korzybski, REBT holds that people have a strong innate (as well as acquired) tendency to rate their thoughts, feelings, and behaviors as effective or less effective for their goals and purposes and also to overgeneralizedly evaluate their self, their totality, their essence, and their being. Therefore, therapists had better help their clients to stop forcefully and persistently upholding the *is* of identity – 'I *am* what I do'.

This aspect of therapy is particularly emphasized by REBT. It not only, as mentioned above, encourages people to accept themselves unconditionally, whether or not they perform well and whether or not other people (including their therapist!) accept them. It also offers them a unique solution to the pernicious self-rating game: 'Don't rate, measure, or evaluate your highly complex self, essence, or being at all. Only rate your thoughts, feelings, and actions. No self-rating!' (Ellis, 1973, 1994, 1996).

According to REBT, this 'ideal' solution to the problem of unconditional self-acceptance (USA) is difficult to achieve and easy to fall back from. So it also offers people the less elegant solution: 'I'm okay just because I exist, because I'm human, because I choose to view myself as okay.' Its concept of and methods of teaching USA are somewhat unique. If they prevail and become influential they will, I predict, importantly enhance the future of counseling and psychotherapy.

Enhancing high frustration tolerance

Both REBT and CBT have always pointed out that people largely needlessly disturb themselves by, first, self-downing (SD) and, second, indulging in low frustration tolerance (LFT) or by demanding that their life absolutely must be easier and more gratifying than it is and by awfulizing (AWF) and whining when it is not (Ellis, 1957, 1962, 1979, 1980, 1985, 1988, 1994, 1996). Particularly REBT has stressed, in this respect, discomfort disturbance along with ego disturbance, and has shown how the two commonly interact and reinforce each other (Ellis, 1979, 1980, 1985).

Most other popular psychotherapies – especially psychodynamic ones – have played down low frustration tolerance and its powerful tendency, first, to lead to emotional dysfunctioning and, second, to maintain it by blocking people who 'see' what is wrong with them from changing – and continuing to change – their dysfunctional ways. Even the poor results that accompany self-downing (SD) are usually maintained and augmented by people's 'easily' indulging in it and stubbornly refusing to give it up. Similarly, people's LFT and awfulizing about their life difficulties – which, of course, absolutely should not exist! – is often exacerbated by their self-downing (SD) about their laziness and resistance to change.

I predict, therefore, that the future of effective counseling and psychotherapy will see more attention being paid to clients' LFT – including their rage, and how to help them overcome it – as well as a strong emphasis on their achieving unconditional self-acceptance.

Low frustration tolerance can be said to have two main subheadings: (1) people demanding that their life conditions be easier and more enjoyable; (2) their insisting that other people absolutely must treat them more kindly, considerately, justly, and lovingly than they often do, and consequently making themselves intensely angry, enraged, violent, and homicidal against these 'inconsiderate bastards'! This major form of LFT is obviously rampant around the world and leads to much social as well as individual harm.

The future of other forms of counseling and psychotherapy

Assuming that general cognitive-behavior therapy (CBT) and specific rational emotive behavioral therapy (REBT) will flourish in the twenty-first century, what will be the future of the other therapies that are popular today? I predict that certain aspects of them will flourish and be integrated with CBT and REBT but that some of them will die out as schools.

To be more specific, person-centered therapy (Rogers, 1961) will continue in the form of unconditional positive regard. But this will be taught to clients more actively–directively and, as is presently the case in REBT, few counselors and therapists will be as nondirective and passive as many person-centered practitioners now are.

Classical psychoanalysis, as practiced by Freud (1965) and his orthodox followers, will rarely be used. But some of the psychodynamic explorations – such as using the relationship between the therapist/counselor and the client and investigating the connection between early experiences and present disturbances – will be briefly employed. Free association and dream analysis will largely be dropped.

Jungian therapy (Jung, 1954) with its emphasis on exploring archetypes and the collective unconscious will rarely be practiced. But Jung's emphasis on individuation, self-actualization, and creativity will often be incorporated into general counseling and psychotherapy.

Adler's individual psychology (Adler, 1927, 1931) will be more popular than ever but its highly cognitive practice will have many of the effective emotive and behavioral methods of CBT and REBT added and routinely incorporated into it. Its pioneering advocacy of social interest will be increasingly incorporated into other therapies.

Existential therapy (May, 1969; Yalom, 1990) will not be too popular in its own right but some of its main values will be incorporated into general counseling and psychotherapy – as they have already been incorporated into REBT. These values include helping clients to choose their own pathways, live in dialogue with other humans, be more present in the immediacy of the moment, and learn to accept certain limits in life.

Religious, transpersonal, shamanistic, and mystical therapies will continue to exist in the twenty-first century just as they have existed for thousands of years. However, they will be studied more scientifically and some of their cultish and iatrogenic aspects will slowly be dropped. 'Spiritual' therapies will also remain popular but professional counselors and therapists will tend to use more of their purposive and meaningful philosophies instead of their supernatural-oriented aspects (Ellis, 1991c, 1994; Ellis and Yeager, 1989; Frankl, 1959).

Eclectic, multimodal, and integrative counseling and therapy, as I noted above, will become more acknowledged and more popular than it is now. I still think that it will usually be heavily cognitive-behavioral but will include important aspects of other therapies (Ellis, 1994; Lazarus, 1989; Norcross and Goldfried, 1992).

The use of biological methods

Rational emotive behavior therapy (REBT) pioneered a biosocial approach to counseling and psychotherapy in the early 1960s, when I faced the fact that many seriously disturbed people have strong biological as well as learned tendencies to become dysfunctional. Indeed, REBT is still one of the few therapies to hypothesize that all humans are born and reared with the tendencies to defeat and to constructively change themselves and that, with hard work and practice, they can use the latter proclivities to minimize (but not entirely remove) the former (Ellis, 1962, 1965b, 1973, 1985, 1987, 1994, 1996).

Consequently, REBT has always favored integrating biological and medical with psychological methods (Ellis, 1994, 1996). It still does. I predict that future counselors and psychotherapists will increasingly refer many of their clients for medication, exercise, diet, and other health procedures and will often integrate psychological and biological methods of increasing emotional function, and happiness.

Individuality and sociality

Although the enhancement of human individuality, self-direction, and self-actualization has been a prime goal of most counselors and therapists in western countries up to now (Freud, 1965; Jung, 1954; Maslow, 1954), individuals practically always live in social groups; their 'personality' is enormously influenced by their social upbringing; and their survival may well depend on a higher degree of social interest than counseling and psychotherapy often promote (Adler, 1927, 1931; Ellis, 1965a, 1973, 1994; Lasch, 1978; Sampson, 1989). Twenty-first century psychological practice had better, and probably will, effectively abet human individuality and sociality. Not either/or but both/and!

Conclusion

The future of counseling and psychotherapy looks good to me for several reasons.

1 Therapy is being experimentally studied and will continue to be investigated, much more than before. This will tend to make it briefer and more effective for more people more of the time.
2 It is becoming more open-minded and integrative – which again will probably increase its efficiency.
3 It is dealing more fully with people's core disturbances and with the thoughts, feelings, and behaviors that go with them. It is on the way to helping them become less disturbed and less disturbable.
4 It is increasingly helping people to achieve both unconditional self-acceptance (USA) and higher frustration tolerance (HFT).
5 It is increasingly emphasizing the dual goals of helping people enhance their human individuality and their sociality.

All this looks optimistic. But what we don't know about effective counseling and psychotherapy far outweighs what we do know. If we have high frustration tolerance and scientific flexibility, our future as counselors and therapists looks bright!

References

Abrams, M. and Ellis, A. (1994) Rational emotive behavior therapy in the treatment of stress, *British Journal of Guidance and Counseling*, 22: 39–50.

Adler, A. (1927) *Understanding Human Nature*. New York: Greenberg.

Adler, A. (1931) *What Life Should Mean to You*. New York: Blue Ribbon Books.

Atwater, J.M. and Smith, D. (1982) Christian therapists utilization of bibliotherapeutic resources, *Journal of Psychology and Theology*, 10: 230–5.

Barlow, D.H. (1989) *Anxiety and its Disorders: The Nature and Treatment of Anxiety and Panic*. New York: Guilford.

Barlow, D.H. and Craske, M.G. (1989) *Mastery of your Anxiety and Panic*. Albany, NY: Center for Stress and Anxiety Disorders.

Baucom, D.H. and Epstein, N. (1990) *Cognitive-behavioral Marital Therapy*. New York: Brunner/Mazel.

Beck, A.T. (1976) *Cognitive Therapy and the Emotional Disorders*. New York: International Universities Press.

Beck, A.T. (1988) *Love is Not Enough*. New York: Harper and Row.

Beck, A.T. (1991) Cognitive therapy: A 30-year retrospective. *American Psychologist*, 46: 382–9.

Beck, A.T. (1995) Introduction, in J.S. Beck, *Cognitive Therapy: Basics and Beyond*. New York: Guilford. pp. v–vii.

Beck, A.T., Rush, A.J., Shaw, B.F. and Emery, G. (1979) *Cognitive Therapy of Depression*. New York: Guilford.

Beck, J.S. (1995) *Cognitive Therapy: Basics and Beyond*. New York: Guilford.

Bernard, M.E. and Joyce, M.R. (1984) *Rational-emotive Therapy with Children and Adolescents*. New York: Wiley.

Beutler, L.E. (1983) *Eclectic Psychotherapy: A Systematic Approach*. New York: Pergamon.

Bordin, E. (1979) The generalizability of the psychoanalytic concept of the working alliance, *Psychotherapy*, 16: 252–60.

Branden, N. (1970) *The Psychology of Self-esteem*. New York: Bantam.

Broder, M. (Speaker). (1995a) *Overcoming your anxiety in the shortest period of time*. Cassette recording. New York: Institute for Rational-Emotive Therapy.

Broder, M. (Speaker). (1995b) *Overcoming your depression in the shortest period of time*. Cassette recording. New York: Institute for Rational-Emotive Therapy.

Craighead, L.W., McNamara, J. and Moran, J. (1984) Perspective on self-help and bibliotherapy, in S.D. Brown and R.W. Lent (eds), *Handbook of Counseling Psychology*. New York: Wiley. pp. 878–929.

deShazer, S. (1985) *Keys to Solution in Brief Therapy*. New York: Norton.

DiMattia, D.J. (1987) *Mind over Myths: Handling Difficult Situations in the Workplace*. New York: Institute for Rational-Emotive Therapy.

DiMattia, D.J. with Mennen, S. (1990) *Rational Effectiveness Training: Increasing Productivity at Work*. New York: Institute for Rational-Emotive Therapy.

DiMattia, D.J. and Long, S. (1990) *Self directed sales success*. Cassette recording. New York: Rational Effectiveness Training Systems.

Dryden, W. (1994) *Invitation to Rational-emotive Psychology*. London: Whurr.

Dryden, W. (1995a) *Brief Rational Emotive Behaviour Therapy*. London: Wiley.

Dryden, W. (ed.) (1995b) *Rational Emotive Behaviour Therapy: A Reader*. London: Sage.

Dubois, P. (1907) *The Psychic Treatment of Nervous Disorders*. New York: Funk and Wagnalls.

Dyer, W. (1976) *Your Erroneous Zones*. New York: Funk and Wagnalls.

Ellenberger, H.F. (1970) *The Discovery of the Unconscious*. New York: Basic Books.

Ellis, A. (1957) *How to Live with a Neurotic: At Home and at Work*. New York: Crown. Rev. ed. (1975) Hollywood, CA: Wilshire Books.

Ellis, A. (1958) Rational psychotherapy, *Journal of General Psychology*, 59: 35–49. Reprinted: New York: Institute for Rational-Emotive Therapy.

Ellis, A. (1962) *Reason and Emotion in Psychotherapy*. Secaucus, NJ: Citadel.

Ellis, A. (1965a) *Suppressed: Seven Key Essays Publishers Dared not Print*. Chicago: New Classics House.

Ellis, A. (1965b) *The Treatment of Borderline and Psychotic Individuals*. New York: Institute for Rational-Emotive Therapy.

Ellis, A. (1972a) *Executive Leadership: The Rational-emotive Approach*. New York: Institute for Rational-Emotive Therapy.

Ellis, A. (1972b) Helping people get better rather than merely feel better, *Rational Living*, 7(2): 2–9.

Ellis, A. (1973) *Humanistic Psychotherapy: The Rational-emotive Approach*. New York: McGraw-Hill.

Ellis, A. (1976) *Sex and the Liberated Man*. Secaucus, NJ: Lyle Stuart.

Ellis, A. (1979a) Discomfort anxiety: A new cognitive behavioral construct. Part 1, *Rational Living*, 14(2): 3–8.

Ellis, A. (1979b) *The Intelligent Woman's Guide to Dating and Mating*. Secaucus, NJ: Lyle Stuart.

Ellis, A. (1979c) Rational-emotive therapy: Research data that support the clinical and personality hypothesis of RET and other modes of cognitive-behavior therapy, in A. Ellis and J.M. Whiteley (eds), *Theoretical and Empirical Foundations of Rational-emotive Therapy*. Monterey, CA: Brooks/Cole. pp. 101–73.

Ellis, A. (1979d) Rejoinder: Elegant and inelegant RET, in A. Ellis and J.M. Whiteley, *Theoretical and Empirical Foundations of Rational-emotive Therapy*. Monterey, CA: Brooks/Cole. pp. 240–67.

Ellis, A. (1980a) Discomfort anxiety: A new cognitive behavioral construct. Part 2, *Rational Living*, 15(1): 25–30.

Ellis, A. (1980b) Rational-emotive therapy and cognitive behavior therapy: Similarities and differences, *Cognitive Therapy and Research*, 4: 325–40.

Ellis, A. (1985) *Overcoming Resistance: Rational-emotive Therapy with Difficult Clients*. New York: Springer.

Ellis, A. (1986a) Anxiety about anxiety: The use of hypnosis with rational-emotive therapy, in E.T. Dowd and J.M. Healy (eds), *Case Studies in Hypnotherapy*. New York: Guilford. pp. 3–11. Reprinted: In A. Ellis and W. Dryden, *The Practice of Rational-emotive Therapy*. New York: Springer.

Ellis, A. (1986b) Rational-emotive therapy applied to relationship therapy, *Journal of Rational-Emotive Therapy*, 4: 4–21.

Ellis, A. (1987) The impossibility of achieving consistently good mental health, *American Psychologist*, 42: 364–75.

Ellis, A. (1988) *How to Stubbornly Refuse to make yourself Miserable about Anything – yes, Anything!* Secaucus, NJ: Lyle Stuart.

Ellis, A. (1991a) Achieving self-actualization, *Journal of Social Behavior and Personality*, 6(5): 1–18. Reprinted: New York: Institute for Rational-Emotive Therapy.

Ellis, A. (1991b) Are all methods of counseling equally effective? *New York State Journal for Counseling and Development*, 6(2): 9–13.

Ellis, A. (1991c) *The Case against Religiosity*. Rev. ed. New York: Institute for Rational-Emotive Therapy.

Ellis, A. (1991d) How can psychological treatments aim to be briefer and better. The rational-emotive therapy approach to brief therapy, in K.N. Anchor (ed.), *The Handbook of Medical Psychotherapy*. Toronto: Hografe and Huber. pp. 51–88. Also in J.K. Zeig and S.G. Gilligan (eds), *Brief Therapy: Myths, Methodism and Metaphors*. New York: Brunner/Mazel. pp. 291–302.

Ellis, A. (1992) Group rational-emotive and cognitive-behavioral therapy, *International Journal of Group Therapy*, 42: 63–80.

Ellis, A. (1993a) The advantages and disadvantages of self-help therapy materials, *Professional Psychology: Research and Practice*, 24: 335–9.

Ellis, A. (1993b) The rational-emotive therapy (RET) approach to marriage and family therapy, *Family Journal: Counseling and Therapy for Couples*, 1: 292–307.

Ellis, A. (1994) *Reason and Emotion in Psychotherapy*. Revised and updated. New York: Birch Lane Press.

Ellis, A. (1996) *Better, Deeper, and More Enduring Brief Therapy*. New York: Brunner/ Mazel.

Ellis, A. and Bernard, M.E. (eds) (1983) *Rational-emotive Approaches to the Problems of Childhood*. New York: Plenum.

Ellis, A. and Bernard, M.E. (eds) (1985) *Clinical Applications of Rational-emotive Therapy*. New York: Plenum.

Ellis, A. and Dryden, W. (1990) *The Essential Albert Ellis*. New York: Springer.

Ellis, A. and Dryden, W. (1991) *A Dialogue with Albert Ellis: Against Dogma*. Philadelphia: Open University Press.

Ellis, A. and Dryden, W. (1997) *The Practice of Rational-emotive Therapy*. New York: Springer.

Ellis, A. and Grieger, R. (eds) (1977) *Handbook of Rational-emotive Therapy*, vol. 1. New York: Springer.

Ellis, A. and Grieger, R. (eds) (1986) *Handbook of Rational-emotive Therapy*, vol. 2. New York: Springer.

Ellis, A. and Harper, R.A. (1961) *A Guide to Successful Marriage*. North Hollywood, CA: Wilshire Books.

Ellis, A. and Harper, R.A. (1975) *A New Guide to Rational Living*. North Hollywood, CA: Wilshire Books.

Ellis, A. and Yeager, R. (1989) *Why some Therapies don't Work: The Dangers of Transpersonal Psychology*. Buffalo, NY: Prometheus.

Ellis, A., Gordon, J., Neenan, M. and Palmer, S. (1997) *Stress Counselling: A Rational Emotive Behaviour Approach*. London: Cassell.

Ellis, A., Sichel, J., Yeager, R., DiMattia, D. and DiGiuseppe, R. (1989) *Rational Emotive Couples Therapy*. New York: Pergamon.

Foa, E.B. and Wilson, R. (1991) *Stop Obsessing*. New York: Bantam.

Forest, J. (1987) Effects of self-actualization of paperbacks about psychological self-help, *Psychological Reports*, 60: 1243–6.

Frankl, V. (1959) *Man's Search for Meaning*. New York: Pocket Books.

Freud, S. (1965) *Standard Edition of the Complete Psychological Works of Sigmund Freud*. New York: Basic Books.

Gerald, M. and Eyman, W. (1981) *Thinking Straight and Talking Sense: An Emotional Education Program*. New York: Institute for Rational-Emotive Therapy.

Goldfried, M.R. (1980) Toward the delineation of therapeutic chance principles, *American Psychologist*, 35: 991–9.

Goleman, D. (1989) Feeling gloomy? A good self-help book may actually help, *New York Times*, 6 July, p. B6.

Gschwander, G. and DiMattia, D. (1991) The psychology of dealing with recession jitters, *Personal Selling Power*, 11(3): 28–32.

Guterman, J.T. (1994) A social constructionist position for mental health counselors, *Journal of Mental Health Counseling*, 16: 226–44.

Hajzler, D. and Bernard, M.E. (1991) A review of rational-emotive outcome studies, *School Psychology Quarterly*, 6(1): 27–49.

Hauck, P.A. (1991) *Overcoming the Rating Game*. Louisville, KY: Westminster.

Hollon, S.D. and Beck, A.T. (1994) Cognitive and cognitive behavioral therapies, in A.E. Bergin and S.L. Garfield (eds), *Handbook of Psychotherapy and Behavior Change*. New York: Wiley. pp. 428–66.

Huber, C.H. and Baruth, L.G. (1989) *Rational-emotive and Systems Family Therapy*. New York: Springer.

Jung, C.G. (1954) *The Practice of Psychotherapy*. New York: Pantheon.

Kaplan, H. (1974) *The New Sex Therapy*. New York: Brunner/Mazel.

Kelly, G. (1955) *The Psychology of Personal Constructs*, 2 vols. New York: Norton.

Klarreich, S.H. (1990) *Work without Stress*. New York: Brunner/Mazel.

Knaus, W. (1974) *Rational-emotive Education*. New York: Institute for Rational-Emotive Therapy.

Knaus, W. (1995) *SMART Recovery*. Springfield, MA: Author.

Korzybski, A. (1933) *Science and Sanity*. San Francisco: International Society for General Semantics.

Lasch, C. (1978) *The Culture of Narcissism*. New York: Norton.

Lazarus, A.A. (1989) *The Practice of Multi-modal Therapy*. Baltimore: Johns Hopkins.

Leiblum, S.R. and Rosen, R.C. (eds) (1989) *Principles and Practice of Sex Therapy*. New York: Guilford.

Lewinsohn, P., Antonuccio, D., Breckenridge, J. and Teri, L. (1984) *The 'Coping with depression course'*. Eugene, OR: Plenum.

LoPiccolo, J. and LoPiccolo, L. (eds) (1978) *Handbook of Sex Therapy*. New York: Plenum.

Lyons, L.C. and Woods, P.J. (1991) The efficacy of rational-emotive therapy: A quantitative review of the outcome research, *Clinical Psychology Review*, 11: 359–69.

Mahoney, M.J. (1991) *Human Change Processes*. New York: Basic Books.

Maslow, A.H. (1954) *Motivation and Personality*. New York: Harper and Row.

Masters, W.H. and Johnson, V.E. (1970) *Human Sexual Inadequacy*. Boston: Little, Brown.

May, R. (1969) *Love and Will*. New York: Norton.

McGovern, T.E. and Silverman, M.S. (1984) A review of outcome studies of rational-emotive therapy from 1977 to 1982, *Journal of Rational-Emotive Therapy*, 2(1): 7–18.

Meichenbaum, D. (1977) *Cognitive-behavior Modification*. New York: Plenum.

Meichenbaum, D. (1992) Evolution of cognition behavior therapy: Origins, tenets, and clinical examples, in J.K. Zeig (ed.), *The Evolution of Psychotherapy: The Second Conference*. New York: Brunner/Mazel. pp. 114–28.

Mills, D. (1993) *Overcoming Self-esteem*. New York: Institute for Rational-Emotive Therapy.

Norcross, J.C. and Goldfried, M.P. (1992) *Psychotherapy Integration*. New York: Basic Books.

Pardeck, J.A. and Pardeck, J.T. (1984) *Young People with Problems*. Westport, CT: Greenwald.

Peck, M.S. (1978) *The Road Less Traveled*. New York: Simon and Schuster.

Piatelli-Palmarini, M. (1994) *Inevitable Illusions: How Mistakes of Reason Rule our Minds*. New York: Wiley.

Rogers, C.R. (1961) *On Becoming a Person*. Boston: Houghton Mifflin.

Sampson, E.E. (1989) The challenge of social change in psychology. Globalization and psychology's theory of the person, *American Psychologist*, 44: 914–21.

Scoggin, F., Jamison, C. and Gochneaur, K. (1989) Comparative efficacy of cognitive and behavioral bibliotherapy for mildly and moderately depressed older adults, *Journal of Consulting and Clinical Psychology*, 57: 403–7.

Seligman, M.E.P., Revich, K., Jaycox, L. and Gillham, J. (1995) *The Optimistic Child*. New York: Houghton Mifflin.

Shapiro, F. (1995) *Eye Movement Desensitization and Reprocessing*. New York: Guilford.

Silverman, M.S., McCarthy, M. and McGovern, T. (1992) A review of outcome studies of rational-emotive therapy from 1982–1989, *Journal of Rational-Emotive and Cognitive-Behavior Therapy*, 10(3): 111–86.

Smith, M.L. and Glass, G.V. (1977) Meta-analysis of psychotherapy outcome studies, *American Psychologist*, 32: 752–60.

Starker, S. (1986) Promises and perceptions, *American Journal of Health Promotions*, 1: 19–24, 68.

Starker, S. (1988) Psychologists and self-help books, *American Journal of Psychotherapy*, 43: 448–55.

Thorne, F.C. (1950) *Principles of Personality Counseling*. Brandon, VT: Journal of Clinical Psychology Press.

Tillich, P. (1953) *The Courage To Be*. New York: Oxford.

Trimpey, J. (1989) *Rational Recovery from Alcoholism: The Small Book*. Lotus, CA: Rational Recovery.

Vernon, A. (1989) *Thinking, Feeling, Behaving: An Emotional Education Curriculum for Children*. Champaign, IL: Research Press.

Warren, R. and Zgourides, G.D. (1991) *Anxiety Disorders: A Rational-emotive Perspective*. Des Moines, IA: Longwood Division Allyn and Bacon.

Wolfe, J.L. (1974) *Rational-emotive therapy and women's assertiveness*. Cassette recording. New York: Institute for Rational-Emotive Therapy.

Wolfe, J.L. and Brand, E. (eds) (1977) *Twenty Years of Rational Therapy*. New York: Institute for Rational-Emotive Therapy.

Yalom, I. (1990) *Existential Psychotherapy*. New York: Basic Books.

Yankura, J. and Dryden, W. (1994) *Albert Ellis*. Thousand Oaks, CA: Sage.

2

Psychotherapy at the millennium

Jeremy Holmes

My aim in this chapter is to consider the possible contours of psychotherapy in the year 2000. It is bound to be proved wrong. Like long-
range weather forecasters and economists, psychotherapists are in an
'impossible profession' (Freud, 1937), dealing with nonlinear and therefore inherently unstable systems, unable to make accurate predictions
about the future. But psychotherapists are familiar with uncertainty, and
indeed, in the Keatsian sense of negative capability – 'the capacity to
be in doubts, uncertainties, mysteries' – actively cultivate it in order to
work more creatively. Indeed, the development of chaos theory (Gleick,
1988) has now made uncertainty a respectable topic for scientific
enquiry.

Psychotherapists might consider why the idea of the year 2000 exerts
such fascination. The notion of two thousand years since the birth of
Christ seems like a solid, rounded, natural phenomenon, but it is in reality
an artefact produced by the mind in order to shape and control reality. Its
psychological function could be seen as the attempt to manage anxiety in
the face of the formless and unpredictable flux of time. The Christian
calendar was devised in the sixth century by the monk Dionysius Exiguus,
for whom the date of the birth of Christ was sheer guesswork (Williams,
1985). In the Islamic calendar we are entering the thirteenth century, a far
less exciting figure. The year 2000 is a narrative, a story, fictive – but none
the less exciting for all that.

Freud was fascinated by numerology and, being an obsessional, he was
prey to irrational fears about numbers. He was convinced he would die at
the age of 62 and became terrified when he was assigned a telephone
number whose last two numbers were 62 (Pedder, 1990). Because they are
arbitrary and abstract signs, numbers attract projections of inner mood
states. The round numbers may evoke primitive images of sexuality – it is
perhaps no accident that bosomy girls appear on page 3 of the popular
press, while male pinups dangle on page 7. The year 2000 could evoke the
many-breasted Hindu goddess of plenty, or alternatively a sterile uni-
formity of identical zeros.

The year 2000 is not 1984. It is too near for Utopian or dystopian
fantasies, more like the day after tomorrow, and yet by looking into the
future we are forced to consider that nothing is permanent, that all we

hold dear can crumble away. With Yeats, we may well ask 'what rough beast, its hour come round at last/ Slouches towards Bethlehem to be born?'.

Millennial fantasies are prevalent; in the brief moment between the ending of the cold war and the onset of the Gulf crisis, the American historian Francis Fukuyama, in a premature orgy of capitalist triumphalism, pronounced the 'end of history'. The convergence of spiritual and ecological concerns has produced a New Age movement that, however much one may approve its aspirations, has to be compared with the Plymouth Brethren who stood upon hilltops towards the end of the nineteenth century, confident in their calculations that the end of the world was at hand. From a psychotherapeutic point of view the advent of the millennium evokes primitive fears of dissolution and destruction, and compensatory fantasies of power or bliss. A pre-industrial society could balance these fears with images of continuity: the succession of saint's days, the cycle of the seasons and the orderly sequence of birth, maturation, decay and death followed by rebirth provided by the farming year. Continuity was provided not just by the land but by the family, extended both in time and space. Stripped of their religious and agrarian significance, living in a world of almost unimaginable change, no longer constrained by the steadying hand of the past, we are free to invest our feast days and millennia with whatever significance we choose: we celebrate the seventy-fifth birthday of the Institute of Psychoanalysis, the half-century since Freud's death and so on. The professional family replaces the village, community, or even the family itself, as the vehicle of celebration and continuity.

The organization of psychotherapy

The 1990s have been a period of both hope and turmoil for psychotherapy, dominated by three current and interrelated themes: expansion, professionalization and pluralism. The 1980s saw a great expansion in psychotherapy and counselling (Pedder, 1990). Trainings proliferated, new forms of psychotherapy emerged – ranging from the now fully established cognitive-behavioural therapy to the wilder fringes, a subculture of complementary therapies varying enormously in depth and respectability. The result has been that psychotherapy is available to a far wider spectrum of the population than ever before, but often in a form which would make some of the psychoanalytic pioneers turn in their graves – although not necessarily Freud, who in 1919 predicted that if the misery of the masses was to be addressed, the 'pure gold of psychoanalysis' would have to be alloyed with the 'copper of suggestion' (Freud, 1919).

Hand-in-hand with this proliferation has been psychotherapy's attempt to organize itself into a profession. The formation of the United Kingdom Council for Psychotherapy (UKCP) in 1991 was a landmark in a process which had been germinating throughout the last quarter of the century. The background to this has been a struggle to produce an organizational structure which catered for the vast range of different psychotherapies, all with varying entry and training requirements, while at the same time maintaining standards that would inform and protect the general public. The 'federal' structure of the UKCP was an inspirational answer to this problem, with the various 'sections' – psychodynamic, cognitive-behavioural, systemic, integrative-humanistic and so on – having the responsibility for setting standards and monitoring the trainings of their member organizations. Personal registration as a psychotherapist is achieved through accreditation of one's member organization.

Many problems remain, which are likely to rumble on into the next century. First, the UKCP and its register has no statutory status, and any member of the public who wishes to set up as a psychotherapist is still free to do so without infringing the law. Second, 'status wars' have broken out between the UKCP and a second organization, the British Confederation of Psychotherapists (BCP) comprising the Institute of Psychoanalysis and some other psychoanalytically oriented organizations. The BCP fastidiously feels that the umbrella of UKCP is too broad, with too diverse a membership, for it to be associated with. At the same time established professions already delivering psychotherapy – the British Psychological Society and the Royal College of Psychiatrists – are preparing their own register of psychotherapists. Pedder (1990) has compared these battles – which in the end boil down to who is, or is not, on a list – with the registration of medical practitioners in the mid-nineteenth century which unified a diversity of doctors from the Harley Street grandees to the unqualified provincial physicians and barber-surgeons who served the poor. Whether such developments will lead to greater unity and a raising of standards, or to dilution and 'discreditation by association' of the hard-won rigour of the tougher and more established trainings in the BCP is a matter for debate.

Pluralism, integration and eclecticism

Underlying the political battles between the various psychotherapy organizations lies the question of integration versus purity in psychotherapy (Albeniz and Holmes, 1996). Since integration in psychotherapy is not easy to define some of this tension is semantic. The debate should be seen in the context of two polarities: purity versus integration, and integration versus eclecticism. Beitman (1989) delineates a spectrum of integration ranging from (a) *rapprochement*, or cordial relations between different approaches, (b) convergence of ideas and practice, (c) eclecticism, a pragmatic stance in which therapists use whatever they think may be helpful to the patient and (d) integration proper, as seen in self-proclaimed 'integrative therapies'.

Prochaska and DiClemente (1992) distinguish sharply between eclecticism which produces mosaic therapies combining elements from many different sources, and integration which attempts to produce a new approach based on the blending of different ideas. Beitman (1989) describes eclecticism as both a 'worn out synonym for theoretical laziness' and 'the only means to a comprehensive psychotherapy'. The therapist must be an 'authentic chameleon' (Garfield and Bergin, 1994), yet eclecticism can be little more than a 'mish-mash of theories, a hugger-mugger of procedures, a gallimaufry of therapies'.

There are strong arguments on both sides of this debate. Integrationists emphasize the fact that, in general, research has failed to demonstrate the superiority of any one therapy over any other, suggesting that 'common factors' such as instillation of hope and the provision of a therapeutic relationship and routine are the main curative elements in psychotherapy. They also point out that most successful psychotherapies for major psychiatric disorders tend to be integrationist. Thus family work in schizophrenia combines systemic, education and behavioural components; interpersonal therapy in eating disorders is a similarly integrationalist therapy combining support, suggestion, and where appropriate, dynamic interpretation; dialectical behaviour therapy (Linehan, 1993), an effective treatment for deliberate self-harm in borderline personality disorder, combines cognitive therapy and a humanistic emphasis on the here-and-now derived from Buddhism.

Advocates of purity, by contrast, argue from the research evidence suggesting that therapists who show good 'adherence' to a particular model of therapy produce better results than those who veer away from standard procedures. Psychoanalytically oriented therapists further suggest that a therapist who hops from model to model may be driven by transferential or countertransferential forces, and thus avoids unconscious conflict and pain.

An emphasis on purity or integration in part reflects the developmental life of a particular psychotherapy: in infancy uniqueness and differences from other types of therapy tend to be emphasized, but with maturation similarities and overlaps can be allowed to emerge The same is true at the level of the individual therapist who usually needs to start by mastering one specific technique, but with experience becomes more flexible and integrative, illustrating Piaget's digestive metaphor of 'accommodation' and 'assimilation' as a model for intellectual maturation. The millennium is likely to see both tendencies reinforced as there is increasing *rapprochement* between different modalities, and new strains of therapy emergence.

The attempt to match patient need and therapeutic approach will continue. Patients need a variety of therapeutic approaches if their differing problems, personalities and situations are to be accommodated, but a mishmash of half-assimilated techniques can produce poor therapy and may lead to a backlash of purism. It remains to be seen how much psychoanalytic psychotherapies will be prepared to compromise their standards (especially the 'gold standard' of three or more times a week analysis) in order to widen their applicability and accessibility (Bateman and Holmes, 1995).

Implications for psychotherapeutic psychiatry

The reverberations of this pluralistic expansion of psychotherapy will have important implications for psychiatry. Tension between psychodynamic and organic psychiatry continues to plague Anglo-Saxon psychiatry. On the one hand many are attracted to psychiatry as a branch of medicine because it is concerned with fundamental problems such as nature of mind, how people should lead their lives and how change of personality comes about. The general public expects and wants psychotherapeutic understanding as well as the fruits of modern technology. On the other hand, health purchasers often view psychotherapy as an unproven and indeterminate and indefinite form of treatment that can best be dealt with by counsellors in General Practice (GP) rather than by costly specialized psychotherapy services.

There is a real danger of fragmentation, with psychiatrists running what is essentially a psychosis service, while the psychotherapeutic needs of the population are met by a diverse group of psychologists, private psychotherapists, GP-based counsellors and so on. The alternative is an integrated psychological treatment service in which psychotherapeutically minded psychiatrists, psychologists and non-medical registered psychotherapists work collaboratively, each contributing their own area of interest and expertise, thus providing a matrix of different treatments which collectively can cater for the varying needs and expectations of patients (Holmes and Lindley, 1997).

Interprofessional rivalries are likely to intensify as resources diminish. Medical hegemony will continue to be challenged, especially by psychologists and nurses who will be able legitimately to claim more psychotherapeutic expertise than many of their psychiatric colleagues. There will be a great temptation for psychiatry to concede the territory of psychotherapy and to retreat into a narrow bunker of scientism and rejection of all that cannot be quantified. But even a narrowly defined psychiatry will continue to need psychotherapeutic skills across the range of psychiatric disorders: in the management of schizophrenics and their families; patients with depressive illnesses for whom antidepressants are ineffective, unwelcome or insufficient; patients with eating disorders in whom medical complications are an ever-present possibility; suicidal patients; those with somatization disorders; and patients with borderline personality problems or unstable mood states, who so often gravitate towards psychiatric services and who, on the whole, are so ill-served by them (Margison, 1991). Furthermore, community psychiatrists will need psychotherapeutic skills both to help in the understanding of the meaning and content of their patients' illnesses, and to provide symbolic containment and integration in the face of increasing administrative fragmentation.

These shifting professional boundaries are but one manifestation of the economic and political pressures that will shape the pattern of our work in the future. It seems likely, whatever the political future, that the introduction of market forces into the health service, in one form or another, is here to stay. Although we may deplore this move politically (psychotherapists tend to be on the liberal wing of the psychiatric party), it may, paradoxically, have the effect of raising the status and morale of psychotherapy, since psychotherapy is what many patients want and are prepared to travel distances to get. Hitherto this tendency of psychotherapy departments to serve a wider population than their immediate district has been frowned upon as an example of an inessential 'luxury'. In future it may be seen by managers as a useful money-spinner while general psychiatric services are increasingly squeezed. Nevertheless psychotherapy departments remain soft targets, vulnerable to cuts if resources diminish.

Meanwhile there will be increasing discouragement of 'analysis interminable', as auditors and managers are prepared to fund only the briefer 'validated' forms of psychotherapy. For some this will undoubtedly be a benefit, widening the availability of therapy and concentrating the minds of the therapists. The danger is that it will encourage a form of psychotherapeutic consumerism whose outlines are already visible, in which 'customers' sample varieties of different therapies, each with its transitory immediate appeal and impact on surface problems – a potpourri of anxiety management, psychodrama weekends, cognitive therapy courses, sessions of self-assertiveness training and awareness programmes, which may act as a defence against facing the central hollowness of the patient's life and the need for an enduring, intimate relationship with a therapist in which trauma, negativity and destructiveness can be accepted and transcended.

The psychoanalytic paradigm of a prolonged, intense, neutral therapeutic relationship, with its potential for long-term benefit but low short-term cost–benefit pay-off, contrasts with the need for validated and realistic forms of psychotherapy for the National Health Service (NHS). Creative conflict between the two extremes will lead to concessions on both sides. Psychoanalysts will become more flexible, while brief or cognitive therapists will acknowledge the need in many patients for more prolonged, open-ended therapeutic encounters than they currently endorse. There are already signs (Teasdale et al., 1996) that some cognitive therapists are beginning to acknowledge the difficulty of modifying the core beliefs that fuel deep depressive illness or personality disorders, and are turning to longer-term methods ranging from 'attention control training' (i.e. a modified form of meditation), to working explicitly with transference.

Themes for the millennium

No science operates in a social or cultural vacuum, least of all a part-scientific, part-pedagogic, part-artistic discipline such as psychotherapy. Numerous examples testify to the intimate relationship between technical and cultural change in society and developments in the field of psychotherapy. Freud's lifework must be seen in the context of the assimilation of the Jewish intelligentsia in the nineteenth century. There is an obvious link between his concept of the death instinct and later elaborations of it by Melanie Klein and others, and the terrible impact of the First World War. The spread of psychoanalysis to the USA and UK in the 1930s (and its conspicuous absence from the Soviet Union) is a direct result of the rise of Nazism and Stalinism in the 1930s. The development of group therapy in this country derives mainly from the impact of the Second World War on a group of psychoanalytically minded military psychiatrists including Bion, Main, Rickman, Trist and others (Pines, 1991). The ideas of cybernetics and the study of communication systems, developed as part of the military effort in the Second World War, laid the foundations for Bateson's work (Bateson, 1973) which led on to the development of family therapy in the 1960s. The current vogue for cognitive therapy can be seen as a response to the first oil crisis of the 1970s, and the consequent need for briefer, cheaper forms of therapy.

I shall pick out five themes which are likely to influence the climate of psychotherapy at the turn of the century: science, religion, inequality, gender and trauma. I shall suggest in particular that trauma and its sequelae will continue to provide a paradigm for psychotherapeutic work in the foreseeable future.

The impact of contemporary science and technology

Psychotherapy, like psychiatry itself, is both a science and an art. Scientific developments have undoubtedly had their impact on psychotherapy. Sulloway (1979) described Freud as the 'biologist of the mind'; he showed how Darwinian ideas were an indispensable precursor of Freudian notions of the evolution of the psyche, and the relationship between our adult conscious minds and the 'primitive' instinctual forces from which consciousness has emerged in the course of development. Slavin and Kriegman (1992) have extended these ideas based on psychobiology. For example in the first year of life the interests of the child's 'selfish genes' are identical with those of the mother, and therefore the child's 'primary narcissism' is likely to evoke her devoted altruism. This contrasts with the situation in the subsequent years of infancy where the mother will want once again to reproduce, thus setting up a genetic as well a psychological 'oedipal situation' in which there is direct competition for her 'resources' with the father and any potential or actual siblings. Similarly Slavin and Kriegman see transference and projective identification as psychological probes with which the individual tests interpersonal situations to see if there is a psychological 'fit' which will lead to acceptance as partner or friend and the possibility of reciprocal altruism.

Communications theory and cybernetics provided a language for the development of family therapy. Ryle's cognitive analytic therapy (Ryle, 1995) – which has become increasingly popular among NHS psychotherapists over the past ten years – is couched in the language of artificial intelligence. Attachment theory (Bowlby, 1979; Goldberg et al., 1995; Holmes, 1993, 1996) brings together ideas from psychoanalysis, ethology and cognitive science, has generated a vast field of empirical research in developmental psychology which is directly relevant to psychotherapeutic work. Thus the finding that parental attunement is a precursor of secure attachment has obvious analogues for the psychotherapeutic relationship. The adult attachment interview (Main, 1995) is a psychodynamically meaningful research instrument that can be used to track changes in the narrative coherence and accurate self-appraisal in therapy, for example in the treatment of patients with severe personality disorders (Fonagy et al., 1995).

Two decades of research have established beyond all doubt the effectiveness of psychotherapy, but the question of how change comes about remains a central issue for psychotherapy research. Sophisticated computer-based methods of analysing the myriad of interactions that take place in psychotherapy sessions are becoming available (Thoma and Kachele, 1986), and mathematical models that are adequate to undertake this task are being developed (Langs and Badalamenti, 1994), although their clinical relevance remains a matter of debate. Chaos theory (Gleick, 1988) which studies the laws which underlie the behaviour of complex systems such as the weather, stock markets, or paroxysmal cardiac arrhythmias, looks like a promising paradigm for psychotherapy researchers. The 'butterfly effect', which suggests that small differences can have big impacts on outcomes of complex processes, has become something of a cliché, but nevertheless is a useful metaphor for aspects of the psychotherapy. For example, early apparently trivial events in a session – where the therapist puts her coat for example, or a chance remark about the weather – may turn out to have a determining impact on the overall shape of the therapeutic encounter. Chaos theory, through its notion of 'fractal geometry', paints a holographic picture of complex systems, showing how all heaven *can* be found in a grain of sand, or how the close texture of a coastline can be related to its overall shape in an atlas. This is relevant to the psychotherapeutic observation that no one part of a therapeutic encounter is privileged, and that each session in a sense 'contains' the whole of the patient's pathology. The notion of 'strange attractors' may help to understand the nodal points that develop in psychotherapy: the recurrent themes and mood states to which the patient regularly returns, the understanding and overcoming of which often prove to be turning points in therapy.

The spiritual quest and the search for meaning

At the opposite pole to the scientific aspect of psychotherapy is the hermeneutic project of decoding meanings, the need to deepen understanding and so increase the significance and richness of lived experience. Many authors have seen psychoanalysis and psychotherapy as providing a response to spiritual needs, especially among the intelligentsia and middle classes, in an increasingly secular world. An upsurge of interest in psychotherapy is taking place in Eastern Europe, filling the vacuum left by the collapse of Marxist-Leninist ideology. Psychotherapy provides an account of personal meanings and a method by which they can be explored and healed that complements the religious impulse. The millennium will see an increasing dialogue between psychotherapy and religion. The impact of Eastern religion may be particularly significant: Zen Buddhism, for example, can itself be seen as a secularized religion, with its absence of theism, its stress on paradox and spontaneity and its use of breathing techniques, which are now a standard part of psychological methods of anxiety control (West, 1990). How this spiritual dimension to psychotherapy (Cox and Thielgaard, 1987) will fit in with the new market economy of the health service is uncertain; but it will remain one of the most important tasks of psychotherapy to be a bastion of human values, of 'being with' the patient as well as 'doing to' him (Wolff, 1971) in an increasingly technologized and commercialized medical world.

Psychotherapy and inequality

Despite its increasingly widened availability, psychotherapy within the NHS, the 'YAVIS' (Young, Attractive, Verbal, Intelligent, Successful) image of psychotherapy as a pleasant pastime for the mildly troubled comfortably off persists (Holmes and Lindley, 1989). The typical patient attending a psychotherapy department may well be between 20 and 40, white, of above average educational achievements, with middle-class aspirations or connections. In themselves, these demographic features are unexceptionable. Perhaps there is more motivation and opportunity for change in younger patients; and since most psychotherapies depend on putting feelings into words they are likely to appeal more to the educated and aspirant. There has been a gradual, but still too hesitant, recognition by psychotherapists that they are not reaching disadvantaged groups. If publicly funded psychotherapy is to have a future there will need to be increasing attempts to cater for the psychotherapeutic needs of those suffering from major mental illness and their carers; the elderly; members of ethnic minorities; the unemployed; the poor; and those living in isolated communities such as large housing estates or in rural areas. Urgent efforts must be made to train those who are working in these communities in psychotherapeutic skills, and also to learn from such workers about how psychotherapeutic techniques can be modified and adapted to a less rarified environment. An integrative, broad-based, nondogmatic approach is needed, without abandoning the essential psycho-therapeutic requirements of a secure, holding environment and a recognition of the role of the unconscious as a reservoir of creativity and energy, but also defence, destructiveness and perversion (Holmes, 1996).

Gender and power: the politics of the psyche

Women's health, including mental health, has been a major social issue over the past two decades. Feminist psychoanalysts have criticized Freudian patriarchy, while accepting that psychoanalysis provides a language for discussing the ways in which a patriarchal society inscribes itself on the female psyche. Psychotherapy has the potential to articulate and perhaps redress feelings of powerlessness and suppressed anger within the individual, the family and in society at large. The issue is complex, since to the extent that psychotherapy is concerned with infantile feelings, *all* will have feelings of powerlessness in relation to adults. This 'necessary weakness' has to be distinguished from socially constructed powerlessness which results from the abuse of adult and/or patriarchal power.

Within a patriarchal society, caring is 'women's work'. The upsurge of interest in psychotherapy and counselling, while not confined to women, is statistically much more prevalent among females. This in turn has been accompanied by a focus on women clients, sometimes explicitly to the exclusion of men. It is becoming increasingly clear that there is a similar need to focus on men's health, especially psychological health. There has been an epidemic of suicide among young men over the past twenty years, many of whom have had no contact with psychiatric or any other helping agency. How to reach them remains a challenge for public health and social psychiatry. In-patient psychiatric units are increasingly dominated by psychotic men, who, despite the polemic of community care, cannot adequately be contained outside hospital. A common theme seems to be the pressure to achieve sexual maturity (at an emotional rather than a physical level) and their failure to do so, with breakdowns in which fears of inadequacy, homosexual panic, regressive demandingness and at times violence towards their mothers are prominent. Often brought up with weak or absent fathers, this constellation cannot be understood in classical Oedipal terms, but seems based on an infantile fear of the overwhelming power of the mother, reactivated in young adulthood when faced with the possibility of a real relationship with a woman and the lack of identification with a potent father. These emotional problems are often exacerbated by difficulties in finding work in an economy in which unemployment, especially for the unskilled, is endemic.

Working psychotherapeutically with men married to women who are often much more emotionally expressive than they are, highlights the conflict that many men in our society experience. In order to function at work they need to suppress feelings, but their partners expect and demand intimacy and affective liveliness at home. Soldiers, offshore oil-workers, long-distance drivers and salesmen, who travel away from home and who habitually deal with the pain of separation and the difficulties of re-entry into families by repressing feelings of grief and loneliness, are particularly vulnerable. They are expected to be emotionally available by wives who are themselves often cut off from traditional intimacy and whose hunger for closeness focuses more and more on their spouses as the strength of traditional family and social networks diminishes. The result of these pressures is often domestic violence and a split-off sexuality in the form of affairs, sexual perversions or sexual abuse.

Trauma as an organizing principle for psychotherapeutic work

Psychotherapists can be divided into those who emphasize the impact of environmental failure in producing emotional difficulty, and those who stress the contribution of the inner world to neurosis and psychological breakdown. Freud belonged at different times to both camps. At first he viewed hysteria as a result of sexual seduction in childhood (rather as he saw the traumata of the Franco-Prussian war leading to battle neurosis), but he later came to think that it was fantasies of infantile seduction that were important and universal, rather than their reality. His early emphasis on and later abandonment of the 'seduction hypothesis' has led to attack from both sides: for betrayal of the large numbers of women who have in reality been sexually abused (although this usually occurs much later in childhood than infancy), and for fostering the idea that abuse lies at the bottom of all emotional disorder and therefore for the creation of 'false memory syndrome'. A violent controversy has broken out over the reality or otherwise of the emergence of memories of abuse in psychotherapy, with ethical, clinical and legal consequences. The next few years should see a more balanced position emerge, acknowledging that 'memories' can be artefacts, especially in the intense atmosphere of a psychotherapeutic relationship, but that such 'false memories' are rare, and that the majority of people who have been abused do remember it, albeit in a split-off or distorted way.

The environment versus inner world debate continued throughout the post-Freudian period. Authors like Bowlby, Winnicott and Kohut emphasized environmental failure as a determinant of neurosis, seeing the therapists' role as providing corrective, non-traumatic counterbalancing experience; while in a curious alliance Kleinian and cognitive theorists consider the inner world with its distorted perceptions as the key issue, viewing the therapists' role as one of correcting misperceptions through interpretation or instruction.

The past two decades have seen an increasing awareness among psychotherapists of the impact and sequelae of individual and group trauma, and this is likely to continue into the millennium. The psychological needs of the survivors of disasters is beginning to be recognized (Garland, 1991); so too is the prevalence of the sexual abuse of children and its long-term consequences for mental health. The recognition of post traumatic stress disorder as a psychiatric entity, and its increasing invocation as a basis for compensation claims, is one manifestation of this awareness. Psychosis itself can be considered as a trauma, needing psychotherapeutic skills alongside pharmacological skills, to help its victims and their families cope with its impact.

The next few years will see a continuation of this emphasis on the impact of real trauma, but also pay increasing attention to its effects on the inner world: thus bringing together the two tacks of psychological thought. When the external world fails so decisively as it does when a vessel drowns its passengers or a parent abuses a child, the survivor will initially (and sometimes permanently) be unable to trust the environment which has let him down. External failure will be mirrored in his inner world which 'contains' the memories of the trauma but also internal attachment figures now felt to be unavailable or irremediably unreliable. Excessive use is made in this situation of projective identification as a defence. Feelings of abandonment and hatred engendered by the trauma, so overwhelming that they cannot be contained, are split off and projected into the environment which is then experienced as hostile and unsafe. A fragmented individual thus faces a fragmented and persecutory world. His fantasies confirm and reinforce his traumatic experience. The traumatized individual sees the world as chaotic and traumatizing and maintains a partial sanity by doing so. Clinical examples of this process are to be found in borderline patients who show unstable mood states, self-loathing, tendency to split, need to seek help and then be unable to use it, to idealize and to feel persecuted, and whose childhood is so often characterized by the traumata of confusion, abandonment and sexual abuse.

In working with traumatized and borderline patients, psychotherapists are beginning to recognize some of the steps needed if some hope for the future is to be found. The first – and often it is not possible to get much further than this – is the full recognition of the extent of the damage, its disclosure and articulation. Next comes the need to deal with the repressed affect associated with the trauma: the rage, fear and guilt. Then – and this is the most difficult part – coming to understand the long-reaching effects of the trauma: how the mental mechanisms used to deal with it can perpetuate the trauma and continue to influence and distort current relationships, including those with the therapist or therapeutic institution. Difficulty arises because the therapist cannot distance himself from the process, but will inevitably be caught up in it himself, be experienced by the patient as unreliable or even traumatizing. This is equally true at an institutional level of hospitals and other psychiatric units that try to work with these patients. Finally there is the possibility of reparation, of making good the damage done both to and by the traumatized individual, the overcoming of guilt and the finding, if not of forgiveness, then at least of acceptance. There is no short cut to reparation and attempts to find one may merely lead to further denial and disillusionment.

In working with traumatized patients a balance has to be struck between firmness and concern, between limit-setting and loving kindness, aiming to produce a safe container which can survive the disappointments and attacks it will inevitably provoke, and within which growth can take place. At present there are two distinct approaches to working with traumatized patients. The analytic approach emphasizes the impact of trauma on the transference, and the inevitable breaks, mistrust, idealization, suppressed rage and seductiveness that characterize the therapeutic relationship with such individuals. The cognitive-behavioural approach adopts a supportive 'debriefing' model in which the traumatic event is seen as a phobic object towards which the sufferer needs to be desensitized. This means a much more directive stance in which the patient is asked to rehearse traumatic memories so that they are no longer so painful, to use distraction techniques to avoid intrusive thoughts, to express anger via writing letters to perpetrators, and so on. A major task for the next decade is to identify which patients are most suitable for which approach, and to develop integrative paradigms that cull the best from both methods. For the more damaged, less psychologically minded, patients sessions can be usefully divided into three phases. Initially attention is paid to the issues of the moment, then follows a period of directive work, moving finally to a more free-flowing psychoanalytic phase in which underlying themes are linked to present-moment tasks – hard work for a therapist who has to be able simultaneously to be active and to monitor her activity from a psycho-dynamic perspective.

In the longer term

Historical change takes place dialectically: conflicts arise, are resolved, only to be replaced by new theses and antitheses. How will psychotherapy look fifty years from now? An imponderable question perhaps, but some of the battle lines are clear. Certainly the need for psychotherapeutic help will not have disappeared, indeed if present trends remain, psychological distress and confusion may well have increased. Psychotherapy as a response to such distress will continue to compete on the one hand with the huge advances in the understanding of the brain that will inevitably take place in the next half century, and on the other with a turn towards religion as a solution to people's ills.

The tension between tradition and innovation within psychotherapy will also continue. New leaders will appear, and the conflict between those who follow them and the iconoclasts will not abate. Psychotherapy as a profession has a particular tendency to look to the past and to venerate its elders. Whether this will seem an anachronism, or as a core value that differentiates it from the increasing pace of change that surrounds it, remains to be seen. Another tension which may have been resolved concerns psychotherapy as welfare: either it will have been incorporated into a welfare/health system that recognizes every citizen's right to psychological help when needed, or it will have been hived off as a preserve of the rich and privileged. Another key issue will be the role of psychodynamic therapy *vis-à-vis* cognitive-behavioural therapies. Here a much clearer trend is emerging and it seems likely that there will be increasing convergence between the two camps (Albinez and Holmes, 1996). The academic status of psychotherapy is another issue that will have been resolved over the next few decades, or sooner. Most psychotherapy trainings will be university-based, emerging finally from the cottage industries that they now are. That in turn will allow a much cooler appraisal of the status of psychoanalysis as a discipline that is to some extent *sui generis*, neither science nor pseudoscience, nor relegated to the arcane world of hermeneutics and postmodernist (or postpostmodernist) discourse. It will be seen as making a fundamental contribution to the theory and practice of human interaction at the emotional and interpersonal level.

Psychotherapy is a necessary counterweight to the dominant values of contemporary society: industrialization, commercialization, urbanization, the pre-eminence of science. At the same time, especially as it becomes professionalized, it partakes of those values. Thus research is essential if psychotherapy is to maintain credibility, and to compete successfully with physical methods of treatment for mental distress. But research often seems to miss the very heart of psychotherapy: the human encounter. Struggling with that tension may be the greatest challenge for the decades to come. More and more people are attracted to psychotherapy, both as clients and practitioners. It seems a good and even pleasant activity. But how can such an apparently unproductive activity be justified? Perhaps psychotherapy earns its right to exist through its capacity to look fearlessly at the dark side of humans, the unsettled society we have produced, and the traumas they entail.

Concern for the environment has become one of the major political and social themes for the coming century. Here the psychological processes associated with trauma can be observed at a social and political level. The earth itself is traumatized. Pollution is based on splitting: unwanted products are expelled into the environment – the atmosphere, the seas, the rivers, Third World countries – at first disowned, later experienced as persecutory. The earth can be seen as a living mother, spoiled, dying even, through the hostile projections of her omnipotent and greedy inhabitants. The green movement is an attempt at therapy and reparation: helping the community to face up to the cycle of trauma in which it is trapped.

There are some encouraging signs that, despite an increasing capacity for destruction and disaster, the world community can move, in Bion's (1962) terms, from a 'fight-flight' group to a 'pairing' group. The shape of the millennium may depend on whether it can transform itself into a work group. If the 'butterfly effect' is to be believed, the increasing importance of psychotherapy, both as an art and a technology, not just in medicine and psychiatry, but also in commerce and government, may be a vital factor in that transformation.

References

Albinez, A. and Holmes, J. (in press) Psychotherapy integration: implications for psychiatry, *British Journal of Psychiatry.*

Bateman, A. and Holmes, J. (1995) *Introduction to Psychoanalysis: Contemporary Theory and Practice.* London: Routledge.

Bateson, G. (1973) *Steps to an Ecology of Mind.* London: Paladin.

Beitman, B. (1989) The movement towards integrating the psychotherapies; an overview, in J. Norcross and M. Goldfried (eds), *Psychotherapy Integration.* New York: Basic Books.

Bion, W. (1962) *Learning from Experience.* London: Heinemann.

Bowlby, J. (1979) *The Making and Breaking of Affectional Bonds.* London: Tavistock.

Cox, M. and Thielgard, A. (1987) *Mutative Metaphors in Psychotherapy.* London: Tavistock.

Fonagy, P., Steele, M., Steele, H., Leigh, T., Kennedy, R. and Mattoon, G. (1995) Attachment, the reflective self, and borderline states; the predictive specificity of the adult attachment interview and pathological emotional development, in S. Goldberg, R. Muir and J. Kerr (eds), *Attachment Theory: Social, Developmental and Clinical Perspectives.* New York: Academic Press.

Freud, S. (1919) Lines of advance in psychoanalytic therapy, *Standard Edition 17.* London: Hogarth.

Freud, S. (1937) Psychoanalysis terminable and interminable, *Standard Edition 23.* London: Hogarth.

Garfield, S. and Bergin, A. (1994) Introduction and historical overview, in A. Bergin and S. Garfield (eds), *Handbook of Psychotherapy and Behaviour Change.* Chichester: Wiley.

Garland, C. (1991) Working with survivors: external disasters and the internal world, in J. Holmes (ed.), *A Textbook of Psychotherapy in Psychiatric Practice.* Edinburgh: Churchill Livingstone.

Gleick, J. (1988) *Chaos: Making a new Science.* London: Penguin.

Goldberg, S., Muir, R. and Kerr, J. (1995) *Attachment Theory: Social, Historical and Clinical Perspectives.* New York: Analytic Press.

Holmes, J. (1993) *John Bowlby and Attachment Theory.* London: Routledge.

Holmes, J. (1996) *Attachment, Intimacy, Autonomy: Using Attachment Ideas in Adult Psychotherapy.* New York: Jason Aronson.

Holmes, J. and Lindley, R. (1989) *The Values of Psychotherapy.* Oxford: Oxford University Press. New edn (1997), London: Karnac Books.

Langs, R. and Badalamenti (1994) A formal science for psychoanalysis, *British Journal of Psychotherapy,* 11: 92–104.

Linehan, M. (1993) *Cognitive Behavioural Treatment of Borderline Personality Disorder.* New York: Guilford Press.

Main, M. (1995) Recent studies in attachment: overview with selected implications for clinical work, in S. Goldberg, R. Muir and J. Kerr (eds), *Attachment Theory: Social, Developmental and Clinical Perspectives.* New York: Academic Press.

Margison, F. (1991) Learning to listen, in J. Holmes (ed.), *A Textbook of Psychotherapy in Psychiatric Practice.* Edinburgh: Churchill Livingstone.

Pedder, J. (1990) Lines of advance in psychoanalytic psychotherapy, *Psychoanalytic Psychotherapy,* 4: 201–17.

Pines, M. (1991) A history of psychodynamic psychiatry in Britain, in J. Holmes (ed.), *A Textbook of Psychotherapy in Psychiatric Practice.* Edinburgh: Churchill Livingstone.

Prochaska, J. and DiClemente, C. (1992) The transtheoretical approach, in J. Norcross and M. Goldfried (eds), *Handbook of Psychotherapy Integration.* New York: Basic Books.

Ryle, A. (1995) *Cognitive Analytic Therapy: Developments in Theory and Practice.* Chichester: Wiley.

Slavin, B. and Kriegman, M. (1992) *The Adaptive Design of the Human Psyche.* New York: Basic Books.

Sulloway, F. (1979) *Freud: Biologist of the Mind.* New York: Basic Books.

Teasdale, J., Segal, Z. and Williams, M. (1996) How does cognitive therapy prevent depressive relapse and why should attentional control (mindfulness) training help? *Behavioural Research and Therapy,* 33: 25–30.

Thoma, H. and Kachele, H. (1986) *Psychoanalytic Practice.* London: Springer Verlag.

West, M. (1990) *The Psychology of Meditation.* Oxford: Oxford University Press.

Williams, R. (1985) *Towards 2000.* London: Penguin.

Wolff, H. (1971) The therapeutic and developmental functions of psychotherapy, *British Journal of Medical Psychology,* 44: 117–39.

3

Then, Now, and Tomorrow

Douglas Hooper

To make some sense of the counselling and psychotherapy scene of today, it is important to go back a little or even quite a lot! Yet we should not allow ourselves to be held to ransom by the past in this field, because the breaks in practice have almost all arisen when a person or a group went outside the current *zeitgeist* and proposed a novel way forward. Freud was initially a minority of one.

But first, a quick run-down on the last two hundred years. Or perhaps five hundred. The shift in the value placed on the individual life and its ability to pursue personal objectives must surely have started the day after Martin Luther nailed his 95 theses to the door of Wittenburg Castle in which he demanded the right for the individual soul to communicate directly with God (amongst many other things). The news spread like wildfire – not an inapposite metaphor for those times – and became the Reformation of Europe. Luther was not unused to debate and discussion about fundamental issues since he was at this time Professor of Philosophy at Wittenburg, but his theses were not mere disputation. They were a direct challenge to the right of authorities to define human nature.

He was not the only one of course. Many others like Erasmus and Francis Bacon used the new-found intellectual freedoms to widen the idea of the 'exploratory person' able to engage directly with the world of experience and in Bacon's case to investigate it empirically. In his celebrated essay *Novum Organum* [1620] Bacon (1960) wrote:

> Man, being the servant and interpreter of nature, can do and understand so much, and so much only, as he has observed in fact or in thought of the course of nature. (p. 39)

Such ideas paved the way for the exploration of the natural world and the great theories which were to accompany it. But our particular engagement with Bacon does not stop there. He was one of the first professionals in the field of counselling because in one of his essays he wrote:

> The greatest trust between man and man is the trust of giving counsel for in other confidences men commit the parts of life, their land, their goods, their child, their credit, some particular affair but to such as they make their counsellors they commit the whole. (Bacon, 1895, p. 126)

Bacon was not, of course, thinking of the common man when he wrote this but of men of state and position. It was to be three centuries at least before the idea of the independent counsellor emerged. Following this renaissance, it looked for a time as if the period called the 'enlightenment' would focus on the psychological development of the individual and the small group. However, this was not to be. The natural world still remained undiscovered both in the local countryside and across the seas and the world of ideas was commonly political and philosophical. Society remained strictly stratified without an intervening professional middle class which was to come rather later. For ordinary people, the rise of Methodism, with a direct appeal to both self-help and mutual association, was able to provide much social and personal care never available from the parish priest.

What the ideas of the enlightenment did bring was a changed view of what we now call mental illness. Institutions for the insane were created in which the atmosphere did become enlightened. This was the era of what was called 'moral treatment' and in which the sufferers were engaged by their attendants in simple forms of counselling aimed at raising morale and self-esteem. These methods spread quite widely during the last quarter of the eighteenth and the first quarter of the nineteenth century, but were swept away by the creation and then the adoption of lunatic asylums by the local authorities of the day. The Victorian authorities looked for economy of operation for which personal care of a psychological kind was simply too expensive.

At the same time the doctors who came to control the institutions were too fascinated with the rapidly developing biological approaches in medicine to attend to the social or the psychological. In addition the stigma of the asylum was so great that people with what we now think of as serious non-psychotic psychological disturbance would never consult the appropriate specialist for fear of being regarded as mad.

But the seeds of change sown much earlier were now having a greater impact in the broader society. The industrialization of work during the nineteenth century led both to the rise of the city and the emergence of a strong middle class of increasingly professional people. This process was intertwined with the rapid increase in educational provision accompanied by the emergence of mass media of all kinds which enabled the newly literate to be informed about the contemporary world. In this newly literate community people were informed not only about events. The popular writers of the day used the medium of the novel in which the emphasis was increasingly on the psychological and intimate social worlds of characters created by writers like Dickens or George Eliot. In most cases the novelists describe the psychological help which their characters needed being provided by an intimate of the individual, often a 'friend' or benefactor and rarely any kind of professional like doctor, lawyer, or priest.

There was no one at hand in these new urban societies obviously fitted to give a helping psychological hand to those casualties of the contemporary world who needed it. Halmos (1965), in discussing the rise of counselling, also believes that the 'critical westerner', as he calls him, rejected the 'betterment' solutions offered by political theorists on the grounds that the reform which was offered would not meet his psychological needs. Further, both the political and social theorists of the turn of the century were (he believed) preoccupied with power, freedom, or the general social edifice expressed in terms of social class or similar concepts. Finally the rise and rise of the large organization meant that people were less and less able to find the personal meaning which they sought for their lives.

The emergence of the counsellor therapist

It seems, then, that there was a vacant professional role filled by no contemporary practitioner who was trusted to meet the psychological needs of modern men and women. Into this role stepped the very unlikely figure of Freud. A man quintessentially of the late nineteenth century, he built upon the paradigm shift already accomplished by Darwin. He was also ready to champion the cause of dealing with the neurotic misery and unhappiness of his day, which the alienist/psychiatrists were not prepared to acknowledge. He was a most unlikely figure. North (1972) describes him as socially and politically authoritarian, elitist, and conservative, and yet he laid claim to a system which (he proposed) would liberate people from the imprisoning aspects of their psyche.

Because he absorbed the anthropology of his day, he believed that the phenomena which he observed in his largely upper-class clientele were universal in human experience, and that in particular the psychological development of individuals, although erratic, followed a similar course. In particular, the conflict and struggle between child and parents in association with and reflecting the inner psychic struggle led to personality structure which would determine the rest of psychological life.

For counselling and psychotherapy, the rest is history in the sense that what Freud was at great pains to demonstrate was that there were ways in which psychological disorder could be understood *and* he thought remedied by using the doctor/patient and then the therapist/sufferer context for the purpose. In addition he did not try to subsume these activities under a more general and inarticulate framework such as that frequently used by spiritual advisers. Rather by using the scientific *zeitgeist* of his era, he recorded the phenomena he was dealing with and then tried to make coherent theoretical sense of both his observations *and* his interventions. However, his methods of training which he and particularly his followers developed could not and would not meet the needs of people which we have identified in the earlier paragraph. The economics of psycho-analytically derived 'treatment' were crazy, but the ideas behind the analytic approach became widespread and in particular were separated out from the medical model.

The surge in the availability of the psychological methods for psychological disturbance of ordinary people probably began with Rogers (1942) and those associated with him because he believed that very extended treatment periods were not necessarily required for effective psychological change. In addition, the methods he developed were more easily applied in a wider variety of settings than was the case with the psychoanalytically derived procedures.

From the earliest of his writings Rogers also emphasized the vital place which research must play in understanding the processes involved in psychotherapeutic activities. This introduction from the more restricted world of academic psychology has also remained a powerful influence in current practice. It, too, marked a sharp break from the Freudian tradition in which research was largely confined to complex theoretical argument or extremely detailed case study.

By the mid-1950s this more heterogeneous approach to counselling and therapy was ready to take off, first within the USA and then within a decade in the UK. The National Marriage Guidance Council was the first organization to train counsellors in any numbers and at that stage was much influenced by a variety of social work practice emanating from schools of social work in the USA known as social case work. Although this work title was rapidly dropped in favour of 'counselling', the concept of the socially active practitioner was (and still is) a potent conceptual idea (Tyndall, 1993). However this agency trained its workers by in-house methods and thus possibly retarded the growth of counselling training for the wider world.

In the collegiate world, the educationists began to recognize the potential value of counselling and set about creating training programmes which were not institutionally bound like marriage counselling. During the ensuing three decades (from 1960 onwards), training programmes spanning the whole gamut of theoretical approaches have come into being, offering both special and generic training to many hundreds of students each year to service both the voluntary and the paid professional demand for the work, much of which has been in the private sector. It is this proliferation of training and practice which led to the quite remarkable output of books, journals, and conferences and to which Windy Dryden has contributed very significantly.

The programme

By the end of the century, then, the psychotherapy business has escalated to the point that some have now called it an 'industry' with many thousands of practitioners drawn from a wide variety of educational and professional backgrounds offering this service to probably hundreds of thousands of people. To take one example, recent estimates of counselling availability in primary health care practice suggest that one third of all

General Practices now have some kind of practice counsellor. In this area alone that must indicate between 400 and 500 thousand interviews each year!

To review the large programme of help now being offered, it should prove helpful to identify the core activities. But where to begin? A useful place is to turn to one of the earliest writers in the three-decade development who was also looking for the concepts of practice and philosophy lying underneath the variety of approaches available. The seminal book by Jerome Frank (1961) not only reviews the bulk of the research available at the time but also looks at the historical roots of practice, especially those of 'healers' in a religious context. Given his own background as a North American psychiatrist, he also offers a surprisingly sharp critique of the psychoanalytic approach to the training and (he believes) indoctrination of their candidates. He argues that the title of 'candidate' for the trainee analyst is a revealing one!

He writes from a medical context and therefore the language is couched in those terms but his definition of psychotherapy easily applies to other settings and is also economical. He argues that distressed people are subject to all kinds of what he calls 'persuasion' and that we have to reserve those types of influence for the title of psychotherapy which are characterized by:

1. a trained, socially sanctioned healer, whose healing powers are accepted by the sufferer and by his social group or an important segment of it
2. a sufferer who seeks relief from the healer
3. a circumscribed, more or less structured series of contacts between the healer and the sufferer, through which the healer, often with the aid of a group, tries to produce certain changes in the sufferer's emotional state, attitudes, and behaviour. All concerned believe these changes will help him. Although physical and chemical adjuncts may be used, the healing influence is primarily exercised by words, acts and rituals in which sufferer, healer, and – if there is one – group, participate jointly. (Frank, 1961, p. 2)

The word 'healer' may surprise but the root of the word is 'whole' and the healer is therefore one who enables wholeness. Crucially the definition is wide-ranging and emphasizes training, mutuality (the therapeutic alliance), societal sanction, special context and place, and finally goals of change which are emotional, cognitive and behavioural.

These six factors are still those which have recurred as many other writers try to define the activity of psychotherapy/counselling, although a common seventh factor has emerged which is that the healer 'respects' the world of the client/sufferer. This additional quality has specifically arisen from the theory and practice of practitioners in the humanistic frame and tradition because it was clearly lacking in the other frameworks.

The problems in offering this framework occur when specific practitioners get into the act and try to appropriate various parts of the task to themselves alone as members of one or other particular guild of practice.

Equally they may define one of the characteristics as belonging exclusively to their guild, and this can just as easily be a matter of the practitioner's title as it is of the really substantive matters. In a recent publication, for example (James and Palmer, 1996) a number of writers of the fourteen chapters dance on the head of the proverbial pin trying to make meaningful distinctions between counselling, psychotherapy, clinical psychology, and (the newest addition to the stable) counselling psychology. Probably the most telling of these contributions is that by James and Palmer (1996) discussing in what ways these role ascriptions can actually prevent people from gaining access to the therapeutic help they need. He does not have an easy solution but provides some suggestions about how the guilds should try and put their houses in some order. In the same volume, both Bond (1996) and Dryden (1996) also argue trenchantly for ignoring the issues, having decided that they are of no substantial consequence. Both writers believe that there are no meaningful differences between the titles – and thus by implication in the activities performed by each group. Bond suggests amusingly that where there are real differences in job title they have real effects; it is not much use calling for a bricklayer if the problem is a burst pipe. No such action differences can be found within the psychological therapists, because the universe of discourse about the problem will be the same. All of these groups of practitioners have developed their patterns of practice within this broad pattern even though clinical behaviour has varied considerably.

Returning to the client, what appears to have happened is that far more people are now willing to define themselves as 'sufferers' (to use Frank's terminology) over recent decades, and that the provision of care has developed accordingly, mushrooming in the last decade. Frank describes the distress and disability experienced by the individual as 'demoralization', which he defines as a sense of failure or of powerlessness to affect oneself and one's environment, and hence the decision to consult a practitioner who may have the means to combat these states. Within the statement above, 'the means' will include all the techniques and theories which any given practitioner may have and these have been subject to extensive research. Since Frank's original publication in 1961 a wealth of research has also accumulated to discover the critical elements of the therapeutic process and their efficacy in bringing the sufferer or client to a better state of being. Thus far no particular means has been shown to be superior to any other, although there is evidence that if the therapist makes stable treatment arrangements and adheres to a specific treatment model, then the results are likely to be better (Orlinski et al., 1994). This is an interesting paradox, but perhaps relates strongly to the sufferer's need for re-moralization. The practitioner who creates a safe and predictable therapeutic environment and then offers techniques which are coherent with a world view of the problem is surely likely to enhance the damaged individual – providing of course that the positive changes are both perceived and experienced by the client.

Practice and research

At present, then, we have a substantial body of training and practice in the UK – undoubtedly of variable quality – matched by a substantial body of research, although the research mostly derives from the USA. The research findings have by no means been routinely translated into practice which is a major issue for the tutors and trainers of the next decade. All too frequently the counselling teacher has also been the experienced practitioner but with no requirement that they are knowledgeable about, let alone engaged in, research. We shall return to this issue later in the chapter, but first there is a need to consider the position which research has currently reached.

In a concise yet wide-ranging review Barkham (1996) has evaluated the research position in counselling and psychotherapy from his position as one of the leading research figures in the UK. One of the most interesting aspects of the review is his description of the temporal sequence of research over the three decades – the lifetime of a single researcher! He describes these as 'generations' of research and in each of the three generations he suggests that researchers have been preoccupied with a particular issue which he states as a question.

The first generation of research, then, tried to answer the question 'Is psychotherapy effective?' which he also calls the outcome issue. The second generation dealt with the question 'Which psychotherapy is more effective?', and the ensuing (and current) generation of research is asking 'How can we make treatments more cost-effective?'. In addition each generation also tried to tease out aspects of the associated therapeutic process and here the associated questions were (in order): 'Are there objective methods for process evaluation?', 'What process components are related to outcome?', 'How does change occur?'.

The title of his chapter also indicates that the earlier modes of research – largely developed within the traditional mode of quantitative science – have now been joined and challenged by a qualitative research stream which asks similar questions but uses a different methodology. Those who support this research approach argue that particularly in counselling and psychotherapy research (but not only there) qualitative methods respect the intrinsic nature of the activity and of the phenomena in a way that the other research does not. And as in psychotherapy theory, so here there are also calls for pluralism of approach.

To return to Barkham: in stating them, the questions appear to be straightforward and, suitably posed, should yield relatively clear answers. This did not prove to be the case because what did become clear is that the deceptively simple act of counselling and therapy is an extremely complicated human transaction which required many research sub-areas to be developed in order to answer the prime question. Not surprisingly too, the practitioners did not wait for the answers but continued to develop their theory and skills which were increasingly in demand regardless of the proof of efficacy of the methods.

Now, however, we have some reasonably firm answers to aspects of the three areas of questioning which should form the basis for the future evolution of practice. These should clearly be the framework for the development of practice and practice learning, even though in the context of a more wide-ranging theory. It has always seemed difficult for personal service practitioners to incorporate and use research in the face-to-face settings and we shall return to this matter shortly. But first it is important to try to set down the main findings of the very extensive research output.

The first 'generation' questions can be firmly answered. Yes, counselling and therapy are more effective than doing nothing or using some form of placebo procedure, and yes, the process can be reliably measured. Next, the answer to the second generation questions is no, there is no firm evidence that any one method is more effective than any other, although for some problems cognitive/behavioural therapy has a fairly small advantage over other techniques. The offering of empathy, warmth, and genuineness by the practitioner was the subject of most process research during this period – based on the theoretical concepts of Rogers. The answer to our next question, then, is that there is no unequivocal evidence that these characteristics link to better outcome. But the findings appeared to be too general and at least lead to more closely formulated questions in the next 'generation'.

The current generation is that of cost-effectiveness and change. What can be said here? First, in view of the lack of specificity of outcome linked to particular theory-based techniques a so-called integrated approach might be superior. Thus far this has not been shown to be the case. Next, then, is the question of the efficacy of the length of the counselling package. This becomes especially important with the rise of theories of brief therapy and the quest for economic use of resources. Unsurprisingly perhaps the answer is that the greatest improvement happens in the shorter phase of a treatment process, but that further improvement *can* be achieved by longer programmes – at a cost. So what is the evidence on the final question of how change can be achieved? First a suitable patient meeting a skilled practitioner is related to outcome. First select your client! Next, the maintenance of a therapeutic bond or alliance is facilitating. Of the practitioner's manoeuvres, such as interpretation, reflection, or self-disclosure by the counsellor, those which are most appropriate for the specific client are the most powerful, but specific therapist procedures *per se* are not necessarily related to change. This suggests a nice balance between following closely the client's themes, and breaking into these with re-framing interventions which are consonant with the client's needs – even if unexpressed.

The importance of this research summary is based on its wide range. many of the dimensions are based on 'research on research' in which individual pieces of work are scrutinized and appraised so that the summation is much more powerful than any particular research study.

This means that those practitioners who use a specific study to support their viewpoint (which often happens) should now be regarded with considerable reserve.

Developing research-based practice

How then should we now proceed? There are substantial and complex research findings about almost every aspect of the practice of counselling and psychotherapy which must be distilled and understood by both practitioners and learners. Yet the demanding (and demanded) world of real-life practice requires personal commitment and focus which may seem inimical to the cool appraisal and application of this knowledge. All practitioners in personal service practice need to develop a strong professional identity which is initially derived from the ideology within which they are trained. That is no longer enough, but help is at hand!

Over recent years Schön (1987) together with colleagues has tackled the core issue of training people for professional practice. He believes that there must be a proper balance struck between what he describes as the technical rationality of the disciplines underlying professional activity, and professional artistry. He says that this artistry is a 'high-powered esoteric variant of the more familiar sorts of competence all of us exhibit every day in countless acts of . . . skilful performance' (1987, p. 22). Where the technical rationality has become disproportionately powerful he argues for a professional curriculum which emphasizes what he calls the indeterminate zones of practice in which there is often uncertainty, uniqueness, and value conflict. He could almost be describing the core of any counselling activity here! He believes that the research-based teaching has to be used by the practitioner in framing the practice problems which are presented to them, and he suggests that we give the title of coach to the teacher who works with the student.

I wish to argue here that teachers of counselling and psychotherapy are in a different place to that occupied by the teachers of law, medicine or engineering, in which technical rationality may well have become too powerful, to the detriment of practice-based learning and professional artistry. Often in psychotherapy the 'artistry' has been promoted to a position of supremacy and the fruits of research have been either benignly neglected or even denied. Schön is helpful here in distinguishing between a theory of action which is taught to the neophyte practitioner, and the theory-in-use which the individual uses in real-life situations. In our field, a great deal of research has actually centred on the theory-in-use and is therefore crucial to practice and should be the basis for discussion between what Schön calls the coach, and his/her student. This has been described by Schön as blending the art of practice with the art of research, but clearly this research can be both quantitative *and* qualitative and not simply the former, as argued by Scanlon and Baillie (1994) in their very thoughtful discussion of these issues.

This brings into focus the counselling and psychotherapy teacher and we can return to the critique which was offered earlier in the chapter. If we are not careful we shall commit the baby-and-the-bath-water error. That is, to reject *all* aspects of the technical/rational approach because it has been abused in the past by teachers who were very often *not* researchers. The three communities of teacher, researcher and practitioner are often too distinct whereas all three are essential to modern professional practice. Practice worlds of all kinds constantly need the cool research view which is not only cool but penetrating – sometimes uncomfortably so. This may appear to be inimical to the cooperative work which the learner needs to do with his/her ,oach in developing competent theories-in-use and the subsequent professional identity. But in fact it should infuse this process if the practitioner is to lay claim to being professional. Indeed Schön suggests that what marks professionals out is that they share a common body of explicit, more-or-less systematically organized knowledge. The professional coach/teacher, then, must be grounded both in this field of discourse *and* the confusions and muddle of practice. Neither alone will do. Over-emphasis on one produces the arid 'scientist' and on the other, the woolly 'mystique-monger'!

The 'then' and 'now' of the sufferer

After the excursion into training and research it is time to return to the object of the counselling and psychotherapy – the troubled person or family. Much earlier in the chapter we noted the dramatic rise of the demand for counselling in this particular era. Following Frank (1961) it is clear that the modern therapist is picking up a tradition of psychological help which is probably as old as society itself, in which men of religion were the chief practitioners. They mostly aimed to enable the person to return their mode of being and thinking to the dominant value life-style then in use. In contrast, the new clients were looking for judgement-free assistance in which they were able to understand and then reject or modify blocked behaviour, thought and feeling. Even if this activity was not culture-free (which it certainly was not), nevertheless the client was free from any authoritative view of how s/he should behave in explicit terms. This appears to have been a prime and emergent need in the second half of this century in which other remedies have been tried and failed.

The major changes at least in western society have been those of longevity (particularly of women); control of conception; diminishing amount of physical work and a much-increased requirement for cognitive and conceptual work; a degree of control of infectious disease with an associated rise in chronic and often incurable systemic disease; and finally a marked rise in disposable incomes (for those in work) with a disproportionate drop in cost of manufactured and similar goods.

Some have argued that this has led to a new 'person' – perhaps the postindustrial postmodernist psyche. Whether or not this has had an impact on individuals, within ordinary psychological structure there are still most ancient characteristics with which to face this new worlu. These were largely genetically honed in an environment which is very different from today's contemporary urban society. Consider the following:

1   *Homo sapiens*: between 1/200,000 years.
    With language and culture as follows:
    at least 135,000 years hunter/gatherer;
    about 12,000 years agriculturalist;
    about 200 years (maximum) industrialist;
    about 50 years global village.
2   *Homo erectus*: about 1.5 million years.
    Migratory, tool-using, with culture transmission. No language, but some cognitive structure.
3   *Homo habilis and australopithocenes*: about 2.5 million years.
    Bi-pedalist and therefore ranging (but not migratory). With social and family structure. No effective cognitive structure.

This outline structure is drawn from Donald's (1991) penetrating approach to the psychobiological origin of what he calls 'mind'. He presents a very wide range of evidence and from our point of view he uses the evidence to create a theory of the growth of cognitive structure linked to the biological anatomy of our forefathers and mothers.

The inference which we can draw from the tabular material set out above is that the prelinguistic cognitive structures are both very ancient and very developed and that the rate of acquisition of our modern psychological apparatus is exceedingly swift in view of our capacity for exploration, invention, and manipulation of extrapolated symbols. In psychobiological time, sequential structures were often step-like rather than continuous but then were developed and reinforced over dozens or hundreds of generations. Yet the modern person has moved from settled agriculture to an urban industrial and even postindustrial milieu in just about six!

Although Donald emphasizes cognitive structure and activity he also suggests that the more ancient structures are actually inclusive of emotional states particularly in what he calls mimetic culture and which he says is clearly evident in most human social interchanges and certainly in performing art forms.

Before, however, proceeding to discuss Donald's proposal in detail we need to present the cognitive stages/structures he is proposing. He states that the first humans functioned with what he calls 'episodic culture' which is immediate short-term and stimulus bound, but also includes the idea of concrete time-bound memory structures. These modes are found in our ape cousins as well as *Homo habilis*. What was added (and therefore distinctly human) was social and familial structure but that there is no evidence for additional cognitive complexity, at that stage.

The break came with *Homo erectus* who appears to have had the capacity for what Donald describes as mimesis. This Donald believes is a powerful psychological process – still very relevant to modern psychological experience – and clearly cognitive. His definition of this facility is:

> The ability to produce conscious, self-initiated, representational acts that are intentional but not linguistic . . . [and also] fundamentally different from . . . mimicry in that it involves the invention of intentional representations. (1991, p. 169)

We have already noted that this includes the representation of emotional states when these are nonlinguistic. He further believes that it was pre-linguistic for both neuroanatomical reasons but also in terms of cognitive function. He says that mimetic culture is slow-moving, ambiguous and restricted in subject matter. But most importantly it led to novel methods of social control and coordination but without proper language as the medium of expression.

The break into language – after many millennia of mimesis alone – came with the ability to articulate in complex ways which Donald argues led early on to the development of mythical thought. He describes the myth as the fundamental integrative mind tool which then permeated and regulated daily life of *Homo sapiens* because the myths modelled the entire human universe. The power of myth continues into our own era and not only in remote tribal culture. The final break was away from spoken language and narrative styles of thought to 'theoretic' culture which depends upon symbol and is capable of being stored away from the individual or collective mind.

Donald proposes that three crucial functions were missing throughout the long millennia of oral-mythic culture. These were graphic invention; external memory; and theory construction. Visual images are about 40,000 years old, but writing (which is far more flexible at conveying facts and ideas) is a mere 6000 years old. Biological memory became increasingly inadequate for human living, as external symbolic storage systems were developed. So human memory became increasingly focused on external memory for gaining access to, and then locating, the right material in these systems, although the problem of daily living remained trapped, as it were, in the biological system.

Donald describes the modern mind as the inheritor of all of these methods of understanding and exploring human experiences. He says:

> Our modern minds are thus hybridizations, highly plastic combinations of all the previous elements in human cognitive evolution . . . Now we are mythic, now

we are theoretic and now we hearken back to the episodic roots of experience . . . and at times we slip into the personae of our old narrative selves pretending that nothing has changed. But everything has changed. (1991, p. 356)

He asserts that with the invention of the digital computer all forms of human experience are now refinable and expandable. Paradoxically this then presents people with *greater* possibilities of individuation – and hence probably overwhelming choices of modes of being.

Individuation and therapeutic response

Individuation has been one of the dominant issues in recent sociological attempts to understand the situation of both individuals and individuals in intimate relationships in modern society. Donald clearly argues that our ancient and deeply embedded structures of mind have to be taken into account in an experiential world of great change and impact.

Giddens (1991) refutes the argument that counselling and therapy are simply adjuncts to the confused modern life. He takes further the issues raised by Donald in his definition of the modern mind above, and proposes that the postindustrial individual is certainly engaged in self-reflexive states connected to the sociotechnical changes of our era. He describes the place of counselling and psychotherapy in these terms:

Therapy is an expert system deeply implicated in the reflexive project of the self [as] . . . a methodology of life-planning . . . It participates in that mixture of opportunities and risks characteristic of the late modern order. (1991, p. 180)

But perhaps the most important aspect of the work of Giddens and others is that the activity of counselling/therapy is consonant with our current state, and not simply a response to contemporary problems. It is an activity in which practitioners and patients/clients are finding ways of dealing with the issues which arise from living in the modern world in which 'external symbolic storage systems' (to use Donald's terminology) impinge on consciousness to a greater and greater degree.

From 'then' and 'now' to where?

My argument, then, is that many factors have led to the rise of the counsellor and his/her client. They appear to be the product of the twentieth century but are much older. This century has seen the formulation of a technology which can (hopefully) help resolve the conflicts, and restore wholeness to the broken-down.

However, the theories upon which practice are based do not take sufficient account of the fact that individual (and small group) experience will be presented by a sufferer in a rapidly shifting series of modes outlined by Donald. Some of these seem similar to the primary processes described by Freud early in his psychoanalytic theory, but they go beyond that description. It would even be tempting to some psychoanalytic theorists to use part of this psychobiology to support some aspects of those theories. But this is to suggest that pre-existing theories of human experience and behaviour are more important than theories based on new experience and new evidence. Rather, the stance of Donald, Giddens and others should lead to a radical review of the response by the counsellors to the emergent human nature of the twenty-first century person.

Some of the grander theories of therapeutic endeavour have believed that the transactions in counselling and therapy produce once-and-for-all life change. But it seems more accurate from the clinical research to assume that these transactions, however important, are episodes of a particular kind in a human life. The therapeutic episodes are subsumed into much broader and longer tracts of experience which form the life trajectory of individuals.

Provided that we can take for granted the overall commitment to the betterment of the community, then the therapeutic collegium must respond to the effective and efficient management of this episodic practice work. The priority must surely be to abandon much of the silliness.

Prominent here is the insistence upon professional labels. The important issues are not professionally what one is called, but whether one is competently trained, subject to effective monitoring, and accepting a code of professional behaviour which is client-centred.

Next is the importance of recognizing that 'counselling' and 'psycho-therapy' are essentially the same activity, using very similar methods of approach to human problems. The delivery of the service may be different, and the organization of the service may vary between the two as well. We need to retain aspects of these which are client-centred (such as good access, economic availability, etc.) and allow other differences to wither on the vine. There is a good case for arguing for the creation of a super-ordinate body which would negotiate new structures for the common purpose.

Then there is the silliness of the doctrine. In all areas of human activity where theories are important, the theory is valuable when it coherently orders some aspect of the world. When it ceases to do this, then it is often altered or abandoned in favour of an alternative theory. In the field of counselling and therapy theory, this has not generally been the case. Proponents of a given theory believe that the phenomena they observe as the therapeutic activity unfolds are only available because of teachings based on the theory, and only understandable within that theory. All too often explanations of therapeutic activity fall back on statements of belief about the phenomena which are (by definition) doctrinaire.

The problem with doctrine is two-fold. First, it does seem from the research evidence very important that a counsellor conveys to the client that s/he 'knows what she is doing'. This sense of firm identity seems linked to a coherent view of human behaviour which is generally drawn from a particular theoretical stance at present. But it is probably the firm assurance that the counsellor/therapist offers (regardless of the source) which is the element for change. Troubled people respond to structure offered by a practitioner and which springs from a coherent view of disorder. Unfortunately, if the client then improves, the particular practitioner may well believe that the theory underlying the practice has been confirmed. Which may be quite untrue!

The second problem with therapeutic theory is that it appears that the major phenomena cannot be evaluated easily. Thus each doctrine can claim validity for its propositions. Nesting in this issue is also the problem of the common tongue. Theories of therapy are somewhat like languages in the sense that the student learns to speak a particular language which relates to his/her practice world. S/he then resists learning another language – or even translating from one language to another because it appears to change the conceptual nature of that world.

It is most unlikely that there will be a grand meta-theory which emerges and much more likely that practitioners will learn from researchers the core elements of competent practice. Some writers have called this integrated counselling and therapy, particularly Norcross (1986). There is a problem here which is that this may simply become the next in a very long line of 'therapies'. But at least it is a way by which existing doctrine can be evaluated against effective practice.

The damage is probably done relatively early. The hopeful student practitioner will join a particular training programme because it appears to suit his/her personal style. The particular slant of the training programme then confirms the view already covertly held and the circle is complete. One way forward would be that the registers of counselling and psychotherapy insist that registrants have learned to practice in at least two modes.

Finale

Future development here could actually be instigated by the complaining client. Any client now has access to ways of evaluating their counsellor/ therapist. This will surely lead to formal complaint that the method used, or formulation offered was inappropriate to the problem – and therefore unethical. Time will tell!

Dryden (1993) emphasized many of the aspects of prospective counselling development in a published lecture entitled Thirty ways to improve counselling. Many of these thirty proposals resonate with the arguments in this chapter and emphasize proper preparation for a professional practice which is deeply responsive to client need using those methods which are researched and which are coherent with complex human nature.

Just in case this all sounds too difficult for mere mortals to achieve we can close by quoting Owen's (1993) summary of the qualities of the 'good enough therapist'. In an extended discussion of what such a practitioner should be in order to serve clients and conserve him/herself he comments:

> *Good enough therapists* are neither self-indulgent nor self-obsessed. . . . [They] know that they are not the sole heirs to the knowledge of humanity . . . They can set boundaries, but are not dogmatic or authoritarian . . . Good enough therapists are self-confident, but not grandiose or omnipotent. (1993, p. 261)

If such standards are to be achieved in order to provide competent service in the future, then the contributions of Windy Dryden – and many others – will surely take account of the issues we have highlighted here. Bacon would certainly approve of the new generation of counsellors, able to deal with puzzles of modern experience in ancient minds.

Acknowledgement

My thanks to my niece, Kate Alexander, for contributing to some of these ideas.

References

Bacon, F. (1895) *The Essays* (1597 and 1625). London: Routledge, Morleys Universal Library.

Bacon, F. (1960[1620]) *The New Organum*. New York: The Liberal Arts Press.

Barkham, M. (1996) Quantitative research on psychotherapeutic interventions, in R. Woolfe and W. Dryden (eds), *Handbook of Counselling Psychology*. London: Sage.

Bond, T. (1996) Competition or collaboration within the talking therapies, in I. James and S. Palmer (eds), *Professional Therapeutic Titles, Myths and Realities*. Occasional Papers vol. 2. Leicester: British Psychological Society.

Donald, M. (1991) *Origins of the Modern Mind: Three Stages in the Evolution of Culture and Cognition*. Cambridge, MA: Harvard University Press.

Dryden, W. (1993) *Thirty Ways to Improve Counselling*. School of Education, University of Durham.

Dryden, W. (1996) A Rose by any other name: a personal view on the differences among professional titles, in I. James and S. Palmer (eds), *Professional Therapeutic Titles: Myths and Realities*. Occasional Papers vol. 2. Leicester, British Psychological Society.

Frank, J.D. (1961) *Persuasion and Healing: A Comparative Study of Psychotherapy*. Baltimore: Johns Hopkins University Press.

Giddens, A. (1991) *Modernity and Self-Identity: Self and Society in the Late Modern Age*. Cambridge: Polity Press/Blackwell.

Halmos, P. (1965) *The Faith of the Counsellors*. London: Constable.

James, I. and Palmer, S. (1996) *Professional Therapeutic Titles: Myths and Realities*. Occasional Papers vol. 2. Leicester: British Psychological Society.

Norcross, J.C. (ed.) (1986) *Handbook of Eclectic Psychotherapy*. New York: Brunner/Mazel.

North, M. (1972) *The Secular Priests: Psychotherapists in Contemporary Society*. London: George Allen and Unwin.

Orlinsky, D., Grawe, K. and Parks, B.K. (1994) Process and outcome in psychotherapy, in S.L. Garfield and A.R. Bergin (eds), *Handbook of Psychotherapy and Behavior Change*, 4th edn. New York: Wiley.

Owen, I. (1993) On 'the private life of the psychotherapist' and the psychology of caring, *Counselling Psychology Quarterly*, 6: 231–64.

Rogers, C.R. (1942) *Counselling and Psychotherapy*. Boston: Houghton Mifflin.

Scanlon, C. and Baillie, A.P. (1994) A preparation for practice? Students' experiences of counselling training within departments of higher education, *Counselling Psychology Quarterly*, 7: 407–27.

Schön, D. (1987) *Educating the Reflective Practitioner*. London: Jossey-Bass.

Tyndall, N. (1993) *Counselling in the Voluntary Sector*. Milton Keynes: Open University Press.

4

Hard Heads, Tough Minds and Tender Hearts?

Pat Milner

The tragedy at Dunblane primary school in Scotland, in which a gunman shot dead sixteen children and their teacher was deeply affecting. Whilst sharing in the shock and disbelief through the intrusive lens of television, it was possible at the same time to be impressed by the quality of understanding compassion shown by many of those interviewed – towns-people, civic officials, police, medical staff and clergy. Shortly afterwards I met several people at a counselling conference who had not been impressed by the news, which so often accompanies current tragedies, that a team of counsellors was being made available to work with people affected by the shocking event. Perhaps we can reflect why, when the struggle to gain acceptance for counselling in the UK has taken a generation (thirty years) and when there is greater understanding from lay people, as demonstrated at Dunblane, why is there a resistance from our profession to a team of counsellors being 'made available' so speedily? It is not a simple question, there are many answers and I recall impressing upon students that 'why' questions are seldom the most helpful in counselling. However, because I am a person who does not know how to live without more questions than she will ever have answers for, this chapter is an opportunity to articulate a few of those questions which concern our future.

We do need to ask questions and hard questions, for if there is to be a future for counselling and psychotherapy those of us who practice need to 'wise up', to take stock and to face the twenty-first century with hard heads, tough minds and tender hearts. Hard heads are those which exercise shrewd and intelligent thinking; tough minds demon-strate that thinking through perceptive, challenging, critical analysis based on real study, a study which does not mistake perception for reality. Both these attributes, when combined with that sensitivity which helps us to hold fast to the crucial 'focus on feeling' inherent in our work, our tender-heartedness, keep us balanced when our hard heads and tough minds would assume total cognitive or intellectual control – or vice versa.

Counselling in a social context?

It is stating the obvious to repeat that one of the most powerful strengths of counselling and psychotherapy is the focus on individual people (or groups) in their individual worlds, a strength which allows time, space, skilled attention and support within a relationship structured around respect, genuineness and empathy. However, those experiences in life which are powerful enough to be beneficial are also usually strong enough to do harm. Is a real danger in the therapeutic process that we can and do help clients to examine their individuality within the counselling setting, to the detriment of their equally important shared place in society? Clients, if not counsellors, live the major part of their lives not only outside their therapeutic hours, but also in a society in which age, social class, ethnicity and gender are social categories through which we are all defined and identified and which form an important part of how we see ourselves and how others see us. Whatever happens within the privacy of counselling, both partners, counsellor and client, are an integral part of the reality and wider perspective of a society in which we are defined and identified, with or without our consent. Jane Pilcher, a social scientist, proposes that 'People are never just youths or middle aged but are also "classed", "raced" and "gendered"' (1995, p. 96).

Is a dilemma for both partners in the counselling alliance the occupational hazard of societal amnesia, which creeps into the subjective therapeutic culture and can ensnare counsellors in an over-indulgent tender-heartedness and emotional introspection, which loses touch with the tough-mindedness required to see the wood of society for the trees of individualism? The Jungian analyst Andrew Samuels has no doubt that therapy is a political act in a social context: 'clinical practice may be something other than a bastion of possessive individualism and narcissistic introspection. It is right to criticise myopic (and greedy) clinicians who cannot apperceive that their world has a political and cultural location and implication' (1993, p. 6).

Culture and/or biology?

Counsellors have increasingly grasped the influences of culture and biology and generally appreciate that differences between men and women and between members of various 'races' are understood not to be totally determined by biology, but to have a strong social construction. This appreciation leads to the language of 'gender' rather than 'sex' differences, of ethnic groups and ethnicity rather than racial groups, which is all part of a recognition that 'differences' between groups in society have at least as much to do with culture as with biology. Such a sociological understanding allows those counsellors who have it to combine an empathic comprehension of a client's struggle to establish, determine and take pride in their individual identity, whilst simultaneously supporting them as they suffer the hard knocks of critical personal, social, racist, bigoted or homophobic reactions to that often vulnerable identity in the world outside counselling. Society is composed of many other people who genuinely believe that aspects of human life such as 'sex' and 'race' are not only determined solely by nature or biology, but are also heavily circumscribed into inflexible compartments. In this particular view of life, the divisions are maintained by a power-base of 'us', meaning those who are like we are, and 'them', meaning those who are not like we are. When there is an 'us' group, everyone else becomes by definition part of 'them'. Taking the dispassionate view of a sociologist, the 'us' may be for example a group called 'men'. In particular:

> able-bodied, white, middle-class males in full-time employment, who are probably the most fully adult [and therefore the most powerful] members of British society. Their advantageous structural position enables them to exercise their citizenship rights, their independence and autonomy to a greater extent than can women, elderly or disabled people, children, the working class or members of ethnic minority groups. (Pilcher, 1995, p. 87)

Although it is true that adults dominate the social world by their control of personal, material and institutional resources, some adults are more equal and powerful than others and many counsellors work, not with the men in the 'us' primary power group, but with clients from the 'them' group of women, elderly or disabled people, children or young people, members of ethnic minority groups or those who are economically, socially or psychologically needy. There are realities in the wider world outside the counselling room which require both the shrewd intelligence of hard-headedness and the considered and analytical perspectives of tough-mindedness, to balance the tender-hearted understanding of the counselling encounter. Does a failure to engage with these realities which impinge on a client's life lead to a failure to enter the client's world? Is it enough to enter the world of the client as it is experienced within the counselling environment? Although that may be where a client feels most alive, it is not where they live.

> An individual leads not only his or her own life, but the life of the times. Links have to be made with the culture of each client – its history and traditions – as well as to the client's social, racial, ethnic, religions and national origins. These form the political history of the person, the politics an individual has inherited through family, class, ethnic, religious and national background as well as those accidental, genetic, typological and fateful inexplicable influences on our personhood. (Samuels, 1993, p. 53)

Attitudes to difference

While our clients may be struggling toward a recognition and expression of their own difference, can we as counsellors be aware of the typical 'psychology trap' which ascribes generalized conclusions to particular groups of people? Can our concern focus on the *experience* of difference for clients, not the *defining* of difference? 'Black' psychology does not have to be contrasted with 'white' psychology, nor 'catholic' with 'protestant', homosexual with heterosexual, female with male psychology. Members of these groups do have some experiences in common, but the groups are not homogeneous. Although there are ways in which everyone is like everyone else and ways in which they are different, it is not possible to predict which set of similarities and differences will hold for any one person.

Nevertheless our acknowledgement of difference may be enhanced by a recognition that there are strongly held attitudes amongst ordinary people which we may be wise to be critically aware of. An example of such attitudes is contained in the British Social Attitudes Survey which reported on age-dependent differences amongst women towards a variety of sociopolitical issues which may be raised in counselling.

Stereotypical roles
8% of women aged 18–34 agreed that
'A husband's job is to earn the money; a wife's job is to look after the house and family'
whereas 21% of women aged 55+ strongly agreed

Abortion
57% of women aged 18–34 agreed that
'Abortion should be allowed in all cases where the woman decides on her own that she does not want the child'
and 45% of women aged 55+ agreed

Homosexual relationships
59% of women aged 18–34 said that
'Homosexual relationships were "always" or "mostly" wrong'
whilst 61% of women aged 35–54 agreed
and 82% of women aged 55+ agreed

Pornography
23% of women aged 18–34 said that
'pornographic films and magazines should be banned altogether'
whilst 39% of women aged 35–54 agreed
and 70% of women aged 55+ agreed

(cited in Pilcher, 1995, p. 142.
Sources: Witherspoon, 1985; Airey and Brook, 1986; Harding, 1988)

Estimates of the corresponding figures for the sociopolitical attitudes of 'counsellors' to the above statements can only be speculated upon. Is it unreasonable to assume that they might be nearest to the stated opinions of the 18 to 34-year-old women in the survey, regardless of the age or gender of the counsellor?

The significance of the results of such sociological surveys is that they may represent the attitudes of clients themselves, or of their mothers, sisters, friends or colleagues. They thus represent powerful forces imping-ing on that person's world, which have a bearing on any counselling work connected with these areas of the client's life. Counsellors who are shrewd will be aware of the extent of the existence of the attitudes uncovered by such surveys. This may help them generate sufficient tough-mindedness to help clients to decide how they wish to respond to the people in their lives who genuinely hold such attitudes and have the tender-hearted empathy to be alongside when they get hard knocks. The world of entrenched opposing attitudes is very much the world of hard knocks, a titanic struggle often involving the shedding of emotional and physical blood.

Are the attitudes of counsellors, in so far as they can be generalized, more *avant-garde* than the attitudes of the majority of society, or are they more conservative? Or is it not possible to generalize at all?

Are there groupings within the counselling world which cocoon counsellors into believing that their perception of society is reality and either everyone else is out of step or nobody else is out there? Does it matter? Are counsellors who are in touch with the stirrings, groans and rumblings which signal the onset of changes in our society better placed to help their clients to live effectively in their worlds?

No such thing as society?

'There is no such thing as society' is a phrase which returned to haunt Margaret Thatcher when she was Prime Minister of Britain, but she actually went on to say: 'There are individual men and women and there are families. And no government can do anything except through people, and people must look to themselves first. It's our duty to look after ourselves and then to look after our neighbour' (Thatcher, 1993, p. 626). The idea of looking after oneself, or even one's self, is not an unfamiliar one in counselling work and the encouragement to clients to pursue their own path and get what they want out of life is frequently a central core. This is a legitimate pursuit for many clients for whom life has offered very little of what they both want and need, particularly in emotional terms. Many counsellors, perhaps to their surprise, would agree with Margaret Thatcher that it is our duty to look after ourselves. An equally surprising unawareness of what is happening in the world outside counselling may lead some to agree with her that there is no such thing as society. Recently it has seemed that the gospel of 'getting what I want', has become aggressively overwhelming as a desired outcome of counselling. Does the promotion of self-centredness, social aloofness and indifference to the well-being of others endanger the fabric of society and the psychological balance of the individual? Tough-minded moral fibre is unfashionable because its maintenance so often depends on denial or repression of powerful feelings, with perhaps familiar consequences. But is the senti-mental ethical slurry of tender-heartedness alone an acceptable alternative?

Many fundamental aspects of social life have changed in important ways in the years since the 1960s, years which have also seen an encouraging growth in counselling activity. The expected course of people's lives has become less orderly in so many ways. The service sector of employment has grown as the industrial sector has declined, with a parallel decline in the strong trade unions which characterized industry. We no longer have full employment and may never see its like again. Instead flexible employment patterns are encouraged and the reduction in the strength of organized labour has reduced the power of men in the industrial sector, relative to other areas of work.

In terms of taking care of people, comprehensive public sector provision has been replaced by a stress on reducing that provision, including the scope of the welfare state and it is argued that many people's health and welfare needs are better met by private individual provision, rather than being comprehensively provided by the state.

Family life is increasingly characterized by diversity as fewer people marry and have fewer children, more people cohabit and have children outside marriage and more people live alone. Trends in marriage, divorce and single parenthood fragment the life course of families and they become reconstituted, so that, for example a vast range of people from the age of 35 to 105 may now have the experience of being grandparents (Pilcher, 1995) and we now have an increased likelihood of families like my own, with three generations of adults. The changing employment patterns of women mean that more and more women are having their first babies later in life, which may have implications for the duration and nature of relationships between the generations in future.

Science and religion have become less relevant as sources of meaning for people in their everyday lives, whilst a high degree of cultural significance has been assumed by and accorded to the mass media.

> The gradual erosion of long-standing frames of reference, such as class, family, community and religion mean that people are less secure in their personal and collective identities. Consequently people are increasingly concerned with issues of self-identity, image and fashion and the presentation of self through body-image. All these changes . . . have consequences for individuals, their families and society at large. (Pilcher, 1995, p. 148)

And therefore for counsellors? Lane (1996) suggests that these trans-formations in society have reduced the functions of social systems such as the family, schools, places of work, religion and science, all of which previously acted as defences against anxiety. The impact of this has been to increase the need for counselling for individuals, organizations and other groups.

The comment that some counsellors display an apparent unawareness of what is happening in the wider world is a personal observation that would benefit from a closer analysis. It is not easy to change focus from the minutiae of the individual lives of clients, within which counsellors spend many hours. There has been a tendency in some training courses to encourage counsellors to discourage clients from talking about social/political matters, because these can be used as a distraction from looking at major personal aspects of their lives, as a means of avoiding personal conflicts or of acting them out. It has been a credo amongst psycho-dynamic practitioners to use such topics brought by clients as legitimate material, a source for interpretation of their personal psychology. Yet increasingly modern social theory is concerned with identity and difference and with the relationship between them; its study underlies such questions as 'How am I wholly and unmistakably myself and how am I part of the mass, similar to or the same as others?' (Samuels, 1993).

Social theory emphasizes that the cultural diversity of our society is not a disaster, but a challenge and an opportunity for us to give greater appreciation to contributions made by women, children, the economically disadvantaged, homosexuals and lesbians, members of ethnic minorities and people living in unconventional families. This is not an idea which gains support from people in general, as the extract from the British Social Attitudes Survey shows, but it is a notion which some counsellors promote actively in their work. The difficulty is that clients live out their lives in the world of people in general, not in the accepting world of counsellors. Does this provide fertile ground for yet another 'them' and 'us' power split to arise, with the likelihood of the client becoming 'piggy-in-the-middle'?

Our age has reorganized the categories of time, space and place and overcome their previous boundaries through technology.

> In its overturning of the laws of nature, the age itself more and more resembles the unconscious. The speedy and multi-levelled tone of life at the close of the twentieth century means that we often do not know what it is that has hurt or disturbed us though we do know that we have been hurt or disturbed. We may only know what it was after the event. Such 'deferred action' means that we are condemned to afterwardness and retrospection, required to fashion our response to hurtful and disturbing social changes out of a backward looking stance. No wonder there has been an explosion of nostalgias. (Samuels, 1993, p. 8)

What other practitioners do

In his book *The Political Psyche*, Andrew Samuels (1993) undertook an international survey by questionnaire to seek information on the extent to which 'political' material was being brought to therapists and analysts. He did this because he had noticed that patients in his analytical practice were increasingly introducing political or social themes and not all this material could be validly understood at a symbolic or countertransference level, but needed to be addressed as a concern in its own right. He quotes the example of a patient needing to talk about a public issue such as the Gulf War at a personal-political-psychological level. His book links the inner journey of analysis and therapy and the passionate political convictions of the outer world, such as environmentalism and the market economy, in some startling and unexpected ways.

Samuels distributed 1964 questionnaires to psychoanalysts, Jungian colleagues, psychotherapists, a group of humanistic psychotherapists and graduates of the Westminster Pastoral Foundation courses. The sample involved such people in seven countries and had a response rate of 32%.

The first section of the survey grouped political material into thirteen themes, with an open-ended fourteenth category. These were international politics, national politics, local (community) politics, economic issues (e.g. distribution of wealth, poverty), Third World issues, racial or ethnic issues, gender issues for women, gender issues for men, environmental concerns, nuclear energy, nuclear weapons, issues to do with mass media, violence in society. The top three themes mentioned by all groups of respondents gives the following league table:

1   gender issues for women
2   economic issues
3   violence in society
4= national politics and gender issues for men
6   racial or ethnic issues
7   international politics

There is a sense of a truly 'political history of the person' and a 'political here and now' of the person. As Samuels says, 'The replies show that politics can be subjected to the same kinds of sensitive, psychological enquiry as any other material and, even more important, that analysts and therapists already know how to do it and are doing it' (1993, p. 265).

The profession shows a marked divide between those who assign political/social material to the 'inner world' of the client and those for whom feelings of responsibility for the state of society, social issues and global concerns are not seen to be projections of self-interest, but are valued as authentic responses (Whitmore, 1996). There is a second split, Samuels suggests, between the public face of the profession which he describes as apolitical and hyperclinical, and the private face, consisting of practitioners struggling to find a balance between inner looking and outer looking attitudes to what their clients or patients bring. 'The split is between the professional persona and its own internal reality' (Samuels, 1993, p. 265).

Samuels' study is weighted toward the analytic spectrum. Is it possible that the collective public face of humanistic or cognitive-behavioural counsellors may be less apolitical and in some cases more Political?

Personal observation suggests that those men and women who work in the world of counselling and psychotherapy are more like each other than they are like others who do not inhabit this world. This impression leads to the possibility that the similarities between men and women counsellors have a basis in the reality that this profession, perhaps more than some, is made up of people who through disposition, training and the element of personal understanding inherent in their work, have to a varying degree integrated within themselves what are widely considered to be masculine and feminine qualities. If this is so, they have made a form of internal gender integration which may be both a strength in their work and a model for certain clients. This integration is observably a source of strength in the community of counsellors. The concept of psychological androgyny offers promise for improving and enriching people's relating skills, so long as men and women increasingly adopt the strengths rather than the deficits of the other's gender characteristics (Nelson-Jones, 1996).

Perhaps again, this is a fantasy which mistakes the community of counsellors for the wider society in which clients live, which differs in quite fundamental ways. As Owen says, 'When counsellors from the world of caring and sharing, self-responsibility and professional status meet clients from a world of pain, inability and indecision, the consequences will be difficulties in communication and understanding' (1996, p. 193).

Is there a tradition of tender-hearted idealism amongst counsellors, which, when it is not informed by deeply perceptive, challenging and critical thinking based on real study, and observation, can lead us astray? Is it an idealism which can encourage us to seek to empower clients to re-make themselves and their world in our uncritical or over-critical view, without sufficient regard for the reality of their society as it is? Do we in fact mistake perception for reality?

The counselling tradition

There are those who suggest that the concept of tough minds and tender hearts is a continuing part of the counselling and pre-counselling 'tradition'. Richard Nelson-Jones (1996), who developed the life-skills approach, acknowledges in the preface to his self-help book on relating skills for students, that he has 'tried to write a tough-minded, tender-hearted, sensitive and humane book'.

Ninety years ago, William James (1975[1906]), in a series of popular lectures on philosophy, proposed that there are basically two types of people, the tender-minded and the tough-minded. The two types are dichotomous, the tender-minded characterized by idealism, optimism, dogmatism, and rationalism (following principles), whilst the tough-minded are materialistic, pessimistic, sceptical and empirical (following facts). According to James, the two types think badly of each other; tender minds often find tough minds callous, brutal or unrefined; tough minds think of the tender as soft-headed sentimentalists (cited in Weinrach, 1995).

Weinrach (1995) himself applies James' typology to counselling approaches in a basic way, by describing the rational emotive behaviour therapy of Albert Ellis as a predominantly tough-minded therapy, whilst considering the person-centred therapy developed by Carl Rogers to be a largely tender-minded one. However, he allows that although 'REBT is a predominantly tough minded therapy (it is) sometimes provided by tender minded counsellors, to clients, of whom some are also tender minded' (p. 305).

Is it significant that James and Weinrach, who are both men, refer to tender-minded, rather than tender-hearted people?

A more discriminating typology than James' bipartite view is provided by the Myers–Briggs Type Indicator (MBTI), a descriptive measure of personality, widely used in the USA, which is based on Carl Jung's developmental theory of psychological types. The MBTI questionnaire encompasses eight personality preferences that all people may use at different times and organizes them into four bipolar scales:

Extraversion–Introversion – relating to our source of energy
Sensing–Intuition – relating to what we pay attention to
Thinking–Feeling – relating to how we make decisions
Judgment–Perception – relating to our chosen life-style

The result of the MBTI offers four preferences for each person, one from each scale, which are called the personality 'type' and are given a four-letter designation code such as ESTJ. This indicates a person who is energized by the external world (E), whose preferred way of dealing with incoming information is sensing (S), whose way of deciding is thinking (T) and who adopts a judging and organized style of living (J). Here is a person who is logical, analytical, decisive and tough-minded, who may be overtaken by their feelings and values if they ignore them for too long.

An ISFP however, draws energy from their own internal world (I), their preferred way of dealing with incoming information is sensing (S), their way of deciding is on the basis of feeling (F), and they prefer a spontaneous and flexible life (P). This is a person who is gentle, considerate, compassionate toward those less fortunate, has an open-minded flexible approach and is tender-hearted. They may be too trusting and gullible and need to develop more scepticism and a way of analysing information rather than just accepting it (Hirsch and Kummerow, 1987).

Jung's psychological functions tend to pull in opposite directions, for example:

Sensing points to the reality of the present
Intuition to the possibility of the future

Thinking to decisions based on objective logic
Feeling to decisions based on subjective value

The perceiving functions – Sensing and Intuition are two opposite ways of taking in information, whilst the judging functions – Thinking and Feeling are two opposite ways of organizing information.

Since we each show a natural preference for one of these four, that one becomes our dominant function – the core or guiding focus of our personality, the mental tool we most rely on. The dominant function is balanced by an auxiliary one – if the dominant function is a perceiving one (S or N), the auxiliary will be a judging one (T or F). We use our dominant function in our preferred world – the outer world for Extraverts (E) and the inner world for Introverts (I). Following the principle of opposites, if our dominant function is Extraverted, our auxiliary one will be Introverted and vice versa.

The goal of developing one's personality type is to develop the ability to use each mental process with some facility when it is appropriate. Thus the dominant function provides purpose and consistency, whilst the auxiliary function provides balance and support. Since most cultures appear to have a predominance of Sensing and Judging types and many of society's institutions support Sensing and Judging values and behaviour, children with a preference for Intuition and Perceiving may receive heavy social pressure to suppress their natural way of being. Similarly, women with a Thinking preference and men with a Feeling preference may become resentful and lacking in confidence as a result of consistent feedback that their preferred way of doing things is wrong (Myers and Kirby, 1994).

Is it possible that amongst counsellors there are to be found a considerable number of people with a preference for Intuition and Perceiving, with dominant Feeling functions and fewer who are dominant Thinking and Sensing types? Is it also possible that the recent growth in popularity of the cognitive-behavioural therapies points to a changing emphasis in the balance between the tough-minded and tender-hearted members of our profession? Might this lead to a more realistic understanding of the realities which support the financing of our work?

The hard-headed market economy pays

If there is an idealism of tender-heartedness amongst counsellors, it may be a response to legitimate feelings of guilt and a longing to atone for our culture's social injustices, which so affect clients. Our society is destructive and the nature of our work can lead to a depressive preoccupation with that destructiveness, but such depression makes it almost impossible to find imaginative solutions to social and political problems.

> . . . depression leads to an awful literalism in which fantasy and actuality are hopelessly muddled. Collective fantasies of hate and aggression are taken literally, leading to depressive guilt (for example over the possession of nuclear weapons) and mass delusional self reproach. The problem is how to contain and integrate guilt on this scale without either repressing it or acting it out. (Samuels, 1993, p. 14)

Certainly counsellors share the common feelings of despair and a sense of meaninglessness, fear of a lack of collective well-being, anger at the inequalities of society, perhaps guilt about their own comfortable existence, frustration at a seeming inability to make a difference and sorrow for others (Whitmore, 1996). However, is it, as Samuels (1996) proposes, that those counsellors who are full of guilty contempt for capitalism, in the desire to atone and express their unease and disgust, make a split between the constructive and the cheating aspects of capitalism and the market economy, preferring only to see the negative side? The extreme fantasies of the negative side may include visions of an apocalyptic end, by an AIDS pandemic or the results of the greenhouse effect. These fantasies are rooted in reality but show deep signs of a punishing self-contempt for ourselves, and the suggestion that we deserve to perish like this.

Do counsellors sometimes try to manage their disgust and guilt at the excesses of the market economy by attempting to make it up to the entire planet in an over-literal act of environmental compensation? This is dangerous territory for counsellors because of the hidden authoritarianism in much of current environmental politics, which may take the form of downgrading the whole of humanity to the level of flora or fauna, or issuing proclaiming edicts about what is 'good' or 'right'. Are the one-sided portrait of humanity which is so often the cornerstone of the environmentalist case, and the unremitting litany of humanity's destructiveness too misanthropic for counsellors to collude with? Is it an insult to shrewd intelligence and a contradiction in terms, for counsellors whose professional ethics and integrity subscribe to a positive attitude to people, also to subscribe to those ideas about the environment which reflect humanity in such an exclusively harsh light? There is much thoughtlessness, greed and destructive environmental behaviour to be acknowledged but a myriad of moral decisions arises when people in rich, industrially advanced countries shout for limits and controls on rainforests or birth rates, or conservation of wild animals in poorer countries, without the opportunity for the people actually involved to make their own choices and decisions and face the moral implications of what is being done.

> The argument that trees and rivers have rights, needs to be assessed so that we can distinguish between its potential to inspire action and its gross oversimplification. Does the HIV virus have rights? Is it ethical to destroy dams, or insert into trees spikes that injure loggers? (Samuels, 1993, p. 105)

Many good things are emerging from the environmental movement and one of these is the developing, if long distance, dialogue between hard-headed market economists, such as those at Shell, and tough-minded, but tender-hearted environmentalists at Greenpeace. It is worrying that both their philosophies lack psychological depth and may be too out of touch with the grass roots of the world to have the enduring and beneficial effect which the seriousness of our environmental problems merits.

The market economy can be seen as a rich person's charter or as the road to freedom and dignity, or as both these things at the same time. Free market economics has unfair and ruthless features and these are an essential cost of its benefits. Can counsellors stay outside the economic world, pure and above the market place, and retain their integrity? Market forces have already entered most aspects of all our lives and we depend on them for our continued existence. There are no 'shadow free politics', there is no 'shadow free' place in which we can hide (Samuels, 1993).

We may bemoan the apparent triumph of capitalism as the clear victory of patriarchal exploitation and other reactionary forces, or we may pause for reflection and see the need to work on the development of a sense of community which is caring and compassionate and reaches out to those in need. Can we develop such a community without the resources of capitalism? Do we need to understand market forces, their psychological nature and the powerful imagery involved in them? Market politics is both speculative, calculating and pragmatic and at the same time holds the economic art of the means of making the world and its people better. Community also has its shadow, the dead hand of totalitarianism which some of the people of the former Soviet union have recently forsaken for their version of the free-culture of capitalism, or perhaps in future elections, the 'new' communism.

Is there a therapy of politics?

A therapeutic attitude toward the world is appropriate because: 'politics is the dimension of social reality that contains the world's pathology' (Samuels, 1993, p. 29). Clear injustices such as a grossly unfair distribution of wealth, skewed gender relations, racism, poverty, disease and a wrecked ecology provide the therapist of politics with just as much material to work with as the individual psychology of a client provides for the therapist. It is not surprising that images from personal growth link so frequently with those from environmental concerns. Political and social problems like human clients will respond to our analysis in differing ways, but since we are ourselves part of the political and social world, our thinking and analysis of necessity needs to have a subjective element. Does this mean that it will have a 'feminine' element?

One of the features of a subjective analysis of politics is the necessity for women to find a more collective voice in relation to a male-dominated social reality. Samuels says: 'A subjective politics in which women may have a significant role must surely mount its challenge to injustice and oppression in diverse ways, according to personal, socioeconomic and other circumstances (1993, p. 35). This diversity is needed to lessen the possibility of replacing the hegemony of men by a more varied, but equally undesirable hegemony of women. Making a subjective analysis of politics enables us to look at the ways in which women are denied access to political power whilst also working out a way of interacting which can integrate the subjective and political (Samuels, 1993).

In this sense is feminism a demand for the right to be subjective in politics and socioeconomic aspects of life, so that they become more of a balanced partnership between women and men?

Women and men

The partnership that is most characteristic of the relations of women and men is still that of marriage, despite a recent decline in its popularity. However, in the last four hundred years marriage has been transformed from an essentially economic institution, usually arranged by parents with a view to improving the family financial status and its prospect of physical survival, into much more of a psychological/economic institution. In such economic arrangements the physical and psychological attributes of the marriage partner were rarely considered of major importance, matters of appearance and personality were overshadowed by the vital struggle to preserve or increase economic status. Given the choice between poverty and marriage to someone who was ugly or obnoxious, nearly all young adults chose the latter and because people did not expect much emotional or sexual fulfilment from marriage, they were not greatly disappointed. Life was so harsh and demanding for most people that the idea of relationships providing emotional support and psychological compatibility was largely irrelevant. Most families were tightly run economic units and members were forced to work together closely and cooperatively, not out of pleasure but because their survival depended on it. Human interaction was governed less by love, affection and mutual respect than by the need to work together in order to survive in a tough and often unpredictable world. We get an authentic view of life from the films and television presentations of the books of Charles Dickens and Jane Austen which illustrate different ends of the social scale. The survival skills of our ancestors deserve our utmost respect.

What have been the effects of the increasing substitution of the 'psychology of love' for 'economics' as a basis for marriage? Both men and women have been psychologically imprisoned in society's stereotyped images of their respective identities, but women have suffered enormously from narrow definitions of what it means to be female. Should we seriously question the idea of a universal maternal instinct, which does not appear to be based on human but on animal reality and puts pressure on women to have children and to experience childbirth and child-raising as exclusively pleasant and fulfilling events? The reality for many women is different. Looking after a baby can be messy, exhausting and frustrating and mothers can become very depressed and incapacitated by fears and anxieties and extremely worried about their feelings of anger and hostility toward their babies, even though such feelings are entirely natural. Winnicott (1975) put forward seventeen reasons why mothers might hate their babies. Samuels makes a similar point: 'There is an inbuilt capacity in symbiosis to self-destruct. Babies and mothers have an investment in separation and to overlook this is to insult mothers and babies' (1996, p. 141).

The image of women who are endlessly patient and caring, who put their own needs second to those of their children, who willingly retreat from the world and abandon their own pleasures and interests to devote themselves wholeheartedly and exclusively to the welfare of their children represents an almost impossible goal. Indeed, women have often struggled to achieve it at the expense of their own health and well-being.

Counsellors may find themselves working with women who are struggling to regain their health and well-being after an over-punitive, self-denying period of motherhood. Others work with clients whose very experiences of childhood leave them struggling with the dilemma of being grown up children of 35, still dependent on their parents. Although in both situations the client is the focus, the risk of tender-heartedness alone is that it can lead to illusions of blame, rather than a healing understanding of the reality. Such illusions can seem to justify the self-excuses we use, rather than face the harder work of taking responsibility for what is our responsibility.

For centuries men have used medicine, religion and the arts as a means of trying to solve 'the problem' of women – the other sex, the dark sex. Now that trend is beginning to be reversed and men are being seen as 'the problem' and when they are depicted as sexually abusing, domestically violent, earthwrecking creatures this is a valid perspective. However, we are given to understand that 'new man' is different, supporting the rights of women and children, being ecologically aware and non-violent. Samuels (1993) suggests that this split in the cultural image of man is perhaps potentially so upsetting to the existing social order as to afflict both men and women with an unbearable anxiety which itself foments the split between the bad 'old' man and the good 'new' man. However, old men and new men are made of the same stuff, sex and aggression constitute the good father as well as the bad one. Although a diversity of competing models of masculinity for men to expose themselves to is valuable, social scientists tell us that from a behavioural standpoint nothing has changed significantly. 'Men do not do housework or look after children and the existence of a few pockets of progressive, well heeled masculinity should not blind us to that more pervasive reality' (Samuels, 1993, p. 178). There has been an explosion of books, articles, television and radio programmes on men's issues during the last decade. We can only speculate what might have happened if AIDS had predominantly affected women.

Since men control the sources of economic and political power including the production of ideology and media representations of sexual difference, the influence of male political power on the idea of male change has the potential to result in a social movement as significant as feminism, but with all the power and resources from which feminism has been excluded. This holds the potential for decisive change in two directions, one is a re-evaluation of men's relationships to women, more nurturing models of fathering and change in men's view of their own identity (Samuels, 1993); the other is more reactionary.

It is not just the impact of feminism that has encouraged a new look at men. The effects of the decline in religion have been quite devastating for men and their conceptions of masculinity. Developments in medical or pseudomedical technology which allow postmenopausal women to have children, or scientists in a laboratory to clone Megan and Morag, the sheep, with a jolt of electricity rather than ram's sperm, mean that what were understood as the natural processes of life are increasingly subject to alteration and an element of human control.

So the second direction of potential change in the rise of a 'men's movement' has at its heart a more reactionary and conservative backlash against feminism and an uncritical reverence for the nuclear family that echoes fundamentalist religions. Faludi (1992) points out that this reactionary backlash will be an undermining of the rather limited gains made by women since 1960. Perhaps the question for hard-headed, tough-minded counsellors, when they feel like being too tender-hearted, is can men ever change the system that they created in order to promote themselves to the top of the world tree, in 'a world in which men have power and a power complex whereas women have only the complex' (Samuels, 1991, p. 191).

What of the future?

Whether our preferred personality function according to the MBTI leads us to use a tough-minded or a tender-hearted mental process and whether that process is introverted or extraverted, do we each have the capacity to develop the shrewd intelligence of hard heads; the perceptive critical analysis of tough minds and the sensitivity to hold these in balance, in the service of ourselves and our clients, by incorporating and acknowledging the influences of our society on our individual lives?

The traditional models which have supported counselling are challenged by the need which is all around us. 'The challenge is to ensure that we are part of a service leading to effective outcomes for our clients, rather than simply a service which meets our needs at the expense of our clients' (Lane, 1996, p. 613).

Can we serve the future of counselling and psychotherapy by presenting the nature and value of our work to various sections of our society, including the economically powerful, in ways that can be understood by tough and tender minds, remembering that thinking and feeling are opposite ways of making decisions?

We are being called upon to validate, include and embrace all the concerns and changes touched on in this chapter and that process rep-resents a developmental step for the counselling profession. Perhaps it is time to recognize that Lane's (1996) proposed interactive view of coun-selling which approaches in a holistic way the social, economic and emo-tional issues which face us all, is a change we need to make. As Whitmore puts it, 'If we are to stay abreast of our rapidly changing world today the profession needs to widen its vision, to recognise the issues and concerns of the day and work with them directly' (1996, p. 612). If we do not achieve this, is the danger of tender-heartedness, uninformed by hard-headed thinking and without the strength of tough-minded challenging, that it has the potential to seduce both counsellors and clients into believing that new mythologies and new stereotypes are the new realities? Does wisdom lie in knowing there are two sides to everything? Tender-heartedness alone will not survive in the world outside counselling. Think about it! Postscript: Serendipity is alive and well!

We have a new organization, Psychotherapists and Counsellors for Social Responsibility (PCSR), which has formed study and campaign groups to look at areas such as society, community, social policy and the public domain, work and money, education, families and children, gender, ecology, sexual diversity, the media, professional issues and professional policies. The aim of PCSR is to help psychotherapists and counsellors bridge the gap between therapeutic work and wider social, cultural, racial and political issues, so that what they have learned as a profession is not unnecessarily and damagingly confined in the clinical context. (Details available from BAC, Rugby.)

References

Airey, C. and Brook, L. (1986) Interim report: social and moral issues, in R. Jowell, S. Witherspoon and L. Brook (eds), *British Social Attitudes*. Aldershot: Gower.

Faludi, S. (1992) *Backlash: The Undeclared War Against Women*. London: Chatto and Windus.

Harding, S. (1988) Trends in permission, in R. Jowell, S. Witherspoon and L. Brook (eds), *British Social Attitudes*. Aldershot: Gower.

Hirsch, S.K. and Kummerow, J.M. (1987) *Introduction to Type in Organisational Settings*. Palo Alto, CA: Consulting Psychologists Press.

James, W. (1975 [1906]) *Pragmatism and The Meaning of Truth*. Cambridge, MA and London: Harvard University Press.

Lane, D. (1996), in I. Horton, R. Bayne and J. Bimrose (eds), *New Directions in Counselling: A Roundtable*. In S. Palmer, S. Dainow and P. Milner (eds), *Counselling: The BAC Counselling Reader*. London: Sage.

Myers, K.D. and Kirby, L.K. (1994) *Introduction to Type: Dynamics and Development*. Palo Alto, CA: Consulting Psychologists Press.

Nelson-Jones, R. (1996) *Relating Skills: A Practical Guide to Effective Personal Relationships*. London: Cassell.

Owen, I.R. (1996) Person-centred approach in a cultural context, in S. Palmer, S. Dainow and P. Milner (eds), *Counselling: the BAC Counselling Reader*. London: Sage.

Pilcher, J. (1995) *Age and Generation in Modern Britain*. Oxford: Oxford University Press.

Samuels, A. (1993) *The Political Psyche*. London: Routledge.

Thatcher, M. (1993) *The Downing Street Years*. London: Harper Collins.

Weinrach, S.G. (1995) Rational emotive behaviour therapy: A tough-minded therapy for a tender-minded profession, in W. Dryden (ed.), *Rational Emotive Behaviour Therapy*. London: Sage.

Whitmore, D. (1996) in I. Horton, R. Bayne and J. Bimrose (eds), *New Directions in Counselling: A Roundtable*. In S. Palmer, S. Dainow and P. Milner (eds), *Counselling: The BAC Counselling Reader*. London: Sage.

Winnicott, D.W. (1975) Hate in the countertransference, *Through Paediatrics to Psycho-Analysis*. London: Hogarth Press.

Witherspoon, S. (1985) Sex roles and gender issues, in R. Jowell, S. Witherspoon and L. Brook (eds), *British Social Attitudes*. Aldershot: Gower.

5

The Future of Psychotherapy and Counseling Psychology in the USA: Delphi Data and Beyond

Greg J. Neimeyer and John C. Norcross

The year 2000 – once distant and unfathomable – now looms directly ahead of us on the psychotherapeutic horizon. Fraught with spiritual and metaphorical significance, the start of the millennium brings a sense of new beginnings, untold possibilities, and frightening prospects. Although in one sense an arbitrary milestone, this chronological portal leads us to speculate on what psychotherapy and counseling psychology will be like in the twenty-first century.

However, we confront at least three problems in attempting to forecast the future. First, innovations appear and vanish with bewildering rapidity on the diffuse psychotherapeutic scene. As Yalom (1975) cautioned, only a truly intrepid observer would attempt to differentiate evanescent from potentially important and durable trends in the field. Second, as Ekstein (1972) warned, many predictions in the uncertain world of psycho-therapy tend to be self-fulfilling prophecies or magical wish-fulfillments. And third, forecasts tend to be plain wrong, as anyone who has attempted them knows. Our predictive accuracy is meager, just as it is in our clinical work.

For these reasons, when endeavouring to discern the future, we prefer to rely on Delphi polls: the most sensitive (but still fallible) prognostic method at our disposal. The Delphic method secures the consensus of intrepid observers representing diverse orientations on what *will* occur in psychotherapy during the next decade, in contrast to what they personally would *like* to happen.

In this chapter, we examine the probable futures of psychotherapy and counseling psychology in the USA by reviewing the results of our Delphi polls (Neimeyer and Diamond, 1996; Norcross et al., 1992) and other empirical surveys (e.g. Norcross et al., 1996). Following a brief considera-tion of the Delphi method, we address four topical clusters of contem-porary and future significance: broad directions in psychotherapy; core identity of counseling psychology; the nature of its anticipated research and scientific subscriptions; and finally, professional training. Throughout, the explicit time frame is a five-year span from 1997 to 2001. Delimiting the upper reach of predictions has its disadvantages, of course, but we hope it will engender more reliable and responsible predictions.

Delphi poll

The Delphi methodology was developed in the early 1950s as part of military research concerning the use of expert opinion, and the original polling technique was a classified secret of the US Air Force until the early 1960s. Named in honor of the ancient oracle, Delphi polling structures a group communication so that the process effectively allows a group of individuals, as a whole, to deal with a complex problem (Linstone and Turoff, 1975). A panel of experts answers the same questions at least twice. In the first phase the experts answer the questions anonymously and without feedback. In subsequent phases the experts are provided with the names and views of the entire panel and given the opportunity to revise their predictions in light of the group judgment.

Consistent with the notion that 'two heads are better than one,' the Delphi poll takes systematic advantage of multiple and interactive expert perspectives. The particular virtues of Delphi methodology are (a) that it consistently provides the closest answer to extremely difficult questions compared to other prognostication techniques; (b) that the responses from the second phase are typically less variable and hence less ambiguous than those on the first; and (c) that group consensus has been found to be more accurate than individual opinion (e.g. Anderson et al., 1981; Ascher, 1978; Boronson, 1980; Dalkey and Helmer, 1963; Martino, 1972; Moore, 1987).

Congruent with previous Delphi findings – and consistent with the aim of developing consensus of expert opinion regarding the future of psychotherapy – over 95% of our questionnaire items evidenced a decrease in standard deviation from round one to round two. Providing results of the initial predictions to the panel thus reduced variation and facilitated agreement regarding future directions (see Neimeyer and Diamond, 1996, and Norcross et al., 1992, for details).

Broad directions in psychotherapy

Our earliest Delphi poll attempted to extract the collective wisdom of 75 intrepid observers on the future of psychotherapy in the USA. The panel predicted trends using a 7-point, Likert-type scale where 1 = great decrease, 3 = remain the same, and 7 = great increase. The panelists were repeatedly reminded to predict the future as they perceived it, not as they desired it (tempting as that might be).

These broad directions in the clinical interventions, therapy modalities, and theoretical orientations of the future are summarized in Table 5.1 and

Table 5.1   *Composite predictions for clinical interventions of the future*

Interventions	Mean	SD
Self-change techniques	5.45	0.81
Problem-solving techniques	5.33	0.70
Homework assignments	5.24	0.75
Communication skills	5.19	0.78
Cognitive restructuring	5.12	0.75
In vivo exposure	5.07	0.93
Social skills training	5.04	0.78
Self-control procedures	4.99	0.81
Imagery	4.79	0.78
Behavioral contracting	4.79	0.78
Computerized therapies	4.75	0.93
Teaching/advising	4.73	0.74
Expressing support/warmth	4.64	0.71
Bibliotherapy	4.60	0.94
Behavior modification	4.56	0.98
Relaxation techniques	4.55	0.95
Reassurance	4.24	0.72
Accurate empathy	4.21	0.76
Biofeedback	4.17	0.95
Therapist self-disclosure	4.15	0.86
Confrontation	4.04	0.89
Paradoxical interventions	3.85	1.11
Hypnosis	3.81	0.77
Systematic desensitization	3.75	0.81
Cathartic methods	3.56	1.06
Analysis of resistance	3.55	0.96
Transference interpretation	3.03	0.94
Encounter exercises	2.89	0.92
Dream interpretation	2.84	0.94
Emotional flooding/implosion	2.68	0.76
Free association	2.29	0.92
Aversive conditioning	2.29	0.92

1 = great decrease, 4 = remain the same, 7 = great increase.

Figures 5.1 and 5.2. Each presents item means and standard deviations from the second round of data collection, organized in ranked order.

Our observers first predicted the extent to which specific therapeutic interventions will be increasingly or decreasingly employed over the next five years. As shown in Table 5.1, present-centered, structured, and directive techniques were presaged to increase markedly in the forthcoming decade. Self-change, problem solving, homework assignments, communication skills, cognitive restructuring, *in vivo* exposure, and social skills training were expected to lead the way. By contrast, historically oriented, unstructured, and relatively passive procedures were predicted to decline. Aversive and implosion interventions were also presaged to decrease, as judged from their means of 2.29 and 2.68, respectively.

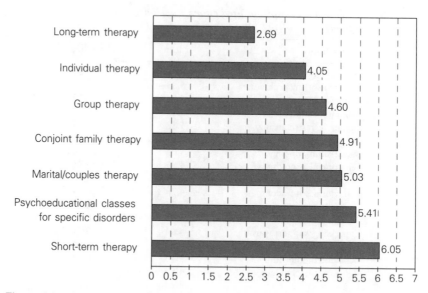

Figure 5.1 *Composite predictions for therapy modalities of the future.*
Ratings reflect mean responses where 1 = great decrease, 4 = remain the
same, and 7 = great increase.

Turning to therapy modalities, the panel expressed strong positive
expectations for short-term therapy (*M* = 6.05 on a 7-point scale) and
concomitant negative expectations for long-term work (*M* = 2.69). Figure
5.1 also shows moderate increases were foreseen for psychoeducational
groups and marital therapy. Conjoint family and group formats were predicted to accelerate more than individual format in professional popularity.

As depicted in Figure 5.2, the systemic, eclectic, cognitive, and integrative orientations were expected to expand moderately next decade in that
all received second round mean ratings of 5.0 or greater. Psychobiological,
behavioral, and feminist perspectives can expect slight growth during the
same time span. By contrast, transactional analysis and (classic) psychoanalysis were predicted to experience marked contraction. In general,
paralleling the patterns in clinical interventions and therapy modalities, the
trend is encouraging for active, present-centered systems of psychotherapy
and discouraging for comparatively passive, historically oriented systems.

These expert composite ratings portend 'what's hot' and 'what's not' as
we approach the millennium. In terms of interventions, our intrepid
observers concur that psychotherapy will become more directive, psychoeducational, present-centered, problem focused, and briefer in the next
decade. Concomitantly, aversive, relatively unstructured, historically
oriented, and long-term approaches are predicted to decrease. In terms
of theoretical orientations, integrative, systemic, and cognitive persuasions
will thrive but neither psychoanalysis nor existentialism. Put a different
way: the future psychotherapist, according to Karasu (1987), will be

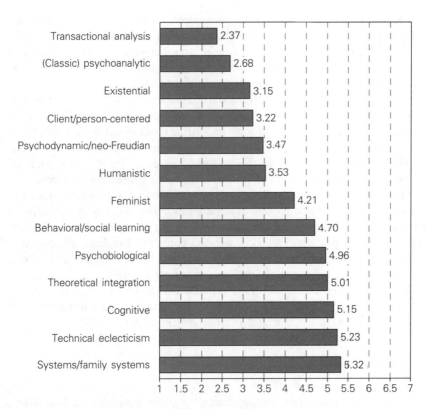

Figure 5.2 *Composite predictions for theoretical orientations of the future.* Ratings reflect mean responses where 1 = great decrease, 4 = remain the same, and 7 = great increase.

increasingly called upon to be eclectic, to treat symptoms directly and efficiently, to deliver psychotherapy within less than 50 minutes in each session, and to see patients infrequently and for a limited duration overall.

Although this Delphi poll did not directly address the settings of psychotherapy, the findings have direct implications for where psychotherapy of the future will be rendered, at least in the USA. In an age of diminishing resources, the ongoing transformations in psychological services portend that a decreased proportion will be provided in individual independent practice. Recent changes in health care delivery models and reimbursement mechanisms will pose major challenges to independent providers of psychotherapy. Kiesler and Morton (1988) emphasized that systems of service delivery – not independent practitioners operating at an *individual* level – will dominate future policies. Managed care insurance will soon cover the majority of Americans and will threaten and may replace individual practices. Indeed, Cummings (1987) has estimated that by the beginning of the new millennium over half of mental health practitioners in independent practice today will be unlikely to survive.

The economic factor, as Freud recognized, is of all our categories the most neglected, and this pertains to the economics of health care as well. The health care dollar will determine in large measure the type, focus, and availability of psychotherapeutic services (Adams, 1992). Theoretical developments and clinical innovations will be fueled by – and be a consequence of – the demands of 'third parties' in the therapeutic relationship. The industrialization of health care, as Cummings (1987, 1991) sees it, is manifesting two cardinal characteristics of any industrial revolution. First, the producer (in our case, the practitioner) is losing control over the product as this control shifts to business interests. Second, practitioners' incomes will decrease because industrialization requires cheap labor.

Though difficult to accept, these forces will probably transform the way Americans practice and receive psychotherapy. The enactment of managed care and cost-containment measures will result in limitations on private fee-for-service practice, restrictions on patients' freedom of provider choice, intrusion into the formerly private world of therapist and client, and insistence on short-term, problem-specific treatments. Some clinicians will find opportunities in the transformation while others will curse it, but all will be profoundly influenced by these accelerating macroeconomic forces (Norcross et al., 1992; Norcross and Freedheim, 1992).

Core identity commitments

Within the broad arena of psychotherapy, the specialty of counseling psychology has experienced a longstanding effort to define its core features and to distinguish them from those of other mental health professions (see Hamilton, 1987). Foundational features that have enjoyed some enduring currency include the field's allegiance to a life-span developmental approach, its focus on vocational and career concerns, and its distinctive attention to issues of diversity (Meara et al., 1988; Watkins, 1994). But even these foundational features are not without challenges, challenges that are borne from within the specialty as well as those wrought from without. The continuing diversification of function enjoyed by counseling psychologists may at once be boon and bane to a profession tied to traditional roots. 'The major implication of this diversity,' notes Fretz *'is that there is little collective, long-sustained effort by any significant proportion of our profession toward any one goal'* (1980, p. 9, emphasis in the original).

Calls for counseling psychology to align more closely with other health care professions, including neuropsychology and child clinical psychology, encourage an additional kind of elasticity in the field's identity that poses further challenges to the integrity and coherence of its core moorings. The consequence is an enduring dissensus regarding the key features of the specialty. As Fretz noted wryly, 'Counseling psychology, it seems, is in the eye of the beholder' (1980, p. 9).

Efforts at identity expansion have been complemented by efforts at identity reclamation, efforts directed at re-infusing the field with doses of its traditional medicine. The role of vocational and career counseling figure pre-eminently in this regard. While the history of counseling psychology clearly documents the centrality of vocational concerns to the field's early development (Whitely, 1984), interest in career concerns seems to have diminished significantly in recent years, at least in certain respects (Fitzgerald and Osipow, 1986; Watkins et al., 1986a, b; cf. Watkins, 1994). This decline has occurred despite cogent arguments on behalf of the vocational realm by some of the leading scholars in the field of counseling psychology (Blustein, 1992; Watkins, 1987).

One longstanding concern in the field has been the possible role of this identity diffusion in the assimilation of the specialty into other areas, most notably clinical psychology. Many authors have predicted the extinction or absorption of counseling psychology into clinical psychology, particularly given the increasing convergence of the specialties in relation to workplace and function. As Hahn (1980, p. 36) noted, 'the distinction between clinical and counseling psychology is vanishing steadily.' This concern has redoubled the field's efforts to forge a distinct identity. 'It is important that counseling psychology be able to define its uniqueness,' noted Brammer et al., 'if it is to avoid efforts by some to merge the current applied specialties' (1988, p. 411).

Recent data bearing on the distinctiveness of counseling psychology vis-à-vis clinical psychology are particularly revealing in this regard. Norcross et al. (1997) examined data provided by directors of APA-accredited doctoral programs in counseling psychology ($n = 56$; 95% response rate) and clinical psychology ($n = 178$; 99% response rate) regarding the credentials of incoming students, rates of acceptance, as well as the theoretical orientations and research areas of the faculty. In comparison to clinical students, counseling students were more likely to be ethnic minorities and master's degree recipients, but were otherwise similar in academic credentials. The acceptance rates of PhD clinical and PhD counseling psychology programs were comparable (6% vs 8%), despite the higher mean number of applications (270 vs 130) to clinical programs.

Differences between clinical psychology programs and counseling psychology programs become more pronounced in terms of theoretical orientations and research interests. Consistent with previous research, clinical faculty were proportionally more psychodynamic and behavioral, whereas counseling faculty were more inclined toward the humanistic persuasion. Clinical faculty expressed more research interest in psychopathological populations (e.g. attention deficit/hyperactivity disorder (ADHD), autism, affective disorders, anxiety disorders, chronic mental illness, eating disorders, personality disorders, schizophrenia) and in activities traditionally associated with medical and hospital settings (e.g. behavioral genetics, biofeedback, child clinical/pediatric, neuropsychology, pain management, psychophysiology). By contrast, counseling psychologists were disproportionately devoted to research in their traditionally distinctive areas of vocational and career processes, human diversity (e.g. gender differences, homosexuality, minority/cross-culture, women's studies), and professional issues (e.g. ethics, professional issues/training). These differences in faculty research are predictably reflected in their students' perception of professional futures: Davis and Meara (1995) recently found that counseling psychology students saw themselves more often involved in consultation and educational-vocational counseling than did clinical psychology students.

These findings are supported and extended by the results of a Delphi poll of Directors of Training in counseling psychology (Neimeyer and Diamond, 1996). The expert panel of counseling psychologists consisted of the directors of training of all institutional members of the Council of Counseling Psychology Training Programs in the USA. In all, 37 of the directors of training who were solicited agreed to participate in the first round of the Delphi poll; 31 of those also completed the second round of polling and their mean responses constituted the data for the study. In all cases, panelists were asked to envision what they anticipate the field of counseling psychology would look like in ten years from now and to indicate their 'expected or anticipated' predictions 'regardless of how desirable or undesirable these may be to you.'

Results concerning the specialty's core identity were telling, as shown in Figure 5.3. The single greatest future identification was expected to be the field's 'commitment to issues of diversity'; expert panel members in the Delphi poll nominated this issue as the feature most central to the identity of counseling psychology ten years from now. In discussing various themes or trends that characterize counseling psychology, Watkins nominated the attention to diversity and special populations as one of only a select handful of areas that reflect 'much of the real identity and substance of what counseling psychology has been, is, and will be' (1994, p. 327). A commitment to life-span development constituted a second central component of the specialty's future identity, echoing longstanding sentiment regarding the centrality of this feature to counseling psychology. Given this, a life-span developmental orientation may well constitute the most enduring and visible of the specialty's features.

While commitments to diversity and life-span developmental orientations occupied the most central features of the specialty's future, identification with adjustment and preventative mental health models, continued commitment to the importance of supervision skills and a commitment to the scientist–practitioner model occupied middle positions in the field's predicted future.

Interestingly, relatively peripheral roles were accorded traditional areas of strength, particularly vocational and career counseling. The role of vocational counseling in the specialty's future has been a subject of continuing debate for several decades now. On the one hand is work that supports Watkins' recent conclusion that 'The vocational arm of our

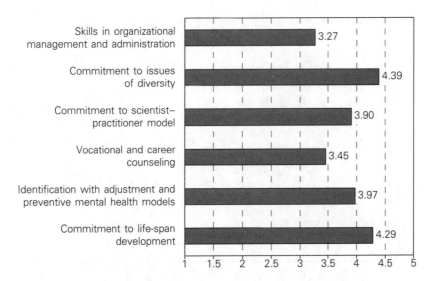

Figure 5.3 *Composite predictions for anticipated core of counseling psychology.* Ratings reflect mean responses to the question 'To what extent do you think each of the following areas will be central or peripheral to the field of counseling psychology ten years from now?' Ratings could range from 5 (highly central) to 1 (highly peripheral).

specialty continues to be a significant part of who and what we are, continues to provide rich, fertile opportunities for practice and research, and continues to thrive and flourish within counseling psychology' (1994, p. 322). On the other hand, available data support a somewhat less sanguine view regarding the centrality of this area to the future of the specialty. Watkins et al.'s (1986b) data, for example, prompted a more somber assessment: 'If subsequent research shows that vocational work continues to be engaged in minimally and is increasingly uninteresting and unattractive to counseling psychologists, a reevaluation of its place in counseling psychology and counseling psychology training may be needed' (p. 307).

One final indicator of the field's distinctive features may be reflected in the initial employment setting of its graduates. A 23-year retrospective review of initial job placements in the field (Neimeyer and Bowman, 1996) suggests three noteworthy things in this regard (see Figure 5.4). First, employment settings for counseling psychologists have generally remained quite stable across time, reflecting the field's tandem commitment to science and practice. Academic settings, for example, have remained among the largest and most consistent employers of counseling psychology graduates (15%). Second, despite this, it is none the less true that the vast preponderance of counseling psychologists are employed in direct service capacities. Community mental health centers (15%), university counseling centers (14.7%) and private practice (12.5%) have jointly accounted for

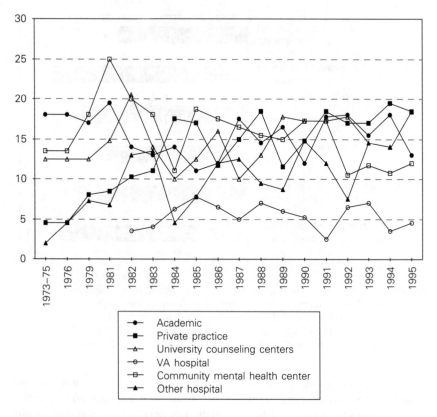

Figure 5.4   *Percentage of counseling psychology first-year job placements over time.*

more than half of the field's initial job placements. Medical settings, including Veterans Administration Medical Centers (5.4%) and 'other hospital' settings (9.3%) have shown a substantial increase across time. A third and final point concerns the meteoric rise in private practice as a work setting. Private practice surpasses all other settings as the first employment setting among counseling psychologists. Overall, initial employment data reflect the general 'professionalization' of the specialty. Enduring commitments to academic and university-based settings are being complemented by growing commitments to medical and private practice contexts.

Scientific subscriptions

As part and parcel of its ongoing self-reflection, the field of counseling psychology has turned special attention to particular facets of its functioning. Nowhere is this reflection more clearly felt than in relation to the role of science and scientific inquiry in the specialty. Nearly a half of a century ago the American Psychological Association officially adopted the scientist–practitioner model (1947), a model that was quickly extended to the training of doctoral psychologists at the Boulder Conference in 1949. With the Northwestern (1951) and Greyston (1964) conferences reaffirming the commitment, it remained for the Vail Conference (1973) to articulate an alternative model based largely on the primacy of the practitioner among the ranks of the field's graduates. While most subsequent authors have again advocated on behalf of the scientist–practitioner model, they have varied widely in their advocacy of which term should receive the greater inflection. An important role was played in this regard by the Third National Conference for Counseling Psychology in Georgia (1987). The conference revitalized the field's twin commitments, emphasizing integration between the tandem terms that comprise the phrase, 'scientist–practitioner.'

It seems likely that part of this broadening may already be underway, at least if a more permissive and permeable notion of science articulates with this objective. For more than a decade, leading scholars in counseling psychology have initiated a critical reappraisal of the field's commitments to what constitutes science. Derived largely from a positivistic world view, earlier 'modern' accounts of science imposed significant restrictions on the conduct of inquiry (Neimeyer, 1993; Polkinghorne, 1984). Awareness of these limitations has prompted recent efforts to harvest meaningful modes of inquiry from disciplines less wedded to objectivist stances. As a result, prominent scholarship has been directed toward issues of postmodernism, hermeneutics and self-agency, and toward theories of intentional action, narrative knowing and constructivism (Neimeyer, 1993; Polkinghorne, 1988). The impact of this critical reflection is clearly registered in renewed calls for methodological diversity in the field, particularly the inclusion of more naturalistic, ethnographic and qualitative methodologies.

Results of our Delphi poll (Neimeyer and Diamond, 1996) support the likelihood of continued diversity in the field's scientific subscriptions in the years ahead. Over the course of the next ten years (as seen in Figure 5.5), the greatest increases were predicted in relation to the development of descriptive and qualitative sophistication, for example, followed closely by attention to methodological diversity and triangulation. Calls for expanding available methodologies are now an enduring feature of the specialty's anticipated future, extending a commitment already visible in the field's scholarship.

The expected attention to diverse and qualitative methods likely articulates with the specialty's broader reflections regarding the nature of science and its role in core training in counseling psychology. Consistent with this notion is the finding that Directors of Training in the Delphi poll predicted that the future would be marked by substantial increases in the exploration of alternative models of training (i.e. practitioner–scientist, professional–practitioner) as well as continued critique of the received

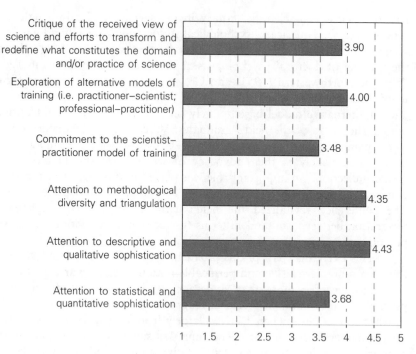

Figure 5.5   *Composite predictions for areas of scientific training.* Ratings reflect mean responses to the question 'To what extent do you think that attention will increase or decrease in relation to each of the areas below?' Ratings could range from 5 (increase significantly) to 1 (decrease significantly).

view of science that has anchored the field's historical methodological commitments.

One consequence of this critique may be an erosion in confidence in the field's future commitment to the scientist–practitioner model of training, and perhaps its associated attention to statistical and quantitative sophistication, since these two areas occupied the bottom positions in terms of their expected attention in the field's future. In neither case, however, were these commitments expected to decrease in an absolute way (i.e. ratings below the midpoint rating of 3), only to remain relatively stable while more vigorous attention was being devoted toward expanding notions of science, scientific methods, and their role in doctoral training.

Professional training

Ongoing debates persist regarding training in psychological assessment and psychotherapy. Both internship and market forces have placed important emphasis on clinical skills, and this emphasis has posed significant

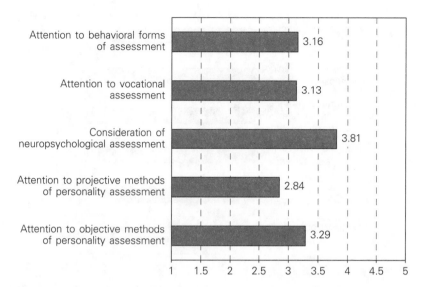

Figure 5.6   *Composite predictions for training in assessment.* Ratings
reflect mean responses to the question 'To what extent do you believe the
field's attention will increase or decrease in relation to each of the
following areas?' Ratings could range from 5 (increase significantly) to 1
(decrease significantly).

challenges to doctoral training programs in counseling psychology. With
practitioner oriented professional schools now generating approximately
50% of the doctoral students in clinical psychology, students and training
programs alike are experiencing pressure to address the quality and
quantity of predoctoral professional training.

Predictions concerning the field's future attention to areas of psychological assessment were widely variable (see Figure 5.6). Out of the five
areas of assessment (objective, projective, neuropsychological, vocational,
and behavioral) studied in the Delphi poll (Neimeyer and Diamond, 1996),
for example, only one was nominated for substantially greater future
attention. This was the area of neuropsychological assessment. By contrast,
relative stasis was predicted in the areas of objective personality and
intellectual assessment, behavioral forms of assessment, and vocational
assessment. These predictions were anchored by predictions regarding
projective methods of personality assessment, the only area in the Delphi
study to reflect an anticipated decrease in future attention within the
specialty.

These findings concerning the future of assessment within counseling
psychology support and extend related studies of the role that psychological assessment plays in the professional lives of current counseling
psychologists. For example, Fitzgerald and Osipow (1986) reported in
their study of Division 17 members that substantial percentages of their

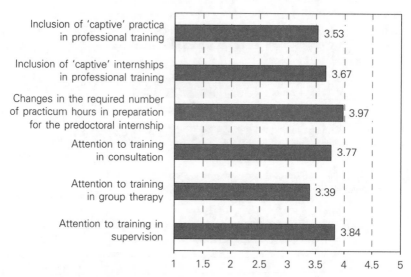

Figure 5.7 *Composite predictions for professional training in psychotherapy.* Ratings reflect mean responses to the question 'To what extent do you expect the field's attention to increase or decrease in relation to each of the following areas?' Ratings could range from 5 (increase significantly) to 1 (decrease significantly).

respondents utilized objective personality inventories (66.7%), vocational interest inventories (61.8%) and intelligence tests (57%) in their practice, with relatively fewer incorporating projective techniques (45.6%). In all cases, however, the amount of time devoted to these activities was minimal (2–3%), and their perceived importance was moderately low. In summarizing his review of more than fifty years of survey data concerning vocational assessment, Watkins (1993) concluded that vocational assessment is still very much alive, still being taught in most counseling psychology programs, and still being practiced by a fair number of counseling psychologists. This optimistic appraisal was tempered by the realization, however, that this 'is not an area in which counseling psychology students seem to be highly interested' (p. 113).

Regarding psychotherapy training, Delphi poll results indicated the single greatest increase was in relation to the number of required practicum hours in preparation for predoctoral internship (see Figure 5.7). Following this, attention to training in supervision and training in consultation were expected to experience the next largest increases in the specialty over the next ten years. These two predictions are supported by independent findings concerning the increasing use of these skills by current counseling psychologists. Approximately 70% of all counseling psychologists engage in supervision and consultation, for example, with the median person spending nearly 10% of his or her time in each of these functions (Fitzgerald and Osipow, 1986).

Concluding comments

It is difficult to fix on a single image that characterizes the future of psychotherapy and counseling psychology, but it seems safe to say that it will reflect tandem commitments to traditional moorings and contemporary demands. In general, issues of diversity and special populations figure especially strongly in counseling psychology's foreseeable future, and the continuing commitment to life-span development seems similarly assured. These predictions cohere to form a focal point for the specialty's future within an increasingly multicultural society dedicated to ongoing personal development and adjustment.

The field's scientific commitments seem equally strong, with increased attention to methodological diversity. This, in turn, may be supported by continued and vigorous explorations of alternative notions of science and, by extension, of scientific training within the specialty. Pressures toward 'professionalization' can be expected to continue, as well, with corresponding increases in the training and placement of counseling psychologists in applied contexts.

To conclude, while we have endeavored to outline the vague contours of a reshaped future for psychotherapy and counseling psychology, the principal value of our efforts may ultimately lie in the process of questioning. The cutting edge of knowledge is not in the known but in the unknown, not in knowing but in questioning. Facts, trends, and data are dull instruments unless they are honed to a sharp edge by persistent inquiry into the unknown. Our Delphi polls and other empirical means of collective wisdom may enable us not only to contemplate and question the transformations confronting us in the next millennium, but also empower us to work toward those transformations in the best interests of our profession, our clients, and our society.

References

Adams, D.B. (1992) The future roles for psychotherapy in the medical-surgical arena. *Psychotherapy*, 29: 95–103.

Anderson, J.K., Parente, F.J. and Gordon, C. (1981) A forecast of the future for the mental health profession, *American Psychologist*, 36: 848–55.

Ascher, W. (1978) *Forecasting*. Baltimore, MD: Johns Hopkins University Press.

Blustein, D.L. (1992) Reinvigorating the vocational realm, *The Counseling Psychologist*, 20: 712–23.

Boronson, W. (1980) The secret of the Delphi oracle, *Next*, 1: 50.

Brammer, L., Alcorn, J., Birk, J., Gazda, G., Hurst, J., LaFromboise, T., Newmann, R., Osipow, S., Packard, T., Romero, D. and Scott, N. (1988) Organizational and political issues in counseling psychology: Recommendations for change, *The Counseling Psychologist*, 16: 407–22.

Cummings, N.A. (1987) The dismantling of our health system: Strategies for the survival of psychological practice, *American Psychologist*, 41: 426–31.

Cummings, N.A. (1991) Out of the cottage, *AAP Advance*, spring: 1–15.

Dalkey, N. and Helmer, O. (1963) An experimental application of the Delphi Method to the use of experts, *Management Science*, 9: 458–67.

Davis, K.L. and Meara, N.M. (1995) Students' perceptions of their future professional behavior, *Applied and Preventive Psychology*, 4: 131–40.

Ekstein, R. (1972) In quest of the professional self, in A. Burton (ed.), *Twelve Therapists: How they Live and Actualize Themselves*. San Francisco: Jossey Bass.

Fitzgerald, L.F. and Osipow, S.H. (1986) An occupational analysis of counseling psychology: How special is the specialty? *American Psychologist*, 41: 535–44.

Fretz, B.R. (1980) Counseling psychology: 2001, *The Counseling Psychologist*, 8: 2–11.

Hahn, M.E. (1980) Counseling psychology: 2000, *The Counseling Psychologist*, 8: 36–7.

Hamilton, M.K. (1987) Some suggestions for our chronic problem, *The Counseling Psychologist*, 15: 341–6.

Karasu, T.B. (1987) The psychotherapy of the future, *Psychosomatics*, 28: 380–4.

Kiesler, C.A. and Morton, T.L. (1988) Psychology and public policy in the 'health care revolution', *American Psychologist*, 43: 993–1003.

Lent, R.W. (1990) Further reflections of the public image of counseling psychology, *The Counseling Psychologist*, 18: 324–32.

Linstone, H.A. and Turoff, M. (eds) (1975) *The Delphi Method: Techniques and Applications*. Reading, MA: Addison-Wesley.

Martino, J.P. (1972) *Technological Forecasting for Decision Making*. New York: American Elsevier.

Meara, N.M., Schmidt, L.D., Carrington, C.H., Davis, K.L., Dixon, D.N., Fretz, B.R., Myers, R.A., Ridley, C.R. and Suinn, R.M. (1988) Training and accreditation in counseling psychology, *The Counseling Psychologist*, 16: 366–84.

Moore, C.M. (1987) *Group Techniques for Idea Building*. Newbury Park, CA: Sage.

Neimeyer, G.J. (ed.) (1993) *Constructivist Assessment*. Thousand Oaks, CA: Sage Publications.

Neimeyer, G.J. and Bowman, J. (1996) *Internship and Initial Job Placements in Counseling Psychology: A 23-year Retrospective*. Unpublished manuscript, University of Florida, Gainesville, FL.

Neimeyer, G.J. and Diamond, A. (1996) *The Future of Counseling Psychology: A Delphi Poll*. Unpublished manuscript, University of Florida, Gainesville, FL.

Neimeyer, G. and Resnikoff, A. (1982) Qualitative strategies in counseling research, *The Counseling Psychologist*, 10: 75–85.

Norcross, J.C. and Freedheim, D.K. (1992) Into the future: Retrospect and prospect in psychotherapy, in D.K. Freedheim (ed.), *History of Psychotherapy: A Century of Change*. Washington, DC: American Psychological Association.

Norcross, J.C., Alford, B.A. and DeMichele, J.T. (1992) The future of psychotherapy: Delphi data and concluding observations, *Psychotherapy*, 29: 150–8.

Norcross, J.C., Sayette, M.A., Mayne, T.J., Karg, R.S. and Turkson, M.A. (1997) *PhD counseling, PhD clinical, and PsyD Clinical Psychology Programs: A Comparison of Admissions Criteria, Student Characteristics, and Faculty Interests*. Manuscript submitted for publication.

Polkinghorne, D.E. (1984) Further extensions of methodological diversity for counseling psychology, *Journal of Counseling Psychology*, 31: 416–29.

Polkinghorne, D.E. (1988) *Narrative Knowing and the Human Sciences*. New York: State University of New York Press.

Watkins, C.E., Jr. (1987) On myopia, rhetoric, and reality in counseling psychology, *The Counseling Psychologist*, 15: 332–6.

Watkins, C.E., Jr. (1993) What have surveys taught us about the teaching and practice of vocational assessment? *The Counseling Psychologist*, 21: 109–17.

Watkins, C.E., Jr. (1994) On hope, promise, and possibility in counseling psychology or some simple, but meaningful observations about our specialty, *The Counseling Psychologist*, 22: 315–34.

Watkins, C.E., Jr., Lopez, F.G., Campbell, V.L. and Himmel, C.D. (1986a) Contemporary counseling psychology: Results of a national survey, *Journal of Counseling Psychology*, 33: 301–9.

Watkins, C.E., Jr., Lopez, F.G., Campbell, V.L. and Himmel, C.D. (1986b) Counseling psychology and clinical psychology: Some preliminary comparative data, *American Psychologist*, 41: 581–2.

Watkins, C.E., Jr., Campbell, V.L. and McGregor, P. (1988) Counseling psychologists' uses of and opinions about psychological tests: A contemporary perspective, *The Counseling Psychologist*, 16: 476–86.

Whitely, J.M. (1984) A historical perspective on the development of counseling psychology as a profession, in S.D. Brown and R.W. Lent (eds), *Handbook of Counseling Psychology*. New York: John Wiley. pp. 3–55.

Yalom, I.D. (1975) *The Theory and Practice of Group Therapy*, 2nd edn. New York: Basic.

6

Stress Counselling and Management: Past, Present and Future

Stephen Palmer

Eventually Homo Sapiens evolved and unlike the others that had come before, they could think about their thinking and disturb themselves about what they thought.

Why stress counselling and management

Why have I decided to write a chapter on the past, present and future of stress counselling and stress management? I have spent many thousands of hours studying, researching, lecturing and writing on stress counselling and management as well as running training/therapy groups and seeing individuals. It has been an all-consuming experience for some years and maybe I wish to share some of my thoughts with others. This chapter will take a historical perspective illustrating how the field has progressed over the years. I have divided this chapter under three main headings: past, present and future. I shall include some of the earlier debates about emotions and also a section on the current understanding on the physiology of the stress response. In each part I shall consider what 'therapies' were, are or will be available during the period in question.

Past (from BC until 1940)

In this section I shall concentrate on the field of stress theory, research and management up until 1940. Although this period may appear to be an arbitrary division of time the next period covered from 1941 until 1994 introduces modern theoretical views of stress and its subsequent management.

The origins of the word 'stress'

The word 'stress' is probably derived from a Latin word, *stringere*, to draw tight, sometimes used to describe hardships. Later it denoted effort or strain. In AD 1303 a poet, Robert Mannyng, used 'stres' in his work, *Handlying Synne*. Cox (1978) has also reported its use in English literature from the fourteenth century onwards in a variety of forms including stres, stresse, strest, straisse and stresce.

Earlier theories of stress and emotion

When looking at the field of stress over the past 2000 years it is important to note that most of the earlier theorists wrote about experiences, passions and emotions and did not necessarily use the word stress. For example, Aristotle (c. 4 BC) wrote about the body and soul including passions, sensations, appetites and thinking and his ideas were further developed by St Thomas Aquinas in the thirteenth century AD. The link between emotions or personality with disease has been widely reported over many centuries. One of the earliest was in AD 400 when the Greek writer, Galen, noted that melancholic women are more susceptible to 'swellings' of the breasts than sanguine women.

In about the seventeenth century Descartes advanced a complex model of passion (emotion) which incorporated a feedback system to the 'Pineal body' which served to reinforce the emotional response. One important factor Descartes included in his model was the idea that passion was triggered by an external environmental event. This idea probably influenced both James and Cannon many years later.

The 1880s were a busy time for theorists attempting to understand emotions. James (1884) and Lange (1885) both explored the relationship between emotional experience and the respective bodily sensations (reactions). To give the reader a flavour of James' ideas let us look at some extracts from his well known later work, *The Principles of Psychology* (1890, vol. II): 'Emotion is a consequence, not the cause, of the bodily expression', and

> Common sense says, we lose our fortune, are sorry and weep; we meet a bear, are frightened and run; we are insulted by a rival, are angry and strike. The hypothesis here to be defended says that this order of sequence is incorrect, that the one mental state is not immediately induced by the other, that the bodily manifestations must first be interposed between, and that the more rational statement is that we feel sorry because we cry, angry because we strike, afraid because we tremble, and not that we cry, strike, or tremble, because we are sorry, angry, or fearful, as the case may be. Without the bodily states following on the perception, the latter would be purely cognitive in form, pale, colourless, destitute of emotional warmth. (p. 450)

> Each emotion is the resultant of a sum of elements, and each element is caused by a physiological process of a sort already well known. The elements are all organic changes, and each of them is the reflex effect of the exciting object. (p. 453)

Essentially, James argued that the emotion-eliciting events evoked bodily changes by a pre-organized mechanism. As each emotion was a sum of the elements which could vary indefinitely, there was a wide range of possible emotions. Due to the emphasis placed on the feedback from the peripheral bodily reactions this theory has been described as a 'peripheral' theory.

The James–Lange theory, as it was sometimes later referred to, was challenged by Professor Ward amongst others. In supplementary volumes of *Encyclopaedia Britannica*, 9th edition, he stated: 'Let Professor James be confronted first by a chained bear and next by a bear at large: to one object he presents a bun, and to the other a clean pair of heels'. Therefore the same person could experience two different emotions and subsequent behaviours on meeting a bear. This seems obvious to us in the 1990s yet to the academics of the time these simple observations were probably of earth-shaking importance.

If we just stick to this one issue of the bears, the story continues as Ward's ideas did not satisfy all other observers. William McDougall commented:

> There is a world of difference between, on the one hand, the instinctive response to the object that excites fear, and, on the other hand, running away because one judges that discretion is the better part of valour. I well remember standing in the zoological garden at Calcutta before a very strong cage in which was a huge Bengal tiger fresh from the jungle. A low-caste Hindu sweeper had amused himself by teasing the monster, and every time he came near the tiger bounded forward with an awful roar. At each of many repetitions of this performance a cold shudder of fear passed over me, and only by an effort could I restrain the impulse to beat a hasty retreat. Though I knew the bars confined the brute more securely than any chain, it was not because the emotion of fear and the corresponding impulse were lacking that I did not show a 'clean pair of heels'. (1919, pp. 52–3)

McDougall and other commentators up to the middle of this century overlooked one extremely important factor that an earlier first-century philosopher, Epictetus has observed: 'People are disturbed not by things but by the views which they take of them'. Later in the second century Marcus Aurelius also commented on this issue in his *Meditations*: 'Put from you the belief that "I have been wronged", and with it will go the feeling. Reject your sense of injury, and the injury itself disappears' (1995, p. 19). He continued with this line of thought:

> For you, evil comes not from the mind of another; nor yet from any of the phases and changes of your own bodily frame. Then whence? From that part of yourself which acts as your assessor of what is evil. Refuse its assessment, and all is well . . . Everything is but what your opinion makes it; and that opinion lies with yourself. Renounce it when you will, and at once you have rounded the foreland and all is calm; a tranquil sea, a tideless haven. (1995, pp. 25, 83)

Notice how he suggests that a relaxed state can be attained if you just change your opinion. No suggestion here of relaxation techniques or other reactive strategies!

The question I often ask is how did the theorists and philosophers manage to overlook these astute observations made many centuries ago? This could be due to my perfect 20–20 vision granted by hindsight. Perhaps the answer is simple: either they had not studied these earlier ideas or did not see the connection. Yet William McDougall was originally a Reader in Mental Philosophy in the University of Oxford and later became

Professor of Psychology in Harvard College. If we assume few people read these works then surely they might have read Shakespeare who noted in *Hamlet*:

> HAMLET: Why, then 'tis none to you; for there is nothing either good or bad but thinking makes it so. (II.ii 259–61)

Returning to this century, Walter Cannon (1927) challenged the James–Lange theory of emotion as it was not compatible with the developing neurophysiological knowledge. He argued that the visceral reactions were too diffuse to produce the many specific patterns of bodily change necessary to produce emotional experience. He also thought that the same visceral changes occurred with different emotions including non-emotional states. Cannon suggested that the thalamus was the main mediating factor as the mechanism of emotion. Thus, when triggered by cortical impulses or sensory input the thalamus fed both the bodily reaction and the experience of emotion. This theory was further developed by Bard (1928) who found that diencephalic and related structures were necessary for emotionally associated behaviours. This 'central' theory became known as the Cannon–Bard theory. Later Cannon (1929, 1931) realized that the sympathetic nervous system was largely responsible for emotionally associated bodily changes. In 1935 Cannon developed the concept of homeostasis which reasserted the earlier views of Claude Bernard from the previous century who suggested that regardless of external changes an individual's internal systems should ideally remain unaltered. A simple analogy would be a modern central heating system which is thermostatically controlled.

Papez (1937) realized that the limbic structures may be involved in the experience and expression of emotion. He formulated a system that included the hippocampus-fornix, mammillary bodies, mammillothalamic tract, thalamocortical radiations, anterior thalamic nuclei, and gyrus cinguli. This modification of the Cannon–Bard theory substituted the limbic system and associated structures as the key emotional control centre and not the thalamus. This basic system has underpinned modern theories of brain function. It is worth noting that the limbic system is associated with the emotions of anger and fear which correspond to the well known 'fight' or 'flight' stress response.

Therapies

So what was on offer to individuals who wanted to manage stress? Very little would be the answer. In fact, in the west, the idea of taking one day a week as a day of rest, i.e. the sabbath, was probably the nearest people came to receiving a regular preventive stress management programme. However, this was not necessarily the intention of religious leaders nor their Gods when the sabbath was recommended. More formally, relaxation techniques and autogenic training were advocated (see Jacobson, 1938; Schultz, 1932). In cases of severe stress such as shell shock, hypnotism was applied (see

Edgell, 1926, p. 268). Freud and Jung focused on the unconscious which may have helped some of their clients deal with stress, 'traumatic neurosis' and 'psychoneuroses' (see Pfister, 1917). In 1907 Dubois included cognitive techniques in *The Psychic Treatment of Nervous Disorders*. Another precursor to Ellis' rational psychotherapy was Adler's (1927) approach to therapy which does include the 're-education of clients' faulty perceptions and social values, and modification of their motivation. It is intended that clients should gain insight into their mistaken ideas and unrealistic goals, both of which are a source of discouragement' (Clifford, 1996, p. 110). In the east, meditation, fragrance, yoga, t'ai chi and massage had been used by many societies throughout recorded history. Interestingly, even though Greek and Roman philosophers two thousand years ago suggested that individuals could take a different view or attitude towards problems, this was not generally advocated as a stress management strategy.

Present (1941–94)

Since 1941 research into stress and latterly stress management has rapidly increased. Although still incomplete, a greater understanding of the psychophysiology of stress has also evolved. This section will reflect current thinking and will cover the physiology of stress, recent theories since 1940, organizational issues, and therapies on offer.

Physiology of stress

If an individual perceives a situation as threatening, two physiological systems are activated. The first involves the autonomic nervous system (ANS), which is responsible for controlling the lungs, heart, stomach, blood vessels and glands. The ANS consists of two subsystems: The parasympathetic (PNS) and the sympathetic (SNS) nervous systems. Messages are conveyed along neurones from the cerebral cortex and the limbic system to the hypothalamus. The anterior hypothalamus triggers the sympathetic arousal of the ANS. The main sympathetic neurotransmitter is called noradrenaline which is released at nerve endings. The adrenal glands are involved with the production of a number of stress hormones and are located on top of the kidneys. The SNS is directly connected via a nerve to the adrenal medulla, the central part of the adrenal gland, which produces adrenaline and noradrenaline. The relative levels of these two catecholamines released into the bloodstream depend upon how the individual appraises a stress scenario, as generally noradrenaline is associated with the anger or fight response whilst adrenaline is associated with the fear and the flight response (see Henry, 1980; Henry et al., 1976). In contrast to the SNS which prepared the body for action, the PNS aids relaxation and conserves energy. For example, the PNS promotes the absorption and digestion of food from the alimentary tract. Pepsinogen, mucus, acid and gastrin are secreted by the stomach whilst saliva is secreted by the mouth. In my experience it is often not realized by stress management practitioners and counsellors that intense emotion can sometimes be associated with both sympathetic and parasympathetic activity (Vingerhoets, 1985). Individuals experiencing extreme fear may suffer from urinary incontinence, diarrhoea and fainting which are manifestations of elevated parasympathetic activity.

The second system is known as the endocrine or pituitary–adrenal cortex system. In this system the hypothalamus instructs the pituitary to release adrenocorticotropic hormone (ACTH) into the bloodstream which then activates the adrenal cortex, which is the outer part of the adrenal gland. The adrenal cortex releases aldosterone which increases blood volume and thereby increases blood pressure. It also synthesizes cortisol which aids glucose and fat mobilization, reduces the inflammatory response and lowers allergic reactions. Individuals who feel depressed and perceive that they have a lack of control over events experience increased levels of cortisol and this reduces the effectiveness of the immune system leading to increased susceptibility of individuals to suffer from minor colds to more life-threatening diseases (see Gregson and Looker, 1996; Irwin and Livnat, 1987; Kiecolt-Glaser and Glaser, 1991).

However, it is worth noting that there is now significant evidence that under acute stress conditions, immune function may be enhanced (e.g. Ader and Cohen, 1993). A good example would be an impending infection that can be held off whilst revising for important exams but resistance crumples as soon as the exams are over. Also Frankenhaeuser (1981) found that stressors such as an extended period of overtime lead to higher catecholamines levels (in particular adrenaline), after the overtime was reduced. This has been called the 'sleeper effect' (see Frese and Zapf, 1988).

The pituitary releases thyroid stimulating hormone which stimulates the thyroid gland to secrete thyroxin. Thyroxin is responsible for increasing the metabolic rate and raises blood sugar levels. Other hormones (or neuromodulators) are also involved. The paraventricular nuclei of the hypothalamus contains neurons that synthesize and release arginine vasopressin, oxytocin and vasoactive intestinal peptide. When the individual perceives that the threatening situation has passed then the PNS restores the person to a state of equilibrium.

What has been described is not the complete picture but hopefully gives an insight into the complex nature of the stress response and reflects current thinking.

It is important for stress counsellors to recognize the symptoms of stress (see Table 6.1). However it is crucial that they do not confuse the symptoms which are directly attributed to the stress-response overactivation for those due to organic causes such as tumours, etc. This is one good reason why stress counsellors should not make a diagnosis unless they are also medically qualified. In my opinion, when in doubt prompt referral to the client's general practitioner (GP) or other specialist should be mandatory as a safeguard. This could be taken a step further by insisting that all

Table 6.1   *Stress-related symptoms*

Psychological	Physiological	Behavioural response
Anxiety/fear	Allergies	Aggressive/passive behaviour
Anger	Angina	Alcohol/drug abuse
Depression	Asthma	Anorexia, bulimia
Guilt	Back-ache/neck-ache	Avoidance/phobias
Hurt	Cancer	Clenched fists
Intrusive thoughts/images	Coronary heart disease	Checking rituals
Morbid jealousy	Diabetes	Compulsive behaviour
Nightmares	Diarrhoea/constipation	Impaired speech
Obsessions	Epilepsy	Increased absenteeism
Reduced self-esteem	Excessive sweating	Insomnia
Shame/embarrassment	High blood pressure/ hypertension	Low productivity
	Lung disease	Nervous cough
	Migraines	Poor time-management
	Muscle tension	Talk/walk/eating faster
	Nausea	Teeth grinding
	Palpitations	Type A behaviour
	Rapid weight loss or gain	Withdrawing from relationships
	Skin disorders	
	Ulcers	

individuals suffering from physical symptoms of stress should initially see their GP before being referred to a counsellor.

Modern theories of stress

This section will focus on the modern theories of stress which have influenced the practice of stress counselling and stress management. The definition of 'modern theories' in this context are those that still had some support after 1940.

Stimulus variable model of stress   The stimulus variable or engineering approach conceptualizes stress as a noxious stimulus or demand that is externally imposed upon an individual which can lead to ill health (see Symonds, 1947; Palmer, 1996a). In this model stress can also be caused by too much or too little external stimulation (Palmer, 1996a, p. 530).

Response variable model of stress   The response variable or physiological approach is based on Selye's (1956) triphasic model involving the initial alarm reaction (sympathetic–adrenal medullary activation), the stage of resistance (adrenal–cortical activation) and the stage of exhaustion (final reactivation of the sympathetic–adrenal medullary system). This response process is known as the general adaptation syndrome, where an individual will eventually suffer from physiological 'diseases of adaptation' to stress caused by aversive or noxious external stimuli if the last stage of exhaustion is reached (Palmer, 1996a, p. 530).

Criticisms of the stimulus and response variable models As noted previously (Palmer, 1996a, p. 530), both the stimulus variable and response
variable models are based on the oversimplified stimulus–response (SR)
paradigm and disregard the importance of perceptions and cognitions
which have a mediating effect on the stress response. Neither model
accounts for existing research findings. For example, 'the effects of noise
on task performance are not a simple function of its loudness or frequency
but are subject both to its nature and to individual differences and context
effects' (Cox, 1993, p. 10). The stimulus variable model does not differentiate between the different factors involved. The response variable model
does not take into account that some noxious external stimuli such as heat
do not necessarily trigger the stress response. Both models do not explain
why plasma catecholamines (adrenaline and noradrenaline) differ according to how the person perceives a situation (see page 86).

In applying the SR paradigm, much research has been undertaken into
the possible effect of specific life events upon individuals. A number of life-
event scales (e.g. Holmes and Rahe, 1967) have been developed which were
based on averaging procedures which totally ignored the personal meaning
of life events for each person and subsequently only weakly predict stress-
related illness episodes (Cooper et al., 1988a; Palmer, 1996a, p. 531).

The only therapeutic interventions these particular models would
suggest are: avoid or change the stressor; avoid life events; use relaxation
techniques to moderate the response; and take medication to control the
physiological response to stress.

Interactive variable model of stress The interactive variable, more commonly known as the psychological approach to stress, attempts to overcome the deficiencies of the earlier models by incorporating the interaction
between the external and internal worlds of an individual. There have been
a number of proposed psychological theories: the interactional and the
transactional. The interactional theories focus on the fit between the
individual and their environment (e.g. Bowers, 1973). Others concentrated
on the interactive nature of job demands and decision latitude (Karasek,
1981), but later studies have only found weak evidence to support real
interactions between specific demands leading to stress-related disease. In
fact, some research discovered that the additive nature of different
demands increased ill health. The transactional theories of stress focus on
the cognitive and affective aspects of an individual's interactions with their
environment and the coping styles they adopt or lack. We will now
examine a number of the proposed psychological theories in more depth.

The breakthrough probably came in 1955 when Albert Ellis first
attempted to explain the nature and cause of emotional disturbance (Ellis,
1955). He developed rational psychotherapy (Ellis, 1958) which was
heavily influenced by the writings of the Greek and Roman Stoic philosophers, in particular, Epictetus and Aurelius. In *Reason and Emotion in
Psychotherapy* (1962) Ellis described the ABC model of disturbance in

which 'A' represents an activating event, 'B' represents an individual's evaluative beliefs (cognitions) about the event, and 'C' represents the emotional, behavioural and physiological consequences. A stressful event such as failing an exam can be analysed as follows:

A = Activating event	Failing exam
B = Beliefs (self-defeating)	'I should have passed'
	'I can't stand failing'
	'It's awful that I have failed'
	'This proves I'm no good'
C = Emotional consequence	Depression
Behavioural consequence	Avoids speaking to family. Loss of appetite.
Physiological consequence	Irritable bowel syndrome

Like the earlier philosophers, Ellis believed that the beliefs and attitudes a person holds about an event largely contribute to his or her level of emotional disturbance. Ellis stressed that dogmatic, inflexible, absolutist, unrealistic, illogical and non-empirical beliefs were more likely to lead to elevated levels of distress. Ellis found that by challenging an individual's attitudes and beliefs through asking logical (how does it logically follow), empirical (where is the evidence) and pragmatic (where is holding onto these beliefs getting you) questions, the person may start to alter their self-defeating beliefs and become less distressed. The new self-helping beliefs and consequences in the previous example could become:

A = Activating event	Failing exam
B = Beliefs (self-helping)	'Although it's strongly preferable to pass, obviously I don't have to'
	'I'm living proof that I can stand failing'
	'It may be bad, but certainly not awful that I've failed'
	'Just because I've failed an exam it does not prove I'm a total failure. I would have to fail at absolutely everything to become a total failure!'
C = Emotional consequence	Sad
Behavioural consequence	Does not avoid interactions with others. Still has good appetite.
Physiological consequence	No irritable bowel syndrome

Ellis's theory of emotional disturbance gave counsellors, psychotherapists and trainers a new approach to helping people either suffering from stress or wishing to learn stress management thinking skills and strategies (see

Ellis et al., 1997). After Ellis, Aaron Beck (see Beck, 1976, 1993) developed cognitive therapy which is similar to rational psychotherapy (see later). Ellis has recently changed the name of his approach to rational emotive behaviour therapy and has revised his theory (see Ellis, Chapter 1, this volume and Ellis, 1994).

Ellis' theory was taken further by Lazarus and Folkman (1984), who defined stress as resulting from an imbalance between demands and resources. They suggested that an individual evaluates a particular incident, demand or on-going situation. This initial evaluation, known as primary appraisal, involves a continuous monitoring of the environment and analysis of whether a problem exists (Lazarus, 1966). If a problem is recognized then the stress response may be activated and unpleasant emotions and physical feelings may be experienced. The next stage, secondary appraisal, follows when the person evaluates his or her resources and options. Unlike either the stimulus variable or response variable models of stress, the crucial issue is whether the individual recognizes that a problem exists. Once recognized, if the demands are greater than the resources only then does stress occur. If the resources are greater than the demands then the person may view the situation as a challenge and not a stress scenario. If the individual is too inexperienced to recognize that a particular problem exists then this would not be considered as a stress scenario. For example, an inexperienced health and safety officer may not foresee the potential dangers of employees using standard 240 volt electrical equipment on a building site, i.e. a short circuit could easily lead to a fatal electrocution. It is worth noting that it is the subjective and not the objective appraisal or assessment of any scenario that may trigger the stress response.

Cox (1978) developed a five-stage transactional model of occupational stress. He describes the stages as follows:

> The first stage, it was argued, represents the sources of demand faced by the person and is part of their environment. Individuals' perceptions of these demands in relation to their ability to cope represents the second stage: effectively primary appraisal . . . stress was described as the psychological state which arose when there was a personally significant imbalance or lack of fit between individuals' perceptions of the demands on them and their ability to cope with those demands. The psychological and physiological changes which are associated with the recognition of such a stress state, and which include coping, represent the third stage of the model. Emotional changes are an important part of the stress state. These tend to be negative in nature and often define the experience of stress for the person. The fourth stage is concerned with the consequences of coping. The fifth stage is the general feedback (and feed forward) which occurs in relation to all the other stages. (Cox, 1993, p. 18)

Therapies

Both the Lazarus and the Cox models of stress would suggest the use of coping and problem-solving skills training in specific areas to help

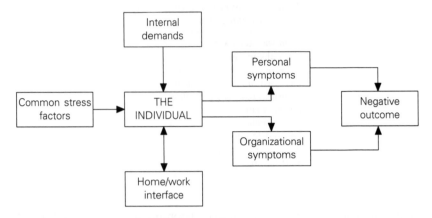

Figure 6.1   *The relationship between stress factors, the individual and the symptoms.* (Source: Palmer, 1993b)

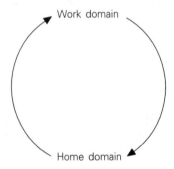

Figure 6.2   *The negative stress cycle.* (Source: Palmer, 1996a)

If this situation is recognized by their manager or occupational health department, then the individual could be referred to a confidential stress counselling service or in-house counsellor to help deal with the problem. Large organizations may be able to afford to employ a counsellor, whereas smaller organizations may need to use either an employee assistance programme or an external counsellor. Whatever intervention is used it is essential that employees are assured of its confidential nature otherwise they are unlikely to use the service.

Internal demands   Individuals often place internal demands upon themselves. In many cases it is not an external pressure or stressor that causes stress but the unrealistic internal demand or pressure.

Palmer (adapted 1993b) highlighted a number of internal demands or beliefs that can exacerbate occupational stress:

Table 6.3 *Other factors*

Boring repetitive tasks
Dangerous work
Deadlines
Excessive travel
Isolated working conditions
Long hours
Shift work
Work underload/overload
Work too difficult for the individual

Source: Palmer, 1993b

I/others must perform well at all times.
I/others must always reach deadlines.
I/others must be perfect.
The organisation must treat me fairly at all times.
I should get what I want otherwise I can't stand it.
Significant others must appreciate my work otherwise I am worthless.
I must be in control of the situation otherwise it would be awful and I couldn't stand it.

Cognitive-behavioural approaches to stress counselling and stress management training, as previously discussed, can help employees to appraise situations more realistically and moderate or change their self-defeating beliefs and attitudes. Yet so often counsellors working in this field of work are not qualified to offer this type of counselling or training.

Factors intrinsic to the job Some of the more common environmental workplace stressors include air pollution, dust/fibres, heat, humidity, lighting, noise, noxious chemicals/nicotine, sick building syndrome, static electricity, uncomfortable chairs/work stations, and visual display unit screen glare. These environmental stressors may come under the remit of the health and safety officer/consultant. Although in the short term changing or modifying environmental stressors can be financially costly, once undertaken there is likely to be less absenteeism due to ill health. This will increase productivity and general morale. Table 6.3 includes other factors that may need to be considered.

It is worth noting that each country tends to have different problems in the workplace that are the major cause of executive stress. However, generally time pressures and deadlines are near the top of the main perceived stressors. In Britain the amount of travel associated with work is considered to be a major problem, although more recently there has been increasing concern about possible redundancy and long-term unemployment. Some occupations are more stressful than others. For example, some of the most stressful jobs are in acting, advertising, building, dentistry, journalism, mining, the police force and prison service, whereas jobs in accountancy, astronomy, biochemistry, geology, insurance, the Church, nature conservancy, horticulture are less stressful (Sloan and Cooper, 1986).

Organizational structure and climate   In some organizations the structure and climate may limit the autonomy of the individual. Employees may feel that they do not have much influence or control over their workload. They may find the work boring and unchallenging and this can contribute to job dissatisfaction, reduced self-esteem, apathy, resentment and a loss of identity. This can lead to increased absenteeism. However, to a large extent loss of identity and self-esteem is dependent upon an individual's belief system and a counsellor may be able to offer assistance with these issues.

Increased participation in decision-making and team work can help to overcome an actual or perceived lack of control. Where appropriate, trade unions can be involved in planning job rotation and employees could elect their own supervisors. This can help to increase job morale and commitment to the work.

Due to the recession and the need of companies to increase their profits, many have already made or are considering making redundancies. Employees living under this fear can suffer from increased levels of stress. Possibly the only way to help alleviate this problem is to ensure that senior management are seen to communicate as quickly as possible on all issues. If a company has a history of making last-minute announcements then employees are likely to be less trusting. In many organizations trade unions or staff representatives are involved at board level to encourage active participation in important company decisions in an attempt to reduce these problems. Unfortunately, with companies 'downsizing', 'right-sizing', 'de-layering' and 're-engineering' (in other words, using less people to do more work) these problems are unlikely to improve for some time.

With the reduced staffing levels, the increased use of technology and job relocations are all possibly life changes that can contribute to stress in employees. Retraining, outplacement counselling and change management seminars or workshops may help to reduce the negative effects of these types of change.

Ageism, sexism and racism can also be prevalent in some organizations. A set policy and procedure to deal with these areas are essential. They must be seen to be proactive as well as just reactive. The policy needs to be displayed on notice boards and enforced whenever necessary.

Career development   Promotion prospects can become increasingly difficult to achieve as an employee moves higher up in an organization and, in addition, older employees may need to retrain to be able to use new technology. This challenge can cause stress and anxiety in some individuals. The fears older employees tend to share are redundancy, demotion, obsolescence, job security, and forced early retirement. These fears can help to reduce an individual's self-esteem and self-worth and thereby lead to depression. In some 'high tech' industries such as computing software, the income earned at the bottom of the career ladder can sometimes be higher than that of management. Once the novelty of the income and the job has worn off, then the employees may feel frustrated. They may perceive that their only chance of improvement is to change jobs. If they do leave this can be very expensive for companies that have invested time and money in staff training. An intricate pay and career structure may be essential to contain this particular problem.

Role in the organization   Individuals who are responsible for subordinates are more likely to suffer from coronary heart disease than those who are just responsible for machines. There are number of different role demands that can contribute to stress:

Role ambiguity	Role conflict
Role definition	Role expectations
Role incompatibility	Role overload
Role sign	Role underload

Often the employees are unaware of the source of their stress and these role demands can be very undermining. Three of the key problems tend to be role ambiguity, role conflict and role overload. These three will now be discussed in more depth. When employees suffer from role ambiguity, they are uncertain about the role expectations that are required of them. Sometimes they receive inadequate or conflicting information about their job. Role objectives are unclear. In some cases they do not know what behaviours will lead to a fulfilment of the role expectations. Induction training and a clear written contract may help to clarify the position for new employees and others with whom they work. Role conflict involves different expectations or sets of expectations made by the following groups on the employee: superiors, superiors' superior, peers, clients, subordinates, subordinates' subordinates. Other forms of conflict include a job in which too many different roles are expected or where the role behaviour is too difficult to perform for the particular individual. One form of conflict can occur when the employee's own value system conflicts with the expectations of the organization. For example, in a recession individuals may take on jobs that they would normally reject such as a vegetarian working for a restaurant serving meat dishes.

Role overload can also lead to stress as individuals may believe that they are not coping with their work. With the advent of 'less people doing more work' this is one of the key problems that counsellors are extremely likely to encounter when helping clients suffering from occupational stress. Apart from changing jobs, in my experience teaching clients time management, problem-solving, assertion and cognitive thinking skills often help them to deal with these very difficult pressures. It is worth mentioning that, conversely, with role underload individuals may not feel challenged and they may become bored. Each job needs to be assessed to avoid both role overload or underload.

Relationships at work   Interpersonal relationship difficulties can be a major cause of stress at work. Often managers or supervisors have received insufficient training in human resources skills. Basic skills such as being able to listen to employees and give instructions in an assertive but non-aggressive manner is sometimes overlooked by management. Unhelpful aggressive behaviour includes: inappropriate anger/hostility, aggressive body postures, pointing finger, angry intonation, and verbal put-downs, e.g. 'you'd better', 'come on', 'you should', 'you must'.

Managers can be taught listening skills and also assertiveness skills if they have skills deficits in these areas. These can form part of a management training programme. Hostile individuals tend to cause interpersonal difficulties in the workplace. They also increase their chances of dying early from CHD. Assertion training can be useful in this instance but often in-depth counselling is required too. Other interpersonal factors to be aware of include abrasive personalities, group/peer pressures, leadership style, social incongruence and social density (Quick and Quick, 1984).

Relationships between co-workers can be negative due to competition, harassment and 'office politics' yet co-workers can also be an excellent source of social support which helps to buffer individuals from stress (Cowen, 1982). Organizations that offer sports and social facilities (Cox et al., 1988) for their employees often unintentionally encourage beneficial social support networks. A good atmosphere in the workplace is likely to lower the incidence of stress-related disorders.

Discussion

Easy and obvious solutions to the resolution or alleviation of occupational stress seldom exist. Usually there is a financial cost if an effective (or ineffective) intervention is going to be undertaken. However, the long-term gains in production and reduced absenteeism may well be worth the initial cost. Jones and associates (1988) found that workplace stress levels in a group of hospitals correlated with the frequency of malpractice claims. Hospitals in the group that implemented a stress management programme significantly reduced the number of claims.

An organizational stress audit is usually a good starting point before any intervention is made. Assessment tools include the Occupational Stress Inventory (Osipow and Spokane, 1987), Occupational Stress Indicator (Cooper et al., 1988b) and the Job Stress Survey (Spielberger, 1994). Once an intervention(s) has been chosen it will need to be assessed and evaluated in a systematic manner (Evans and Reynolds, 1993; Palmer, 1993a,b) to ensure that the intervention actually helped the situation. All too often a stress management workshop is seen as the panacea when in fact it could raise more issues than it resolves. The stress audit may indicate that an employee assistance programme or a stress counselling service (see Allison et al., 1989) could be more effective in the long run.

Some interventions which involve change can lead to increased levels of stress if they are not implemented properly. Specialists in this field may be needed to help evaluate a stress management programme or intervention. Regular annual stress audits involving employee participation may help to keep the subject of stress on the agenda. It can also form part of a total quality management programme. It is recommended that employees from different parts of the organization are included on a stress 'working party' as active participation may be necessary for the employee to take the process seriously. In some organizations that have a 'macho' culture, initially it is preferable to talk about 'managing pressure' as stress may be seen as a weakness that must not be admitted publicly. This can lead to reluctance to attend stress management workshops, to take up stress counselling or support stress management interventions.

Future (1995 onwards)

This last part of the chapter will focus on the future of stress counselling and stress management and will include predictions about what may occur in the twenty-first century. A recent model of stress which has been developed specifically to help counsellors, psychotherapists, stress management trainers and other health professionals to apply theory to the practice of stress counselling and management will be described.

The multimodal-transactional model of stress

In 1995 I described in *Counselling for Stress Problems* (Palmer and Dryden, 1995) a psychological model of stress that I had been developing which not only explains how the stress response occurs but also guides counsellors and health professionals in the selection of suitable interventions which may help an individual to reduce or manage stress. It is a modified version of the transactional model of stress proposed by Cox (1978) and Cox and Mackay (1981) which incorporates Arnold Lazarus' (1989) seven interacting modalities consisting of behaviour, affect, sensory, imaginal, cognitive, interpersonal, and drugs/biology (known by the acronym BASIC I.D.). Figure 6.3 illustrates the most recent version of the multimodal-transactional model.

How a person reacts to a potential stress scenario is more due to his or her appraisal of it and his or her perceived abilities to cope or deal with it than the event or situation itself. Therefore the event can be considered as a potential 'trigger' to activate the stress response but not necessarily the main cause of its activation. Once the event has passed, the individual may remain disturbed about it due to the action or interaction of the different modalities. For example, in extreme stress scenarios such as those leading to the individual suffering from post traumatic stress disorder, the person

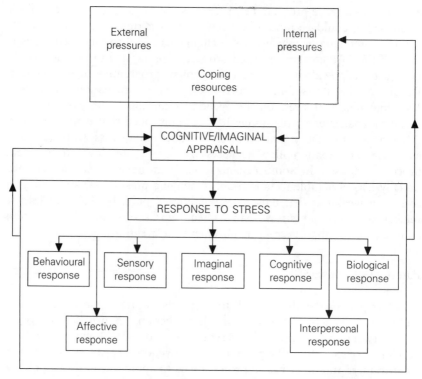

Figure 6.3   *Multimodal-transactional model of stress.* (Source: Adapted from Palmer and Dryden, 1995, p. 5)

may behaviourally avoid specific cues that reminds him or her of the event, feel very anxious, have physiological symptoms or anxiety such as panic attacks, may repeatedly see negative images of the event, may have many negative cognitions, may avoid people, and have raised catecholamine and corticosteroid levels. In many cases this typical response may still occur years after the event.

The multimodal-transactional model of stress can be broken down into five discrete stages to aid understanding and this is explained below.

In Stage 1, a pressure or demand is usually perceived by the individual to be emanating from an external source in the environment, for example, having to complete a project. However, individuals suffering from hypochondriasis have internal bodily sensations (i.e. internal pressures) that may trigger their stress response.

Stage 2 reflects the individual's perception of the pressure or demand and her appraisal of her ability to deal with it. If the individual believes that she can cope, even if she is being unrealistic, then she may stay in the situation; for example, continuing to work on the project. If the individual perceives that she cannot cope, then at that moment she may experience stress. However, other factors are usually involved such as social, family, organizational or cultural beliefs which she may have over time imbibed and now strongly believes in. Thus, if the individual believes that she 'must' always complete important work on projects, an innocuous project may assume great importance. In reality the inflexible 'must' is an internal and not an external pressure as she does not have to hold onto the belief. Many individuals who suffer from stress cognitively appraise experiences as 'extremely stressful' as a result of their beliefs and attitudes which distort the importance of a feared or actual event. In Stage 2, the individual decides whether she has the resources (e.g. skills, time available, etc.) to cope with the external pressures of a specific situation whilst usually unaware of the significant demands her internal pressures are placing on the situation. If she believes that she can deal with the situation then her stress response is less likely to be activated. However, if she perceives that she does not have the coping resources to deal with the situation then she progresses on to Stage 3 of the model. It is worth noting that the appraisal of any given situation may occur almost instantaneously. Thus a cognition, either verbally expressed or just internally thought, such as, 'Oh shit', or 'Oh my God', or 'This is awful', or 'I can't stand it', or 'I'm going to fail', may all constitute as negative appraisals of a situation or negative predictions about the possible outcome and will be sufficient to • trigger the stress response. In addition, the appraisal does not have to be in a cognitive form as sometimes a catastrophic image of the possible negative outcome of an event can also be considered as equivalent to its cognitive counterpart. It is likely that the image and cognitive modalities interact with each other either in parallel or in series when appraising a potential stress scenario and may even be inseparable.

In Stage 3, psychophysiological changes occur (see Table 6.1). Taken together, these comprise what is generally known as the 'stress response'. There is usually an emotion or combination of emotions such as anger, anxiety or guilt. In some cases where a failure has occurred, the person may feel depressed. According to the model, these emotions may have behavioural, sensory, imaginal, cognitive, interpersonal and biological/physiological components (see Figure 6.3). In addition, there will probably be the minimum of behavioural and cognitive attempts to change the environment or escape from the situation and thereby reduce the pressure. Individuals with a range of skills may also use strategies taken from the other modalities too, e.g. coping imagery (imaginal), assertion skills (interpersonal), breathing exercises (sensory). However, like animals some individuals freeze with fear which is not always helpful (see Marshall, 1978).

Stage 4 relates to the consequences of the application or lack of application of the coping strategies or responses of the individual. At this stage the individual's appraisal of the coping strategies applied is important. Thus if he perceives that he has successfully dealt with the crisis then he returns to a state of equilibrium. However, if an individual believes that his intervention is not helping, he may picture himself failing which, in itself, becomes an additional strain in the situation. Actual failure to meet the demand is also detrimental if the individual truly believes that the demand 'must' be met in a satisfactory manner.

Stage 5 is concerned with the long-term feedback or feed forward system. Interventions may be made by the individual which may either reduce stress, maintain the status quo or alter the external or internal pressures. If these produce a positive outcome then the organism may return to a neutral state of equilibrium. However, if the interventions continue to be ineffective, then the individual may experience prolonged stress. For example, an individual is likely to be stuck in Stage 5 of this model when he is experiencing an ongoing problem such as having to deal with many deadlines. If he does not achieve them then this can add to the existing problems he has at work with an additional backlog of projects to complete. This can directly impact upon his and others perceptions of his capabilities to perform well and maintains a negative cycle feeding back into Stage 1. Over a prolonged period this has many psychophysiological consequences which may lead to ill health, mental breakdown, burnout or even death in extreme cases. Each person may suffer from different stress-related disorders due to a genetic predisposition. In addition, there is a psychological-biological breaking point for every person which cannot be easily predicted (see Frese and Okonek, 1984).

Individuals who have managed to cope with difficult life-events or situations may view themselves as possessing coping skills which they can apply in similar situations. This is known as 'self-efficacy' and is a major cognitive component in the appraisal of future events as non-threatening and therefore not stressful. They may hold beliefs such as : 'I know I can do it', 'I'm in control', 'This will not be a problem', 'This will be a challenge and not stressful'. These self-helping beliefs often prevent the individual from going beyond Stage 2 of the multimodal-transactional model of stress. With many individuals in Stage 3 of the model, they quickly calm down when they remind themselves of these beliefs. Generally individuals in Stage 5 of the model suffering from prolonged stress have less belief in these types of cognition. The concepts of coping and control are considered by researchers and theorists as an important part of the stress process (e.g. Cox, 1993; Dewe et al., 1993; Lazarus, 1966; Lazarus and Folkman, 1984; Palmer, 1996a).

Therapies

Multimodal stress counsellors and stress management trainers teach clients how to intervene at the most appropriate stage of the multimodal-transactional model (Palmer, 1996b). Whenever possible, clients or trainees are shown how to improve their coping skills/resources and how to moderate their appraisal of difficult situations. For effective stress management, their internal demands such as 'I must perform well at all times regardless of the resources available' need to be modified otherwise innocuous activating events will still trigger the stress response. Changing

Table 6.4   *Frequently used techniques/interventions in multimodal therapy and training*

Modality	Techniques/interventions	Modality	Techniques/interventions
Behaviour	Behaviour rehearsal	Cognition	Bibliotherapy
	Empty chair		Challenging faulty
	Exposure programme		inferences
	Fixed role therapy		Cognitive rehearsal
	Modelling		Coping statements
	Paradoxical intention		Correcting misconceptions
	Psychodrama		Disputing irrational beliefs
	Reinforcement programmes		Focusing
	Response prevention/cost		Positive self-statements
	Risk-taking exercises		Problem-solving training
	Self-monitoring and		Rational proselytizing
	recording		Self-acceptance training
	Stimulus control		Thought-stopping
	Shame-attacking	Interpersonal	Assertion training
Affect	Anger expression		Communication training
	Anxiety/anger management		Contracting
	Feeling-identification		Fixed role therapy
Sensation	Biofeedback		Friendship/intimacy
	Hypnosis		training
	Meditation		Graded sexual approaches
	Relaxation training		Paradoxical intentions
	Sensate focus training		Role play
	Threshold training		Social skills training
Imagery	Anti-future shock imagery	Drugs/Biology	Alcohol reduction
	Associated imagery		programme
	Aversive imagery		Life-style changes, e.g.
	Coping imagery		exercise, nutrition, etc.
	Implosion and imaginal		Referral to physicians or
	exposure		other specialists
	Positive imagery		Stop smoking programme
	Rational-emotive imagery		Weight reduction and
	Time projection imagery		maintenance programme

Source: Adapted from Palmer, 1996b

the internal pressures can become a proactive approach strategy as individuals keep events or problems in perspective. Unfortunately, this more elegant form of stress management is difficult to achieve with many individuals who will continue to appraise certain situations as stressful and consequently will trigger the stress response. However, with suitable training once the individual is in Stage 3 of the model, he or she may then employ a range of useful strategies taken from the seven BASIC I.D. modalities and quickly short-circuit the stress response. Table 6.4 illustrates a range of techniques and strategies a multimodal counsellor and trainer may use to help a client or trainee.

Individuals suffering from prolonged stress will usually be in Stage 5 of the model and will need a thorough assessment and therapeutic programme. Table 6.5 illustrates a typical assessment and treatment programme that an

Table 6.5 *John's modality profile (or BASIC I.D. chart)*

Modality	Problem	Proposed programme/treatment
Behaviour	East/walks fast, always in a rush, hostile, competitive: indicative of type A	Discuss advantages of slowing down; disadvantages of rushing and being hostile; teach relaxation exercise; dispute self-defeating beliefs
	Avoidance of giving presentations	Exposure programme; teach necessary skills; dispute self-defeating beliefs
	Accident proneness	Discuss advantages of slowing down
Affect	Anxious when giving presentations	Anxiety management (Ellis et al., 1997)
	Guilt when work targets not achieved	Dispute self-defeating thinking
	Frequent angry outbursts at work	Anger management; dispute irrational beliefs
Sensation	Tension in shoulders	Self-massage; muscle relaxation exercise
	Palpitations	Anxiety management, e.g. breathing relaxation technique, dispute catastrophic thinking
	Frequent headaches	Relaxation exercise and biofeedback
	Sleeping difficulties	Relaxation or self-hypnosis tape for bedtime use; behavioural retraining; possibly reduce caffeine intake
Imagery	Negative images of not performing well	Coping imagery focusing on giving adequate presentations
	Images of losing control	Coping imagery of dealing with difficult work situations and with presentations; 'step-up' imagery (Palmer and Dryden, 1995)
	Poor self-image	Positive imagery (Lazarus, 1989)
Cognition	'I must perform well otherwise it will be awful and I couldn't stand it' 'I must be in control' 'Significant others should recognize my work' 'If I fail them I am a total failure'	Dispute self-defeating and irrational beliefs; coping statements; cognitive restructuring; ABCDE paradigm (Ellis et al., 1997); bibliotherapy; coping imagery (Palmer and Dryden, 1995)
Interpersonal	Passive/aggressive in relationships	Assertiveness training
	Manipulative tendencies at work	Discuss pros and cons of behaviour
	Always puts self first	Discuss pros and cons of behaviour
	Few supportive friends	Friendship training (Palmer and Dryden, 1995)
Drugs/biology	Feeling inexplicably tired	Improve sleeping and re-assess; refer to GP
	Takes aspirins for headaches	Refer to GP; relaxation exercises
	Consumes 10 cups of coffee a day	Discuss benefits of reducing caffeine intake
	Poor nutrition and little exercise	Nutrition and exercise programme

Source: Palmer, 1997

individual may need to reduce or manage stress. In multimodal therapy Table 6.5 is called a BASIC I.D. chart or modality profile.

Other related issues over the next 50 years

In this chapter we looked at the development of theories of stress and emotion over many years. In the 1880s and early 1900s the theorists appeared to make simple errors or oversights which is somewhat surprising. Yet this was still occurring in the 1950s and later, for example, in the response variable or physiological approach. Although the transactional models of stress seem to explain the stress response phenomenon, in fifty years from now, they could also receive criticism (see Spielberger and Reheiser, 1994). In recent years research into genes has shown that many physical disorders may have genetic markers. As our knowledge in these areas expands, an accurate prediction of what a particular person may suffer from if he or she is subjected to prolonged stress may be possible.

It may also be possible to predict which person may suffer from stress in a specific job if his or her beliefs and attitudes, coping skills or coping skills deficits are known. At the moment computer hardware and software are probably sufficiently advanced to provide the necessary back-up; what we need is more information. Most of the current models of occupational stress do not go into much depth about the cognitive modality except to state that it is the central factor involved. I believe that one of the problems experienced in the past twenty years in this field of work is due to occupational psychologists researching into occupational stress without necessarily having first-hand knowledge of the type of cognitions that exacerbate stress which are often recognized by cognitive-behavioural therapists attempting to help stressed clients (see Ellis et al., 1997). If and when these cognitions are assessed in a systematic manner then it may be possible to predict how and why one person's stress is another person's challenge. Currently and for the foreseeable future much money will be spent on the study of occupational stress but unless the researchers grasp the nettle and focus on the nature of cognitions, I believe that the research will all be in vain. This would account for why it appears to be difficult to predict what intervention will help reduce occupational stress. Although handbooks exist on helping individuals cope or manage stress (e.g. Palmer and Dryden, 1995), I believe that a comprehensive manual showing how to choose the most suitable organizational stress management intervention(s) will be more difficult to produce as organizations consist of a wide range of people with a diversity of different beliefs and attitudes. Their beliefs largely determine whether a particular problem such as organizational structure and climate or factors intrinsic to the job are stressful.

Many researchers have been critical of the research methodology used in the field of organizational stress management (see Reynolds and Briner, 1996) yet well controlled studies are difficult to undertake as organizations tend to resist organization-focused interventions, preferring employee-focused interventions such as counselling or stress management work-shops. This will continue to hinder research for many years to come.

Research undertaken at the level of the individual may move away from focusing on the effectiveness of particular types of therapy (known as big Ts) towards focusing on specific techniques or interventions (known as little ts). Shoham and Rohrbaugh (1995) recommend the ATI paradigm to undertake research where 'A' (aptitude) represents any client-characteristic or individual-difference variable that may moderate the effects of treatment (T) on an outcome (O). I (interaction) refers to the moderating effect of A on the relationship between T and O. If a large treatment package or therapy is evaluated, there is an increased risk of including, accidentally or otherwise, change mechanisms that may effect or cancel each other's effects. Shoham and Rohrbaugh (1995, p. 85) suggest this would be reduced when:

1   the theory underlying the design clearly states *what* in the T (i.e. its main change mechanisms) should interact with *what* in the A (i.e. the underlying theory of personality, psychopathology, or family dynamics, and other theoretically meaningful problem-maintaining patient's processes);
2   a treatment manual is carefully crafted to keep the change mechanism in focus and to minimize irrelevant or contradictory therapeutic elements;
3   adherence to the principles outlined in the manual is continuously monitored.

However, even if these conditions are achieved, it is unlikely that the risk would be completely eliminated. An important observation is that the most productive research appears to emanate from the 'little t' designs. I suspect that due to the financial pressures placed upon health professionals over the next couple of decades, efficient treatment packages will be demanded by the accountants and administrators of our health service. There will be continued political pressure to reduce the health budget. The most likely outcome of the research will be that treatment manuals based on techniques and strategies and *not* particular therapies will be developed.

These manuals will also recommend what interpersonal approach the therapist may need to take when dealing with a particular type of client in addition to matching the specific techniques to that person. The inter-personal matching process has already been given a name by Arnold Lazarus (1993) who uses the term 'an authentic chameleon'. For example, a person may prefer a very formal relationship with a health professional whereas another person may prefer a more informal relationship with their therapist and the latter may refer to each other by their first names (see Palmer and Dryden, 1995). Some clients may prefer interaction with a therapeutic computer programme in preference to a therapist. Examples of suitable technique selection would be social phobics who are mainly physiological reactors and therefore benefit most from relaxation treatment, whereas behavioural reactors benefit most from social skills training (see Ost et al., 1981). The treatment manual will give guidance on a whole range of these issues. The multimodal-transactional model of stress and the multimodal approach to therapy already cater for these specific procedures in the existing treatment manuals (see Lazarus, 1989; Palmer and Dryden, 1995).

I also predict that if the demand for effective therapeutic interventions by cost-cutting service purchasers continues, this will impact directly upon the hundreds of therapies currently taught and practised in the UK and the USA. I believe that therapies that do not adapt to brief or time-limited settings will become obsolete or relegated to private practice.

I predict that integration of incompatible therapies will hinder the development of treatment manuals whereas systematic, technical eclecticism will become one of the major forces in therapy (see Lazarus, 1997). Therapies such as rational emotive behaviour therapy or cognitive therapy which are multimodal in the application of techniques will also continue to flourish, especially if the practitioners match their interpersonal styles to those that maximize clinical effectiveness for each particular client (see Neenan and Dryden, 1996).

Stress management workshops in industrial and clinical settings are likely to become more easily available as they are cost-effective in comparison to individual counselling. Due to increased litigation for workplace stress (see Earnshaw and Cooper, 1996), employers will be encouraged by insurance companies to run stress management programmes. They might even offer discount on insurance premiums for companies that comply. There would be great appeal to administrators in hospitals to offer workshops or group stress therapy if this would keep costs down especially as large 'stress control' groups have been shown to be effective (see White et al., 1992).

The complex nature of the physiology of stress and the immune system (see Leonard and Miller, 1995; Toates, 1995) may be finally worked out and the transactional models of stress may need additional modification to incorporate the new knowledge. Exactly why an individual may sometimes release more catecholamines (stress hormones) after prolonged pressure in the 'unwinding' period may also be finally explained.

I believe that we will continue to see the professional bodies involved in psychology, counselling, psychotherapy and other related fields continuing to stake their claims on different aspects of work and professional titles, just like the prospectors in the 'gold rush'. However, as therapies become dissected into discrete skills thanks to the (British) national vocational qualifications system, this may lead to a situation where practitioners can be easily trained, or computers programmed, to help clients with specific problems.

This could have an adverse effect on the therapeutic professions. Medication of the future may also be so effective and comparatively cheap, that therapists may become the second option of choice. The very strength of professional therapeutic bodies such as the British Association for Counselling is the free time, knowledge, effort and enthusiasm that the members put into the committees and projects. How long will this continue? With increasing pressure upon employees working in the therapeutic and academic fields from employers to raise productivity, I doubt that many members will have any free time available to sit on external committees!

I hope to be around in fifty years from now to see if these developments have occurred or whether we are still no clearer on the very process of stress and its subsequent management. However, only a few members of my family have reached 90 years of age. I hope I have the right genes and I continue to use stress management techniques on myself.

References

Ader, R. and Cohen, N. (1993) Psychoneuroimmunology: conditioning and stress, *Annual Review of Psychology*, 44: 53–85.

Adler, A. (1927) *Understanding Human Nature*. New York: Greenberg.

Allison, T., Cooper, C.L. and Reynolds, P. (1989) Stress counselling in the workplace, *The Psychologist*, 12(9): 384–8.

Aurelius, A. (1995) *Meditations* (abridged by R. Waterfield). London: Penguin Books.

Bard, P. (1928) A diencephalic mechanism for the expression of rage with special reference to the sympathetic nervous system, *American Journal of Physiology*, 84: 490.

Beck, A.T. (1976) *Cognitive Therapy and the Emotional Disorders*. New York: International Universities Press.

Beck, A.T. (1993) Cognitive approaches to stress, in P.M. Lehrer and R.L. Woolfolk (eds), *Principles and Practice of Stress Management*, 2nd edn. New York: Guilford Press.

Bowers, K.S. (1973) Situationism in psychology: An analysis and critique, *Psychological Review*, 80: 307–35.

Cannon, W.B. (1927) The James–Lange theory of emotion, *American Journal of Psychology*, 39: 106.

Cannon, W.B. (1929) *Bodily Changes in Pain, Hunger, Fear and Rage*. Boston: Branford.

Cannon, W.B. (1931) *The Wisdom of the Body*. New York: Norton.

Cannon, W.B. (1935) Stresses and strains of homeostasis, *American Journal of Medical Science*, 189: 1.

Clarke, P.T. (1996) A person-centred approach to stress management, in S. Palmer and W. Dryden (eds), *Stress Management and Counselling: Theory, Practice, Research and Methodology*. London: Cassell.

Clarke, D. and Palmer, S. (1994a) *Stress Management*. Cambridge: National Extension College.

Clarke, D. and Palmer, S. (1994b) *Stress Management: Trainer Notes*. Cambridge: National Extension College.

Clifford, J. (1996) Adlerian therapy, in W. Dryden (ed.), *Handbook of Individual Therapy*. London: Sage.

Cooper, C., Cooper, R. and Eaker, L. (1988a) *Living with Stress*. Harmondsworth: Penguin Books.

Cooper, C.L., Sloan, S.J. and Williams, S. (1988b) *Occupational Stress Indicator*. Windsor: ASE.

Cowen, E.L. (1982) Help is where you find it, *American Psychologist*, 37: 385–95.

Cox, T. (1978) *Stress*. Basingstoke: Macmillan Education.

Cox, T. (1993) *Stress Research and Stress Management: Putting Theory to Work*. Sudbury: HMSO.

Cox, T. and Mackay, C.J. (1981) A transactional approach to occupational stress, in E.N. Corlett and J. Richardson (eds), *Stress, Work Design and Productivity*. Chichester: Wiley.

Cox, T., Gotts, G., Boot, N., Kerr, J. (1988) Physical exercise, employee fitness and the management of health at work, *Work and Stress*, 2(1): 71–6.

Dewe, P., Cox, T. and Ferguson, E. (1992) Individual strategies for coping with stress at work: A review of progress and directions for future research, *Work and Stress*, 7: 5–15.

Dubois, P. (1907) *The Psychic Treatment of Nervous Disorders*. New York: Funk and Wagnalls.

D'Zurilla, T.J. (1986) *Problem-Solving Therapy: A Social Competence Approach to Clinical Intervention*. New York: Springer.

Earnshaw, J. and Cooper, C. (1996) *Stress and Employer Liability*. London: Institute of Personnel and Development.

Edgell, B. (1926) *Mental Life: An Introduction to Psychology*. London: Methuen.

Ellis, A. (1955) Psychotherapy techniques for use with psychotics, *American Journal of Psychotherapy*, 9: 425–76.

Ellis, A. (1958) Rational psychotherapy, *Journal of General Psychology*, 59: 35–49.

Ellis, A. (1962) *Reason and Emotion in Psychotherapy*. Seacaucus, NJ: Lyle Stuart.

Ellis, A. (1994) *Reason and Emotion in Psychotherapy*, rev. and updated edn. New York: Birch Lane Press.

Ellis, A., Gordon, J., Neenan, M. and Palmer, S. (1997) *Stress Counselling: A Rational Emotive Behaviour Approach*. London: Cassell.

Evans, B. and Reynolds, P. (1993) Stress consulting: A client-centred approach, *Stress News*, 5(1): 2–6, S. Palmer (ed.), Special Symposium Issue: Stress Management Interventions.

Frankenhaeuser, M. (1981) Coping with job stress – a psychobiological approach, in B. Gardell and G. Johansson (eds), *Working Life*. Chichester: Wiley.

Frese, M. and Okonek, K. (1984) Reasons to leave shiftwork and psychological complaints of former shiftworkers, *Journal of Applied Psychology*, 69: 509–14.

Frese, M. and Zapf, D. (1988) Methodological issues in the study of work stress: Objectives vs subjective measurement of work stress and the question of longitudinal studies, in C.L. Cooper and R. Payne (eds), *Causes, Coping and Consequences of Stress at Work*. Chichester: Wiley.

Gregson, O. and Looker, T. (1996) The biological basis of stress management, in S. Palmer and W. Dryden (eds), *Stress Management and Counselling: Theory, Practice, Research and Methodology*. London: Cassell.

Henry, J.P. (1980) Present concept of stress theory, in E. Usdin, R. Kvetnansky and I.J. Kopin (eds), *Catecholamines and Stress: Recent Advances*. New York: Elsevier/North-Holland. pp. 557–71.

Henry, J.P., Kross, M.E., Stephens, P.M. and Watson, F.M.C. (1976) Evidence that differing psychological stimuli lead to adrenal cortical stimulation by autonomic pathways, in E. Usdin, R. Kvetnansky and I.J. Kopin (eds), *Catecholamines and Stress*. Oxford: Pergamon Press. pp. 457–68.

Holmes, T.H. and Rahe, R.H. (1967) The Social Readjustment Rating Scale, *Psychosomatic Medicine*, 11: 213–18.

Irwin, J. and Livnat, S. (1987) Behavioral influences on the immune system: stress and conditioning, *Progress in Neuropsychopharmacological and Biological Psychiatry*, 11: 137–43.

Jacobson, E. (1938) *Progressive Relaxation*. Chicago: University of Chicago Press.

James, W. (1884) What is emotion, *Mind*, 19: 188.

James, W. (1890) *The Principles of Psychology*. New York: Henry Holt.

Jones, R.L., Barge, B.N., Steffy, B.D., Fay, L.M., Kunz, L.K. and Wuebker, L.J. (1988) Stress and medical malpractice: Organisational risk assessment and intervention, *Journal of Applied Psychology*, 73: 727–35.

Karasek, R.A. (1981) Job socialisation and job strain: The implications of two psychosocial mechanisms for job design, in B. Gardell and G. Johansson (eds), *Working Life: A Social Science Contribution to Work Reform*. Chichester: Wiley.

Kiecolt-Glaser, J.K. and Glaser, R. (1991) Stress and immune function in humans, in R. Ader, D.L. Felten and N. Cohen (eds), *Psychoneuroimmunology*. San Diego: Academic Press.

Lange, C. (1885) The emotions (trans. I.A. Haupt), in K. Dunlap (ed.), *The Emotions*. Baltimore, MD: Williams and Wilkins.

Lazarus, A.A. (1989) *The Practice of Multimodal Therapy*. Baltimore, MD: The Johns Hopkins University Press.

Lazarus, A.A. (1993) Tailoring the therapeutic relationship or being an authentic chameleon, *Psychotherapy*, 30: 404–7.

Lazarus, A.A. (1997) *Brief But Comprehensive Psychotherapy*. New York: Springer.

Lazarus, R.S. (1966) *Psychological Stress and the Coping Process*. New York: McGraw-Hill.

Lazarus, R.S. and Folkman, R. (1984) *Stress, Appraisal, and Coping*. New York: Springer.

Leonard, B.E. and Miller, K. (eds) (1995) *Stress, the Immune System and Psychiatry*. Chichester: Wiley.

Marshall, S.L. (1978) *Men against Fire*. Gloucester: Peter Smith Publications.

McDougall, W. (1919) *An Introduction to Social Psychology*, rev. edn. London: Methuen.

McDougall, W. (1922) *An Outline of Psychology*. London: Methuen.

Meichenbaum, D. (1985) *Stress Inoculation Training*. Elmsford, NY: Pergamon Press.

Meichenhaum, D. and Cameron, R. (1972) *Stress Inoculation Training: A Skills Training Approach to Anxiety Management*. Unpublished manuscript. Waterloo, Ontario: University of Waterloo.

Neenan, M. and Dryden, W. (1996) *Dealing with Difficulties in Rational Emotive Behaviour Therapy*. London: Whurr.

Osipow, S.H. and Spokane, A.R. (1987) *Manual for the Occupational Stress Inventory*. Odessa, FL: Psychological Assessment Resources, Inc.

Ost, L., Jerremalm, A. and Johansson, J. (1981) Individual response patterns and the effects of different behavioral methods in the treatment of social phobia, *Behaviour Research and Therapy*, 19: 1–16.

Palmer, S. (1989) Occupational stress, *The Safety and Health Practitioner*, 7(8): 16–18.

Palmer, S. (1993a) Occupational stress: Its causes and alleviation, in W. Dekker (ed.), *Chief Executive International*. London: Sterling Publications.

Palmer, S. (1993b) Organisational stress: Symptoms, causes and reduction. *Newsletter of the Society of Public Health*.

Palmer, S. (1996a) Developing stress management programmes, in R. Woolfe and W. Dryden (eds), *Handbook of Counselling Psychology*. London: Sage.

Palmer, S. (1996b). The multimodal approach: Theory, assessment, techniques and interventions, in S. Palmer and W. Dryden (eds), *Stress Management and Counselling: Theory, Practice, Research and Methodology*. London: Cassell.

Palmer, S. (1997) Modality assessment, in S. Palmer and G. McMahon (eds), *Client Assessment*. London: Sage.

Palmer, S. and Dryden, W. (1995) *Counselling for Stress Problems*. London: Sage.

Papez, J.W. (1937) A proposed mechanism for emotion, *Archives of Neurology and Psychology*, 38: 725.

Pfister, O. (1917) *The Psychoanalytic Method*. London: Kegan Paul.

Quick, J.C. and Quick, J.D. (1984) *Organisational Stress and Preventive Management*. New York: McGraw-Hill.

Reynolds, S. and Briner, R.B. (1996) Stress management at work: With whom, for whom and to what ends? in S. Palmer and W. Dryden (eds), *Stress Management and Counselling: Theory, Practice, Research and Methodology*. London: Cassell.

Schultz, J.H. (1932) *Das Autogene Training-Konzentrative Selbstentspannung*. Leipzig: Thieme.

Selye, H. (1956) *The Stress of Life*. New York: McGraw-Hill.

Sigman, A. (1992) The state of corporate health care, *Personnel Management*, February, 24–31.

Shoham, V. and Rohrbaugh, M. (1995) Aptitude x Treatment Interaction (ATI) research: Sharpening the focus, widening the lens, in M. Aveline and D.A. Shapiro (eds), *Research Foundations for Psychotherapy Practice*. Chichester: Wiley.

Sloan, S. and Cooper, C. (1986) *Pilots under Stress*. London: Routledge and Kegan Paul.

Smith, R.E. (1980) A cognitive-affective approach to stress management training for athletes, in C.H. Nadeau, W.R. Halliwell, K.M. Newell and G.C. Roberts (eds), *Psychology of Motor Behavior and Sport – 1979*. Champaign, IL: Human Kinetics.

Spielberger, C.D. (1994) *Professional Manual for the Job Stress Survey (JSS)*. Odessa, FL: Psychological Assessment Resources, Inc.

Spielberger, C.D. and Reheiser, E.C. (1994) The Job Stress Survey: Measuring gender differences in occupational stress, *Journal of Social Behavior and Personality*, 9: 2, 199–218.

Suinn, R.M. (1990) *Anxiety Management Training*. New York: Plenum.

Suinn, R.M. and Richardson, F. (1971) Anxiety management training: A non-specific behavior therapy program for anxiety control, *Behavior Therapy*, 2: 498–510.

Symonds, C.P. (1947) Use and abuse of the term flying stress, in Air Ministry, *Psychological Disorders in Flying Personnel of the Royal Air Force, Investigated during the War, 1939–1945*. London: HMSO.

Toates, P. (1995) *Stress: Conceptual and Biological Aspects*. Chichester: Wiley.

Vingerhoets, J.J.M. (1985) The role of the parasympathetic division of the autonomic nervous system in stress and the emotions, *International Journal of Psychosomatics*, 32: 28–33.

White, J., Keenan, M. and Brookes, N. (1992) Stress control: A controlled comparative investigation of large group therapy for generalised anxiety disorder, *Behavioural Psychotherapy*, 20: 97–114.

7

The Future of Primal Integration

John Rowan

Primal Integration is a very free-form type of primal work that involves an exploration of deeper levels of experience with a view to being more alive and living more authentically. It is concerned with the recovery and reintegration of split-off parts of the self and works with very early preverbal experiences from the womb, birth and infancy, as well as later experiences. (Brown and Mowbray, 1994, p. 13)

This account of primal integration brings out some of the essentials of the approach, and the authors add that 'The emphasis of the work is on self-direction and self-regulation and allowing spontaneous growth processes to unfold rather than on a highly structured or directed programme'. This of course places this approach squarely within the humanistic tradition, the tradition of Maslow, Rogers, Perls, Moreno, Mahrer and May. The purpose of all the techniques used in their approaches is towards the unfolding and unhindering of the person as a whole.

I would add to this a little more emphasis on the transpersonal aspects of the work. The best image I have come across to illuminate this is the spiral staircase on a mirrored floor. Every step up the staircase is accompanied by a step down in the mirror, and every step down is also a step up (Merry, 1983, p. 108). Similarly, primal work opens people up to their true nature as spiritual beings: just as work in meditation often opens up primal material. Mickel Adzema puts it this way:

Some long-term primallers with whom I have contact have talked of receiving love, helping, strength or bliss that seemed to be coming from a place beyond the scope of their current physical existence, to be emanating from a 'higher power' of some sort. Their descriptions have many parallels to some descriptions of spiritual experience. (1985, p. 95)

The opening up, the dropping of defences which happens in the best depth work, is parallel to the opening up and dropping of defences which is necessary in transpersonal work. In the one case it is defences against our lower nature, our impulses, our traumas, our early pain and so forth: in the other it is defences against our higher nature, our spiritual awareness, our sense of the sublime. Frank Haronian wrote a celebrated paper in which he said:

We orient ourselves toward the sublime when we disinterestedly seek to know things as they are; when we nurture others for the pleasure of seeing them grow; when we arrange physical events so that they are seen as beautiful or artistic. Then there is the tendency towards community, brotherliness, and caring. (1974, p. 52)

His paper is entitled 'The repression of the sublime' (a phrase which he took from Desoille), and the point he makes is that in our culture it is all too common to say that living up to the sublime is too much to ask. We shy away from the sublime as too demanding, too impossible. As soon as we think of growth into new and higher areas of our life, new fears, new anxieties, stop us from going further. We put away such thoughts – we repress them. Here we are squarely in the transpersonal tradition, of people like Assagioli, Hillman and Wilber. Indeed, Wilber (1995) devotes some important space to showing historically how any interest in the sublime was dismissed and regarded as 'pride' in the days of John Locke. Anything not empirically provable was metaphysical and to be ignored. Similarly, Abraham Maslow wrote about 'the Jonah complex', and said that:

We are generally afraid to become that which we can glimpse in our most perfect moments, under the most perfect conditions, under conditions of greatest courage. We enjoy and even thrill to the godlike possibilities we see in ourselves at such peak moments. And yet we simultaneously shiver with weakness, awe and fear before these very same possibilities. (1973, p. 37)

Again, a strange process of repression takes place, whereby we cut things down to size and make them ordinary. Maslow calls this 'desacralization' and says that our culture regularly strips everything of its spiritual source and meaning, and tells us not to concern ourselves with such matters. Ken Wilber's recent book (1995) goes into this in great detail, showing how it gives us the current 'flatland' approach to the world. Just as our culture also tells us not to be concerned about our infancy, our birth, our prenatal life – all this is to be repressed, disowned. Maslow is here moving, as he did through his life, from the humanistic towards the transpersonal.

For this reason primal integration 'pays due regard to the spiritual and transpersonal aspects of the primal process, and values primal joy as well as the primal "Pain" that is Janov's sole focus' (Brown and Mowbray, 1994, p. 16).

This means that when we think about the future, five main areas come up for consideration: (a) humanistic work; (b) transpersonal work; (c) integrative work; (d) training; and (e) cultural trends. Table 7.1 can be used as a guide, which should make it easier to follow. My position is that the humanistic approaches are concerned most centrally and character- istically with column 2, and the transpersonal approach in psychotherapy is concerned most centrally and characteristically with column 3. Primal integration is mainly in column 2, but reaches out in certain important ways into column 3.

Table 7.1 *A comparison of four positions in personal development*

Wilber level Rowan position	1 Persona/shadow Mental ego	2 Centaur Real self	3 Subtle self Soul	4 Causal self Spirit
Self	I am defined by others	I define who I am	I am defined by the Other(s)	I am not defined
Motivation	Need	Choice	Allowing	Surrender
Personal goal	Adjustment	Self-actualization	Contacting	Union
Social goal	Socialization	Liberation	Extending	Salvation
Process	Healing – ego-building	Development – ego-extending	Opening – ego-reduction	Enlightenment
Traditional role of helper	Physician Analyst	Growth Facilitator	Advanced Guide	Priest(ess) Sage
Representative approaches	Hospital treatment Chemotherapy Psychoanalysis Directive Behaviour mod Cognitive-behavioural Some TA Crisis work REBT Brief Therapy	Primal integration Gestalt therapy Open encounter Psychodrama Neo-freudians Bodywork therapies Some TA Person-centred Co-counselling Regression	Psychosynthesis Some Jungians Some pagans Transpersonal Voice dialogue Some Wicca or Magic Kabbalah Some astrology Some Tantra Shamanism	Mystical Buddhism Raja Yoga Taoism Monasticism Da Love Ananda Christian mysticism Sufi Goddess mystics Some Judaism Advaita

Focus	Individual and Group	Group and individual	Supportive community	Ideal community
Representative names	Freud Ellis Meichenbaum Beck Eysenck Skinner Lazarus Watzlawick Wessler Haley	Maslow Rogers Mahrer Perls Lowen Schutz Moreno Stevens Argyris Bugental	Jung Hillman Starhawk Assagioli Gordon-Brown Mary Watkins Jean Houston Bolen Grof Boorstein	Eckhart Shankara Dante Tauler Suso Ruysbroeck Nagarjuna Lao Tzu George Fox Julian of Norwich
Research methods	Qualitative	Collaborative	Transformative	None
Questions	Dare you face the challenge of the unconscious?	Dare you face the challenge of freedom?	Dare you face the loss of your boundaries?	Dare you face the loss of all your symbols?
Key issues	Acceptability Respect	Autonomy Authenticity	Openness Vision	Devotion Commitment

Humanistic work

One of the most important ideas in the field of humanistic psychology is self-actualization (Maslow, 1987). In recent years doubt has been cast on the idea because of the attacks which have been made by postmodernism on the very idea of the self. If everything is constructed, if everything is an appearance, if everything is a simulacrum, then there is no place for an authentic self. But if Wilber is right – and he has a detailed examination of postmodernism in his recent book (Wilber, 1995) – there is a place for an authentic self at the level of development he calls the Centaur (see Table 7.1).

I regard self-actualization as belonging very much to the Centaur level of development. This means that I see humanistic psychology as centring on that level and addressing itself mainly to the problems of that level. It is not all things to all people, but quite specific and limited. It is also possible to move into a different level, the subtle level for example, and try to do justice to the subtle self as well. Similarly with the Causal self and the Causal level. But that is a different level and a different task. So I don't want to give in to the postmodernists and redefine self-actualization theory, I just want to rid it of excrescences and misunderstandings and possible inflations.

There is nothing wrong with the idea of self-actualization. I wrote an article some time back which appeared in *The Humanistic Psychologist* (Rowan, 1992a) showing that the major philosopher Hegel was in favour of the idea and could even clarify some of the puzzles connected with the concept. Recently I have seen a paper by Hester Solomon (1994) which links Hegel with Jung, and of course Jung's notion of individuation is very close to Maslow's idea of self-actualization. According to Samuels and his co-workers (1986), individuation is 'the key concept in Jung's contribution to the theories of personality development' (p. 76). But I think the person who has done most to revive the concept in a fuller form is Ken Wilber. He has suggested that the self which is to be actualized in Maslow's theory is only one particular version of the self, which he calls the Centaur self. Further on, in the process of psychospiritual development, comes the Subtle self (soul). Further on again comes the Causal self (spirit). This framework makes a lot more sense to me than the original version, which mixed up self, soul and spirit, and did not allow for such distinctions to be made.

It will be easier to differentiate it from the subtle and the Causal and the Nondual (beyond the Causal but lumped with it in Table 7.1) as we become more familiar with these levels. I think the Centaur level has a unique part to play, both for the individual and for society. It is remarkable that it is this century which has seen the discovery of the Centaur level and the real self on any wide scale: these things are just not described at all in the eastern literature or in the earlier western literature. They are very much of today, though of course there were precursors like Kierkegaard (1813–55).

Humanistic psychotherapy is not very different from other forms of therapy. Most humanistic therapists, like others, are faced with people who just want to get back to being the way they were before. But the more interesting work, and the work which humanistic psychotherapists are best at, is that where the person wants to work through to the point of discovering their real self (existential self, body–mind unity, true self, etc.). In order to do that job, which Jim Bugental (1987) describes as life-changing, the therapist has to be authentic. We cannot lead people to the real self if we have not yet got there ourselves.

Any approach which does not value authenticity is not going to be compatible with the humanistic approach. So those psychoanalysts who believe that everything happening in the session is transference or counter-transference cannot be humanistic. And those cognitive and behavioural therapists who have no notion of the real self cannot be humanistic. On the other hand, those psychoanalysts who do believe in the real self (Winnicott, Guntrip, Balint, Horney, Fromm, etc.) are perfectly compatible with the humanistic approach. And those cognitive and behavioural therapists who acknowledge the importance of the real self are quite acceptable too.

A humanistic creed

I believe:

- human potential is more important and more interesting than basic functioning
- real personal transformation can happen, and not mere adjustment to society; celebration and ecstasy are desirable and possible
- personal growth is something which happens with the help of society up to a point, but which at a later point needs to be pursued consciously, even perhaps sometimes in contrast to the pressures of society
- autonomy and spontaneity are desirable goals for the individual, understood as including a recognition of our interdependence and our responsibilities to one another, to society and culture, and to the future
- authoritative guides are preferable to authoritarian experts
- we can aim for empowerment rather than control of people around us, and that this is particularly important when doing research
- that emotional competence and the ability to negotiate are essential to genuine partnership in groups and organizations
- our own experience is central; and we therefore have a special respect for experiential learning
- body, feelings, intellect, soul and spirit form a single action system

Humanistic psychology is more successful in England at the moment than at any time in the past, and has been growing steadily in recent years. The Association of Humanistic Psychology (AHP) in Britain has over 1000 members, and the journal *Self and Society* comes out bimonthly. There is a professional wing, the Association of Humanistic Psychology Practitioners, with about 150 members, all of whom have been rigorously examined and accredited. The accreditation of psychotherapist members automatically gets them on to the National Register of Psychotherapists which has existed now for several years, and which includes therapists of every camp – a real achievement, which took fifteen years to get together. I am quite proud of this effort, which I helped to pioneer.

The humanistic impact on academia is small but growing. There are no formal records of which courses are operating, but I know of at least half a dozen. One exciting development is that existing training centres in psychotherapy and counselling are linking up with universities to provide MA or MSc programmes. One of them has even now developed a PhD programme.

I don't think there are any important distinctions between humanistic psychology as it has developed in this country and in the USA. This is largely because I and others have taken great care to keep in contact with the AHP over there and to stay in line with it. I have been to about eight annual meetings of the AHP and a couple of smaller meetings organized by chapters, and I know many of the people in the USA personally.

If Wilber is right in his argument (1981) that the Centaur level is the next stage of development for the whole human race, then humanistic psychology is due for a huge increase in its effectiveness and its influence. But there are counter-forces too. Two in particular concern me.

First, there is the counter-force of fundamentalism. Whether it takes the form of religious fundamentalism or nationalist fundamentalism, it is intolerant and narrow.

Second, there is the counter-force of postmodernism. The emphasis on relativism and fragmentation is hostile to any idea of a real self or its actualization. We shall be looking again at both of these currents in a later section.

Transpersonal work

One of the most neglected areas in the field of psychotherapy is the transpersonal. Probably even now most psychotherapists have no idea what it is or why it is important. Even those who have heard of it often get it wrong. In psychoanalysis the word is sometimes used to mean interpersonal, but this usage is not to be found in any dictionary. In the *Dictionary of Counselling* it is defined as:

> Transpersonal therapy – any form of counselling or therapy which places emphasis on spirituality, human potential or heightened consciousness. The 'transpersonal' is concerned with what is beyond purely individual, problematic everyday experience. The transpersonal is often known as 'fourth force

psychology' (after the psychoanalytic, behavioural and humanistic) and is considered by many to represent a higher stage of human evolution. (Feltham and Dryden, 1993, p. 198)

The important word here is 'beyond'. It is very easy to mix up and confuse the pre-rational with the trans-rational: children and some indigenous peoples are pre-rational, in the sense of not having advanced to the level of science and formal logic. Authentic people, yogis, saints and sages are trans-rational, in the sense of having advanced to the level of science and formal logic, and then having gone beyond it. The difference is that the trans-rational person has reached full rationality and the ability to handle even difficult logical relations but has then gone beyond that, finding formal logic insufficient and too limiting (see Table 7.1 again).

Possibly the biggest challenge in psychotherapy today is this spiritual aspect of the work. If we can take Wilber and his co-workers seriously, we have to devote much more attention than we normally do to this type of approach. The argument is that people operate on something like nine different developmental levels, some of which are completed, some of which are still in process, and some of which are as yet not visible at all. My own belief at present is that anyone who wants to be a psychotherapist who can do justice to the whole person has to have their own spiritual discipline which they follow. Otherwise there are important and crucial human areas, such as for example spiritual emergencies (Grof and Grof, 1990), where they cannot help their clients. This is to cheat people of part of their humanity, and it won't do.

The transpersonal, which was originally contained within humanistic psychology, and still has a close relationship with it, has now differentiated itself out. It has its own conferences, its own journals (*Journal of Transpersonal Psychology, Transpersonal Review*), and so forth. This is the process of evolution, which proceeds by successive waves of differentiation and integration. We shall be looking more at integration in the next section.

But the great achievement of Ken Wilber's version of the transpersonal has been to clarify the many confusions which can occur in our thinking about such matters. His basic distinction between the prepersonal, the personal and the transpersonal, and his acute remarks on what he calls the pre/trans fallacy – reducing the transpersonal to the prepersonal, or elevating the prepersonal to the transpersonal – are so simple and yet so challenging that they have still not been digested even by most of those deeply involved with the transpersonal (Rowan, 1993).

For example, he points out that magical and mythical thinking is prepersonal in the first place: it comes before rational thinking in the history of the planet. Later spiritual development into the subtle level can call once again on mythical themes, but in effect reworks them and revises them. The same symbol can then mean one thing on a prepersonal level and something very different on a transpersonal level. The same ritual can serve prepersonal purposes in uniting the group and staving off the fear of death, or transpersonal purposes in pointing to deeper or higher spiritual realities beyond the group. This means that not everything which comes from indigenous peoples is automatically related to the deeper or higher levels which have to do with the subtle – and many people do make this faulty assumption, including at times Jung and Joseph Campbell. This is an area which I am very interested in and writing about at the moment (Rowan, 1996).

The most useful summary of Wilber's whole position is to be found in *The Atman Project*. Good stuff for psychotherapists is to be found in *No Boundary* and in the book he put together with some other people, called *Transformations of Consciousness*. The book on cultural development down the centuries is *Up From Eden*, and the one on the sociology of religion is *A Sociable God*. The masterwork, the first of three volumes which are now appearing, is *Sex, Ecology, Spirituality*, which really has everything in it, in an up-to-date form.

Over the next 25 or 50 years, I see the transpersonal approach being far more recognized and understood. It will become more and more obvious that any psychotherapy which aims to deal with the whole person cannot ignore it. Primal integration already does not ignore it, and can cope very well with the new demands which may be made in this respect. It can even help to lead the way into this fuller realization of what human beings are like.

Integrative work

Now we come to the question of the future of the integrative approach. In general, it looks as though this is a growth area, and there is now a *Journal of Psychotherapy* coming out of Arizona. But there are some hidden difficulties, for which we shall again have to consult Table 7.1.

Basically I follow Ken Wilber in saying that at each level in our psychospiritual development we have a different notion of the self. At first it is undifferentiated, then it becomes a body–self, then a magical self, then a mythic-membership self, then a mental ego, then a Centaur self, then a subtle self, then a Causal self and then a Nondual self or no-self. At each of these levels the notion of the self changes. At each level it seems to us as if there is just one possible definition – the one we hold at the moment. All the previous ones were inadequate, and all the future ones unthinkable.

Subpersonalities are found at most of the levels mentioned, first as imaginary companions, then as inner conflicts, then as ego states and so forth. At the real-self stage we are very rejecting of subpersonalities, and see no place for them, because they would get in the way of authenticity. Then if we move on to the subtle stage, we find a use for them again, but now as high archetypes, as goddesses and gods, and so forth.

The implications of all this are devastating. What we have to say now is that while it is always possible to integrate therapies within a single column of Table 7.1 – and by integration I mean moving in and out of them in a free-flowing kind of way so that they become part of a single coherent therapeutic effort – it is not possible to integrate therapies in different columns. The reason for this is clear: the whole notion of the self changes from column to column. Hence the aim of the therapy is different in each column, as is clearly stated in the table. To switch from one column to another is to switch from one set of aims to another. This is not integration, it is alteration, which is quite different.

Let us look, in the light of this idea, at the question of which combinations of therapies are most popular. The study of Norcross and Prochaska (1983) showed that the cognitive and behavioural approaches were the most favoured team mates. This fits with column one. So does the third favourite, which is psychoanalytic and cognitive; there is a practical difficulty here about the unconscious, but it seems that this can be overcome. This again fits with our diagram. But what about the second favourite, which is humanistic and cognitive? According to the argument above, this would be impossible.

What I would suggest here is that when the attempt is made to integrate the humanistic and the cognitive, one of two things will happen. Either the cognitive will be transformed into a mere adjunct to the humanistic, or the humanistic will be transformed into a mere adjunct to the cognitive. In other words one will be assimilated into the other, rather than staying with the assumptions of its own heartland in one column or the other. For example, take the Erskine and Moursund (1988) book. In it they put together the theory of transactional analysis (TA) with the techniques of gestalt therapy. But in doing so they force TA to remain within column 1, and the same with gestalt. None of the outcomes in the case histories so fully given in the book are discoveries of the real self. They are all triumphs of adjustment, whereby the person is rendered able to take up customary roles with greater success. There is no ecstasy in this book, no discovery of the real self.

The implication of this is that therapists, in their own training, need to have moved at least into column 2 of Table 7.1 before doing much work there, and preferably need to have moved into column 3 as well, if they are not going to be thrown by some spiritual emergency (Bragdon, 1990; Grof and Grof, 1989, 1990).

All I am contending is that we be clear about what we are doing, and don't confuse ourselves or our clients.

Some of the implications of what I am saying are quite surprising. For example, I am saying that it should be possible to combine classical psychoanalysis and behaviour therapy, the Kleinian and the cognitive, because they are both in column 1. This means, of course, that several times in recent years successful attempts have been made to combine the psychoanalytic with the behavioural approaches (Wachtel, 1977; Arkowitz and Messer, 1984). At the same time, the development of cognitive analytical therapy was to be expected, and has now arrived on the bookstalls (Ryle, 1990). And the Brussels programme of an integrative model in psychotherapy training (Roose et al., 1991) also fits well with this analysis, combining as it does the psychodynamic, the behavioural and the systemic approaches.

It is very revealing that both psychoanalysis and cognitive-behaviour therapy relate very well to the National Health Service and to medicine generally. This is because they share with medicine the basic model of restoring people to health, by one means or another.

On the other hand, it also explains why people in column 2 find it so difficult to relate to medicine, unless it is complementary or holistic medicine. They do not hold to the basic medical model, and indeed criticize it regularly. I myself have been known to say things like, 'Anyone who wants to cure a client is deeply into countertransference!' (Rowan, 1994).

It also explains why psychoanalysts of the classical school in column 1 often say that everything that happens in therapy is transference or countertransference, while psychoanalysts of a more liberal kind in column 2 want to make clear distinctions between different relationships which are going on in therapy, of which transference and countertransference are only two. For example, it is crucial for people in column 2 to have a notion of authenticity, and if everything is transference or countertransference, there is no room for authenticity (Clarkson, 1995).

It is of course always possible to alternate methods, but that is not the same thing at all. Some of the attempts at integration which have been made, as for example Douglas (1989) and Fonagy (1989), seem to me to fall into this trap, and to believe that they are integrating when they are only alternating. By alternating I mean that the same therapist uses one approach with one client, and another with another, or with the first on another occasion.

It may also be possible to devise some very subtle forms of integration, where the attempt is made to see different approaches as complementary rather than unified, or where bridges are built between disparate schools of psychotherapy. There is a very full discussion of all these matters in the magisterial book by Mahrer (1989) on this topic. Of course I am not saying that there are not all sorts of interesting questions as to how, when and why a therapist would want to move from one column into another. All I am trying to say is that there are certain approaches which cannot be melded, moulded or fused into one, and that there are others which can.

Some objections have been made to this view by Michael Wilson (1994). He says that someone working at the highest level can operate eclectically at any other level. He says that too many things are mixed up together in my column 4, so that it looks as if I am lumping together types of pure spirituality which are really rather different from each other, such as Christianity and Taoism. This is quite true. The reason for this is that I wanted mainly to talk about columns 1, 2 and 3, which I believe are the main ones which therapists actually use – mostly column 1, in fact, column 2 to a lesser extent, and column 3 only occasionally. I don't think many therapists use column 4 much in their actual work, though they may find such a spiritual discipline very useful for their own development. If we wanted to talk more about column 4 as such, as I believe Wilson is trying to do, we should have to distinguish, as Ken Wilber (1995) does, between the lower Causal, the higher Causal and the Nondual. But for that the rubrics on the left of the chart which I have used to distinguish between the different levels actually used in therapy would be more or less irrelevant. So a different approach would have to be used, and a different article written, which would be very interesting to those embarked upon a spiritual quest, but not so interesting to the everyday therapist I am trying to address.

All in all, then, there is much to agree with in what Michael Wilson has said, and in fact I find his views quite compatible with my own. It seems to me that we have here more a difference of emphasis than a real difference of opinion.

To sum up, then, if two forms of therapy in a single column want to come together, they may construct something which may look as unlikely as a duck-billed platypus, but which may well be viable and productive. From such a union a new school of integrative psychotherapy may spring up. But if two forms of therapy in two different columns try to come together, the result will be more like a Sphinx, with parts which never quite fit, and do not lead to any successful school or training. The only apparent exception to this would be a training which assimilated something in one column to something in another, changing its nature in the process.

The way primal integration fits in to this analysis is very interesting. Its main focus, as we have said, is in column 2 on our chart. But once the client has got in touch with the real self, and come to terms with all the implications of that for daily life, it does not have to call a halt. It can say to the person: there is more. And at that point it can move into column 3 and start to work there, at that new and different level. It can then help the person to own up to their spiritual nature, their subtle self. It can use ritual and ceremony where appropriate. It can open up the use of symbols, myths and images to cultivate the imagination and the soul of the client. This is a rich and colourful area to work in, and I have written about it at greater length elsewhere (Rowan, 1992b).

Training

At the moment there is no centre offering training in primal integration itself in this country, though some training takes place at the Amethyst centre in Dublin, and some in the USA, under the auspices of the International Primal Association. But there are some considerations which seem relevant, not just to primal integration but to any therapy which aims to be integrative. I have some experience, over twenty years or so, of working with integrative training programmes, and am at the moment involved with one at the Minster Centre in London.

I would argue that every therapist who works in depth must be able to handle infant stuff when it comes up, must be able to handle perinatal stuff when it comes up, must be able to handle prenatal stuff when it comes up, must be able to handle spiritual stuff when it comes up. Many training courses avoid some of these areas, and the beginning therapist will just have to get them somewhere else, or face being inadequately equipped.

Similarly, many training courses have quite an inadequate coverage of group work, and the aspiring therapist will probably need to go elsewhere for work on psychodrama, encounter, t-groups and so on. This work is needed to produce the kind of authentic human being which is needed if the person is to work in what we have been calling the discipline of column 2. It has often been pointed out that certain problems, as for example insensitive talkativeness, are never going to come out in one-to-one therapy, and need a group to become at all accessible. So I feel very strongly that a good training course absolutely needs to cover group work in some detail. And if an otherwise good course is not adequate in this respect, the aspiring therapist is just going to have to go elsewhere for such training and experience.

On the whole, the therapists I know myself are very conscientious in this respect, and do continue to work on themselves and expose themselves to new ideas and new experiences. But there should be more facilities for established psychotherapists and counsellors to be properly taught about the new work as it comes along. Probably there are today more therapists who have never enabled their clients to go back to their early experiences before 5 years old than there are any other kind. And yet all the implications of the work which has come along in the past few years, both in psychoanalysis and in the humanistic approaches, are that clients often need to go further back than that if we want to see substantial changes in the basic character structure. Further, it seems to me that any course which avoids any discussion of the social context is going to let its students down. There is so much opportunity for manipulation by psychotherapists that it is crucially important to make sure that students are made aware of the necessity for this not to happen in their work. I believe that psychotherapy is a political act, and has to be taken seriously as a political act if it is not ultimately to do more harm than good. Andrew Samuels says:

> Amidst the tragic anomie and baffling atomization, amidst the dreadful con-
> formism of 'international' architecture, telecommunications and cuisine, amidst
> the sense of oppression and fear of a horrific future, amidst war itself, there is an
> equally fragmented, fractured and complex attempt at a *resacralization of the
> culture* going on. (1993, p. 11)

Psychotherapy is either on the side of this resacralization or it is not. My own view is that it can and should be.

I don't know what will happen over the next many years, but I do know what I want to happen. The one main thing I would like people to learn is a negative one – don't put all your eggs in one basket. I hate the narrow kind of therapist who was trained in one school, analysed by one analyst, and practises in one mode. I hate even more the narrow kind of so-called 'therapist' who has never done any self-therapy at all. I very much like the open kind of therapist who has had many teachers and tried many modes, and has then settled on his or her own combination.

And this is not just a personal preference – there is a theoretical rationale for it too. It is that, as Freud said, therapists can only operate up to the limit of their own resistances. These resistances tend to be strongest in the areas which have not been reached by the type of therapy they did in their training. So when they get clients bringing up material which they did not cover in their training, they distort it and treat it as something else, which must be ineffectual.

It is amazing, when one brings up this sort of point in mixed company, the way in which there will always be one or two people who say at this point, 'Where is the research to prove this?' And it virtually always turns out that when I ask such people for their own experience, they will say that, sure, their own experience shows that their own therapy was very important to them, and did help them become more balanced and more adequate in their work. But they would rather ignore their own experience and indulge in this fractious demand for empirical research evidence. Yet as soon as we really think about this, we can see that such research would be so hard to do that it is no wonder that researchers have steered clear of it and stuck to things which they think are simpler. The research which has been done has been shallow and simplistic, and far from helping us, has only made us more confused (Matarazzo, 1978). Much of it, indeed, has not been done using real therapists or real clients, and this surprises non-researchers when they discover it.

It seems crystal clear to me that the most important influence on any therapist is the personal therapy they have experienced themselves: on themselves and for themselves. The second most important influence is the supervision they have had. And the third most important influence is the clients they have had; but this third one can be crucially and sometimes cruelly limited by the first two.

As I go around the world, I often find myself introducing people to the idea of self and peer assessment, which entails watching people do short sessions of 15–20 minutes using their own form of psychotherapy or counselling. And I am struck by the almost uniformly dismal level of expertise which I see and hear. I have come to believe that most psychotherapy and counselling that goes on in the world is pretty bad. I want it to be better. But it seems obvious to me that unless psycho-therapists and counsellors are continually and quite humbly working on themselves to improve and develop further as professionals no improvement will happen. As far as I can see, the reason for the lack of quality is that people do not really question themselves very much, once the training years are over. Jeffrey Kottler (1986, 1989) has been writing well about this in recent years.

Of course supervision has a most important part to play in all this, and in recent years there have been some excellent contributions to the literature, notably the work of Peter Hawkins and Robin Shohet (1989) and Elizabeth Holloway (1995).

I had my first important breakthrough in therapy after five years of working on myself, and other major breakthroughs in the five years following. From that point on I was what Rogers calls a 'fully functioning person' and my spiritual path and growth became more important than my therapy. It seems to me that therapy really does take this long – something like a ten-year stint. And I think the experience of someone like Jenny James (1983) in this country, who had almost continuous access to psychotherapy for long periods, and who still took ten years about it, bears out this view.

Obviously no training course could take this long, and this means that any psychotherapist, no matter how well trained, must continue to engage in personal growth for a considerable time after the end of any training course. What I am arguing for is a substantial change in the way this further work is regarded – not as further deepening in the same method, but rather an extension into new and different methods and approaches which were not covered, or hardly covered, in the original training. Only in this way can we get the fully trained, fully functioning psychotherapists that clients so desperately need.

I do not yet see the training courses which I think are needed. But the general movement towards modularity in education, and the much greater ability to pick one course from here and another from there which I do see now, point in the right direction. So this is how I see the future in this respect.

Cultural trends

There now seem to be some general things to be said about the context within which all this is taking place. It seems to me that the whole of western civilization is going through a reaction to the optimism of the 1960s. The main form this takes is postmodernism and deconstruction. In other words, there is a scepticism about metanarratives. The great theories, the great dreams of the past are now seen as untenable or actively harmful, and what we are left with is fragmentation. This general and widespread tendency has affected humanistic psychology too. Decent writers like Walt Anderson (1990) have taken up the postmodernist banner, and many people in the AHP have been influenced, to the point of trying to revise the

AHP mission statement in a postmodern direction. Luckily this effort failed!

If we can come out of the extreme positions here with our heads and our hearts intact, I think we can talk in terms of a valid form of pluralism, which avoids monism at one end of the spectrum and relativism at the other. John Kekes has been writing well about this recently, though I do not claim him for humanistic psychology: he is a philosopher. But I think he has much to say which can help us. Pluralism, according to Kekes (1994), says we can have a fundamental set of values, each of which can support the others, and this, I believe, is exactly what we have always had and always needed, in humanistic psychology.

In the *AHP Perspective*, published in San Francisco, the issue of January/February 1995 contains an article by Maureen O'Hara sounding a 'wake up call for humanistic warriors'. She warns of the trends in the field of psychotherapy particularly.

In California and New York, and increasingly elsewhere, managed care is well under way. What this means is that insurers, healthcare purchasers and governmental agencies appear to have decided that in the interests of cost containment they must control therapeutic practice, controlling what therapists can and cannot do, for how long, and for what reasons. 'One managed care company I work with wants a symptom checklist and therapeutic intervention report after *every single session*!' And she says that most humanistic therapists cannot twist their practice to fit into such a mechanistic system.

She tells us that the American Psychological Association has embarked upon a project to create a diagnostic manual of its own, distinct from the psychiatric manual (DSM-IV) which is now so well known. This will enable clear distinctions to be made between acceptable care and sub-standard care. Again this will probably be to standards other than those which humanistic psychologists espouse.

A third threat to humanistic psychology, she says, is the tightening up of accreditation criteria in various states. Increasingly 'graduates from humanistically oriented schools are being refused licensing'. This has bad implications for those who are running humanistic types of course.

And a fourth threat comes from the backlash against therapy which is now going on from the False Memory Society and its associates, from the religious right, and from books such as those attacking Freud and Robyn Dawes' *The House of Cards*, which purports to demonstrate that there is no correlation between outcomes in psychotherapy and requirements for training and licensing in clinical psychology. Some humanistic and trans-personal psychologists have already been charged with ethics violations and malpractice for using experiential or shamanistic practices.

Do we have to worry? Is the same thing going to happen in this country? It seems to me that the mental health field is dominated by accountants and attempts at standardization. There is a version of science, dominated by empiricism and cognitive psychology, which says that cost–

benefit analyses can always be conducted. Everything worthwhile can be measured at the level of ordinary consciousness. There is no need to worry about the unconscious or the spiritual. As for the oppressions of class, race, gender, age, disability and the like, all that can be taken care of within the standardization procedures.

The prime example of all this is the movement towards devising National Vocational Qualifications for befriending, advice, guidance, counselling, therapeutic counselling and psychotherapy. By means of a functional analysis, all these activities are broken down into elements, which can then be combined in various ways to form requirements for certain positions in employment. The thinking behind this comes from cognitive psychology and empiricist science, which are very limited when it comes to dealing with human beings.

Now there is in statistics a thing called the Gompertz curve, which applies quite regularly to innovative practices. After a slow start, the innovation speeds up and starts an exponential period of growth, such that if the trend continued, the earth would be totally taken over by it. But at a certain point, the curve inflects, making it more like an S – in fact, it is sometimes called the S-curve. At that point the phenomenon slows down, and some new innovation comes on the scene. I assume that the process of progressive control and centralization, of which some examples have been given above, will also go the same way. How far it still has to go is uncertain.

After it I suspect there will be a period of fragmentation, very much in tune with the postmodern ideas which at the moment are only popular in the universities. In this more postmodern atmosphere, humanistic and transpersonal approaches would fit very well. In fact, these approaches, with their full appreciation of the multiplicity of things, might be more at home in such a world than most others. And we might be able to teach something about pluralism. The whole thrust of the chart in Table 7.1 is to say that there is not just one right way, not just one great truth: there are different truths at different levels. This is a pluralist vision, not a relativist one. Yet it does not deny the important truth of relativism, which is that dogmatism and the One Great Truth are oppressive and inhuman.

Personally I have no great problem with this, as I don't think it is a good idea to have certainties in the first place. One of the strengths of the humanistic approach, it seems to me, is its restless refusal to stay content with the received wisdom. 'Let's find out' seems to me its watchword. This is the upside of the lack of interest in grand theory, which elsewhere can look like a weakness.

Somebody once said that the mark of an intelligent person was the ability to hold two ideas in the mind at the same time. In the present age this makes more sense than ever before. I think we are all wary of the authority who offers us THE TRUTH. Before you know it, he has followers who are all trying to put everyone else down because they do not have THE TRUTH and are therefore in error and probably wicked and evil. Most of the problems in the world come from people who know they are right. Some people have criticized Ken Wilber for having a grand theory, but his theory subverts itself in this respect, because it says so clearly that there are different 'truths' at different levels, and at the highest level the idea of truth drops out entirely.

I know I have myself put forward a credo of a kind, but I assure you that I hold its tenets very lightly, and would not excommunicate anyone who did not hold any one of them.

I think we in humanistic psychology just have to keep on fighting our corner and not letting go of what we believe. We can give up the idea some of us once had of being the majority. We shall always be a minority, because our requirements are really very strong. We insist on self-knowledge, we insist on authenticity, we insist on the value of autonomy. We oppose authoritarianism, we oppose black-and-white thinking, we oppose the meek following of leaders and the simple playing of roles. And this makes us unusual. On good days I think we shall never be less than two standard deviations from the mean; on bad days I think we shall never be less than three standard deviations from the mean. (In case you don't speak statistics, this can be roughly translated as 'quite a bit different' as against 'really far out'.) Even more particularly, I don't think primal integration will ever be the most popular therapy in the world. It is too demanding, it asks too much from its therapists, its educators, its clients: it asks them to be nothing less than complete human beings. How simple, and how hard.

I don't know how society will develop in the next quarter century. G.K. Chesterton used to say that the majority of people had a simple game which they loved to play: they would notice carefully what the experts said they were going to do, and then they would go away and do something different. All I know is that humanistic psychology has contributed something enormous to society, something that can never be forgotten or lost, and which it is up to all of us who care about such things to keep whole. And I believe that primal integration not only does justice to the humanistic approach, but to the transpersonal approach and the integrative approach as well. I don't know if the majority of the people of the future will practise primal integration, but I hope they do and I know some will.

References

Adzema, M. (1985) A primal perspective on spirituality, *Journal of Humanistic Psychology*, 25(3): 83–116.

Anderson, W.T. (1990) *Reality isn't what it used to be: Theatrical Politics, Ready-to-wear Religion, Global Myths, Primitive Chic, and Other Wonders of the Postmodern World.* San Francisco: Harper and Row.

Arkowitz, H. and Messer, S.B. (eds) (1984) *Psychoanalytic Therapy and Behaviour Therapy: Is Integration Possible?* New York: Plenum Press.

Bragdon, E. (1990) *The Call of Spiritual Emergency*. San Francisco: Harper and Row.

Brown, J. and Mowbray, R. (1994) Primal integration, in D. Jones (ed.), *Innovative Therapy: A Handbook*. Buckingham: Open University Press.

Bugental, J.F.T. (1987) *The Art of the Psychotherapist*. New York: Norton.

Clarkson, P. (1995) *The Therapeutic Relationship*. London: Whurr.

Douglas, A. (1989) The limits of cognitive-behaviour therapy: Can it be integrated with psychodynamic therapy? *British Journal of Psychotherapy*, 5(3): 390–401.

Erskine, R.G. and Moursund, J.P. (1988) *Integrative Psychotherapy in Action*. London: Sage.

Feltham, C. and Dryden, W. (1993) *Dictionary of Counselling*. London: Whurr.

Fonagy, P. (1989) On the integration of cognitive-behaviour therapy with psychoanalysis, *British Journal of Psychotherapy*, 5(4): 557–63.

Grof, S. and Grof, C. (1989) *Spiritual Emergency*. Los Angeles: Jeremy Tarcher.

Grof, C. and Grof, S. (1990) *The Stormy Search for the Self*. Los Angeles: Jeremy Tarcher.

Haronian, F. (1974) The repression of the sublime, *Synthesis* 1(1): 51–62.

Hawkins, P. and Shohet, R. (1989) *Supervision in the Helping Professions*. Buckingham: Open University Press.

Holloway, E. (1995) *Clinical Supervision: A Systems Approach*. Thousand Oaks: Sage.

James, J. (1983) *Room to Breathe*. London: Caliban.

Kekes, J. (1993) *The Morality of Pluralism*. Princeton: Princeton University Press.

Kottler, J.A. (1986) *On Being a Therapist*. San Francisco: Jossey-Bass.

Kottler, J.A. and Blau, D.S. (1989) *The Imperfect Therapist: Learning from Failure in Therapeutic Practice*. San Francisco: Jossey-Bass.

Mahrer, A.R. (1989) *The Integration of Psychotherapies*. New York: Human Sciences Press.

Maslow, A.H. (1973) *The Farther Reaches of Human Nature*. London: Penguin.

Maslow, A.H. (1987) *Motivation and Personality*, 3rd edn. New York: Harper and Row.

Matarazzo, R.G. (1978) 'Research on the teaching and learning of psychotherapeutic skills', in S.L. Garfield and A.E. Bergin (eds), *Handbook of Psychotherapy and Behaviour Change*, 2nd edn. New York: Wiley.

Merry, E.C. (1983) *The Flaming Door*. Edinburgh: Floris Books.

Norcross, J.C. and Prochaska, J.O. (1983) Clinicians' theoretical orientations: Selection, utilization and efficacy, *Professional Psychology*, 14: 197–208.

Roose, K. et al. (1991) An integrative model in psychotherapy training. Paper presented at the SEPI congress in London, July 1991.

Rowan, J. (1992a) 'Hegel and self-actualization', in *Breakthroughs and Integration in Psychotherapy*. London: Whurr.

Rowan, J. (1992b) 'Spiritual aspects of Primal Integration', in *Breakthroughs and Integration in Psychotherapy*. London: Whurr.

Rowan, J. (1993) *The Transpersonal in Psychotherapy and Counselling*. London: Routledge.

Rowan, J. (1994) Do therapists ever cure clients? *Self and Society*, 22(5): 4–5.

Rowan, J. (1996) 'Transpersonal psychotherapy', in W. Dryden (ed.) *Developments in Psychotherapy: Historical Perspectives*. London: Sage.

Ryle, A. (1990) *Cognitive-Analytic Therapy: Active Participation in Change*. Chichester: Wiley.

Samuels, A. (1993) *The Political Psyche*. London: Routledge.

Samuels, A., Shorter, B. and Plaut, F. (1986) *A Critical Dictionary of Jungian Analysis*. London: Routledge.

Solomon, H. (1994) The transcendent function and Hegel's dialectical vision, *Journal of Analytical Psychology*, 39: 77–100.

Wachtel, P.L. (1977) *Psychoanalysis and Behaviour Therapy: Toward an Integration*. New York: Basic Books.

Wilber, K. (1980) *The Atman Project*. Wheaton: Quest.

Wilber, K. (1981a) *Up from Eden: A Transpersonal View of Human Evolution*. Garden City: Anchor Doubleday.

Wilber, K. (1981b) *No Boundary*. Boston: Shambhala.

Wilber, K. (1983) *A Sociable God*. New York: McGraw-Hill.

Wilber, K. (1995) *Sex, Ecology, Spirituality*. Boston: Shambhala.

Wilber, K. et al. (eds) (1986) *Transformations of Consciousness*. Boston: New Science Library.

Wilson, M. (1994) Spiritual terrain, *Counselling News*, 16, December: 24–5.

8

Pluralism and the Future of Psychotherapy

Andrew Samuels

Introduction

The roots of this chapter on the future of psychotherapy lie in a number of recent political developments with which I have been closely involved. I have carried out a number of consultations with politicians in Britain and the United States designed to explore how useful and effective perspectives derived from psychotherapy might be in the formation of public policy and in new thinking about the political process. It is difficult to operationalize psychotherapeutic thinking about politics so that mainline politicians – for example, a Democratic Senator of a Labour Party Committee – will take it seriously. For instance, I have found that issues of gender and sexuality are particularly effective in concentrating minds. Partly this is due to the perennial fascination and excitement carried by such topics. Partly it is because gender is itself a hybrid notion from a political point of view. In the social world of lived experience, gender and sexuality are everyday realities, suffused with experiences of power, powerlessness, vulnerability and misunderstanding. Gender has its own socioeconomic dimensions and set of electoral significances. But gender is also an exceedingly private business, part of a story that people tell themselves and are told in attempts to create or discover identities and relationships with others. Gender and sexuality are therefore liminal, sitting on the threshold between internal and external worlds, contributing to and partaking of both.

I have also been involved in the creation of three organizations whose mission statements are relevant to the context of this chapter. Psychotherapists and Counsellors for Social Responsibility is a professional organization, intended to facilitate the desire of many therapists and analysts and counsellors to intervene as professionals in social and political matters making appropriate use of their knowledge and, it must be admitted, whatever cultural authority they possess. The second organization is a psychotherapy-based think tank, Antidote. Here, the strategy has been to limit the numbers of mental health professionals involved so as to reduce the chances of psychotherapy reductionism and foster multi-disciplinary work in the social policy field. Antidote has undertaken research work in connection with psychological attitudes to money and economic issues generally, and is also involved in work in the area of 'emotional literacy' but expanding the usual remit from personal relationships and family matters to include issues in the public domain. The third organization is a broad front based at St James's Church in London. The St James's Alliance consists of individuals from diverse fields such as politics, economics, ethics, religion, non-governmental organizations, the media, and psychotherapy. The goal is to incorporate ethical, spiritual and psychological concerns into the British political agenda and to facilitate a dialogue between non-governmental organizations, single issue groups and progressive political organizations. It is an experiment in gathering in political energy that is split up and dissipated under current arrangements.

It might be thought that the increasing numbers of psychotherapists and analysts such as myself who are interested in politics are making these moves from an on-high and detached position, careless of the political issues affecting our own profession. If this were so, then the project would have little or no future. However, all three organizations have been profoundly affected by the acrimonious yet successful campaign waged by elements of the psychotherapy profession to end discrimination against lesbian and gay men candidates for training in psychoanalytic psychotherapy and psychoanalysis. When psychotherapists get involved with politics they need to do so with a degree of self-mockery over the appalling mess in which their own professional politics are usually to be found, as well as over the counter-intuitive and slightly mad tone of what they have to say.

In fact, psychotherapists can learn a good deal from politics as it is practised and theorized these days. Much of what I have to say about pluralism is taken directly from political theory and praxis. One political theme that seems to me to be very relevant is what the political philosophers call the 'identity/difference theme'. This means that, in some ways, everybody is identical, and in some ways everybody is different. Now, there are no votes in such an unsexy formulation. But I invite my readers to consider it for its very complexity and ambiguity. When you journey across Europe today, visiting the different countries, do you find similarity or do you find difference? It would be much more emotionally appealing to say: 'Everyone is the same these days in the new Europe without frontiers'. Or, 'In fact everybody is very different. National identities are not at all eroded'. How much more difficult, and yet how much more in tune with the kind of detailed complexities of therapy work is it to say: 'In some respects the countries of Europe are all the same, and in some respects the countries of Europe are different'.

I want to relate the professional concerns raised in this chapter to the ongoing work in the psychology–politics field described earlier. I am attempting to bring a psychological perspective to the political issues of the day, and to a re-invention of the political itself. For example, I am interested in the psychological implications of the strategies adopted by nearly all the parties in the west, not just the more social democratic parties, to rethink labour economics in terms of retraining and then retraining again throughout a lifetime of work. Because of the speed and pace of technological innovation, changing demands of the labour market mean that the old pattern in which one acquired a knowledge pool, and then had a job based on that knowledge pool for the rest of one's life, has gone for ever. What psychotherapy brings to this particular discussion is how different retraining is going to be for males and females. There is a gender dimension to consider here. Women are already familiar with a certain amount of labour flexibility. How will they react to being told from on high what to do with that flexibility? Men, on the other hand, have traded off their *in*flexibility in relation to employment. How are they going to react to being told that what they know is no longer of any use? There are different agendas for the two sexes.

Moving onto a more clinical level, I am also involved in working out the details of what I call the 'politicization of therapy practice'. Everybody these days says they want to work with the political and social dimensions in therapy. It has become a kind of cocktail-party truism or slogan. Yet there are absolutely no detailed texts on how to do this. So I am trying to write such detailed texts that explicate the political person as he or she appears in the clinical situation (see Samuels, 1993).

Pluralism and psychotherapy

My interest in pluralism and psychotherapy dates from the publication of *Jung and the Post-Jungians* in 1985. In that book I commented that it was not easy to find one's way around in the contemporary Jungian world. This was because very little had been written on the various competing schools of analytical psychology that have grown up. Moreover, Jungians had been encouraged by Jung himself not to think of themselves as belonging to a recognizable discipline in the first place – an attitude of Jung's and a situation which I questioned severely in the book.

The book and my whole approach rest on a fundamental paradox – that, by concentrating on debate, dispute and difference, we could get the best possible conception of what psychotherapy as a whole really is.

Traditionally, the ways in which one defines a field involve looking for that which everybody agrees with – the consensus approach. These core values and core practices are usually regarded as defining the field. This is old-fashioned thinking. We need instead to think of a radical way of defining the field by references to the differences of opinion in and around it. What will continue to define the field of psychotherapy in the future is, in my view, dispute. How does this actually work out in practice?

If some psychotherapists, of whatever orientations, are having an argument about what psychotherapy really is, and you have some idea what they are talking about, and you are in some way stirred by their argument, then you are in a sense in the field. The field can be defined by the emotional ripples its arguments generate. This is a very complex and difficult idea that lies at the heart of much that I shall be proposing in this chapter. We should start our profession-defining work at the outer limits of the envelope. We should stay with dispute, argument, disagreement, miscommunication, misunderstanding, betrayal and onslaughts on the other, rather than staying with the core, the centre, the consensus. The philosopher A.N. Whitehead put this beautifully in a nutshell when he said: 'A clash of doctrines is not a disaster, it is an opportunity'. But first you have to *find* the clash, and *use* the clash to *define* what you are doing.

There is a cultural change to consider here as well. I want to mention this, lest my stress on dispute sound like an exclusively male perspective. I do not like the term, but there is what could be called a 'feminization of knowledge' going on in the west today involving a boundary blurring between disciplines and within disciplines. There is a new valuing of subjectivity and intuition even within the hard sciences, and certainly within the social sciences and the humanities. It is my belief that altering the angle from which we define the field to one of difference and dispute, and away from one of consensus and agreement, is in a sense aligned with such new approaches to knowledge that I would reluctantly call the 'feminization of knowledge'.

Of course, any work on psychotherapy as a field is bound to be a creative falsehood in that there will be large discrepancies between countries and according to the background and orientation of the writer. But there is an imaginative and metaphorical aspect to the mapping of psychotherapy. These imaginative and metaphorical aspects have gradually become more and more interesting and important to me. In fact I focus on them, amongst other things, in a later book *The Plural Psyche: Personality, Morality and the Father* (1989). The different modalities of psychotherapy can also be envisioned as *separate strands existing in the mind of a single practitioner and even as having a certain imaginal autonomy therein*. In that case, their strident and polemical debate becomes an unavoidable, urgent, internal matter for each and every one of us.

So – what is 'pluralism'?

Pluralism is an attitude to conflict which tries to reconcile differences without imposing a false resolution on them or losing sight of the unique value of each position. Hence, pluralism is *not* the same as 'multiplicity' or 'diversity'. Rather, pluralism is an attempt to hold unity and diversity in balance – humanity's age-old struggle, in religion, philosophy and politics, to hold the tension between the One and the Many. My use of the term 'pluralism' is also supposed to be different from 'eclecticism' or 'synthesis'. As the paper unfolds, the distinctions should become clearer. Here, at the beginning, I would merely say that the trademark of pluralism is competition and its way of life is bargaining.

We need a psychological working out of the idea of pluralism and, in order to do this, I will make two suggestions.

First, on a personal level, each of us is faced with the pluralistic task of aligning our many internal voices and images of ourselves with our need and wish to speak with one voice and recognize ourselves as integrated beings. So it is an issue of intense feeling. But it is also an issue of thinking – for psychological theory also seeks to see how the various structures, conflicts, complexes, objects, attitudes, functions, self-objects, part-selves, subpersonalities, deintegrates, internal objects, psychic *dramatis personae*, areas of the mind, subphases, gods – how all of these relate to the personality as a whole. The extent of the list demonstrates the universality of the problem and its inherent fascination.

My second suggestion is that a pluralistic approach may be of immense help in dealing with issues of unity and diversity as they affect psychotherapy, with its massive ideological differences. By 'psychotherapy' I mean all psychological endeavours which seek to help individuals and small groups. We need a term which refers to the social context of *the whole field*, psychoanalytic, Jungian, humanistic, family and marital, cognitive-behaviourist, rational emotive, etc., and, at the same time, to *the divisions within the field*. (Of course, we should not forget that the field itself is composed of individual psychotherapists.)

The fragmentation and dispute within psychotherapy, as each group fights for the general acceptance of its viewpoint, seem, on the surface, to be the very opposite of what is usually regarded as pluralism. However, as I said earlier, this competitive aggression is at the heart of any attempt to build up a pluralistic approach. The idea of unconscious compensation (in Jungian terms) or the idea of reaction formation (in Freudian terms) suggest that we should look a little more deeply into the warlike situation. If we do so, then it is possible to see psychotherapy as struggling, and as having always struggled towards pluralism. As Herakleitos put it, 'that which alone is wise both wishes and does not wish to be called Zeus'. What seems like a flight from pluralism may also be a yearning for it and an acceptance at some level of a pluralistic destiny for psychotherapy.

A pluralistic attitude can hold the tension between the claims of and tendencies towards unity *and* claims of and tendencies towards diversity. Psychotherapy as a cohesive discipline with right and wrong approaches – *and* psychotherapy as containing a multiplicity of valued approaches. It would not be pluralistic, as I understand it, to assert that there are many diverse truths but that these are merely aspects of one greater Truth. In that religious and élitist approach, entry into the greater Truth, which would do away with all the lesser and seemingly contradictory truths, is reserved for the elect. This is not pluralistic, it is condescendingly casuistic. From a pluralist standpoint, Truth (with a capital T) and truth have to compete. Sometimes passionate and aggressive expressions of and adherence to the truth can (even should) be the right way to live and function. But sometimes we need a more partial and pragmatic vision, equally passionate and aggressive in its way. Aggression, which is so characteristic of debates between psychotherapists, often contains the deepest needs for contact, dialogue, playback, affirmation.

Now, many psychotherapists are probably committed to dialogue but the psychological difficulties associated with maintaining a tolerant attitude cannot be minimized. Psychotherapists, being human, will continually fail to be as tolerant as they would like to be. In part, this is because of their passionate devotion to their own psychological approach, to their own particular vision, or 'personal confession'. *But where is a programme to combine passion and tolerance in psychotherapy?* We know about and concentrate on the opposites of tolerance – envy, denigration, power, control, and so forth. But we usually pathologize these. My intent is to do something positive and realistic with the incorrigible competitiveness and argumentativeness, mining the envious shit for the tension-rich gold it might contain. Competition that is open, competition that is brought into the open, and into consciousness, competition that is psychologically integrated and valued, could lead to a new tough-minded tolerance. My approach is psychologically realistic here, staying close to and trading off what Jung called the shadow – the thing each of us has no wish to be. To paraphrase Lacan, if the unconscious is indeed structured like anything, it is structured like an argument.

Through competition and argument with others we may come to know ourselves and our ideas better and more deeply. This is an example of the importance of the mirroring other whose presence glimmers in so many dialectical psychologies – Jung's, Winnicott's, Neumann's, Lacan's, Kohut's. This other is a creative other and needs nurturing. What is more – and I mention this as an example of the realism of pluralism – you cannot annihilate the other who is your opponent. He or she will not go away. The opponent is omnipresent and indestructible. The opponent resists the false way in which we all try to describe him or her. Sure, you can describe your opponent as narcissistic, religiose, mechanistic, idealistic, transference-bound – but he or she will bounce back, rejecting that distortion and returning to the argument: *la lutta continua*. Like it or not, the dialogue and confrontation go on, as they always have in psychotherapy. And, amidst the seemingly ridiculous institutional splits, a kind of exchange is constantly being crafted. We should recall that when we project onto an other, it is often the good or positive things about ourselves that are projected (for whatever reason). Re-collection of projected contents is vital for the health and integrity of the self.

I think that this kind of exchange – and let us remember that Hermes is the god of trade – can be illustrated by reference to Jungian analysis, which is obviously the field I know best. My view is that, already for quite some time, Jungian analysis has been pluralistic, employing many diverse metaphors such as alchemy, infancy, mythology, but remaining one discernible enterprise. The problem is that our thinking has not caught up with what we are doing or can do. So, if a Jungian analyst seeks to place so-called classical 'Jungian analysis' and analysis of the infantile components of personality in eternal opposition, then both the history and the future of Jungian analysis are passing him or her by. Reductive analysis can be a *part* of Jungian analysis.

Similarly I have come to see that it is possible to link the monotheistic/integrative/*unus mundus*/élitist concerns of the classical Jung and the classical school with the polytheistic/interactive/microscopic/democratic concerns of the other post-Jungians – without losing the value and heartfelt truth of both sets of concerns.

Psychotherapy is a social phenomenon which, viewed over time, has shown itself able to withstand clashes and splits and generate new ideas out of them. This capacity lies alongside the far better known tendency for the splits to become institutional and concrete, and hence somewhat unproductive. Psychotherapy continues to be desirous of entering a pluralistic state but lacks the ideological and methodological means to do it. It could even be possible that we are all pluralists but the prevailing ideology in the world we live in forces us to deny it. The tendency towards multiplicity and diversity is as strong – and creative – as the search for unity or a striving for hegemony.

As we proceed, we shall see again and again how these two suggestions of mine are really the same suggestion. That is to say, the experience of the One and the Many in relation to one's own psyche and personality, and the argument about the One and the Many in relation to disputes in the professional area of psychotherapy are, in a sense, the same thing. However, the vicissitudes of psychotherapy as a cultural movement, the splits, plots, alliances, gossip and power struggles – all these reveal that, in their professional lives, therapists are participating in a mighty projection of the psyche. For, when therapists argue, it is the psyche that is speaking. Differing points of view reflect the multiplicity of the psyche itself. And when therapists recognize what they have in common, often through discussions of clinical experiences, then it is psyche in its monistic, unified vein that is revealed.

My point is that when therapists look at themselves – and they should always be looking at themselves – how they think, feel, behave, organize themselves, they are, perhaps without knowing it, also gazing at and participating in the world of the psyche.

Similarly, the books that therapists write, and candidates and colleagues read, are not what they seem to be. Texts of psychological theory can constitute for us what alchemical texts constituted for Jung. A deconstruction of psychotherapy parallels his of alchemy. Just as the alchemists projected the workings of the unconscious into chemical elements and processes, becoming caught up in the pervasive symbolism of it all, so the texts of the psychotherapists, taken as a whole and understood psychologically, may unwittingly provide us with documents of the soul. I think this is a radical re-reading of what books on psychotherapy are about. What was intended to be *about* psyche is *of* psyche. The conscious aim may be to plumb the past for its truths, or to connect past and present, or to reveal the workings of cumulative psychopathology. But what gets revealed, according to this analysis, are the central characteristics of psyche itself. This is where clashes between theories are so useful, because the *actual clash itself* contains the definitive psychic issue, not the specific ideas which are in conflict. Not psychological dialectics, but psyche's discourse given dialectical form. The warring theories and the particular points of conflict speak directly of what is at war in the psyche and of what the points of conflict might be therein.

Now, sometimes it is claimed that differences of opinion could not have such deep implications because they only show differences in the psychological type of the disputants. I agree that some therapists will tend constitutionally, to prefer, see and search for multiplicity and diffusion. Others will be more inclined to favour and to find integration and unity. But this typological approach contains the seeds of its own contradiction. For, as with typology, to become truly himself or herself, the psychotherapist cannot 'belong' to one school alone. There is an interdependence with all possible manner of divergence and convergence.

Pluralism is a perspective in which various therapists or the various schools of psychotherapy have to take note of each other, without necessarily having unity as a goal, a modular, conversational approach in which different world views meet but do not try to take over each other.

Pluralism, diversity and professional politics

When theories and fantasies of the psyche are in competition, what attitudes are possible? None seems really satisfactory. We can choose between theories – but that may lead to blind partisanship and possibly to tyranny. We can synthesize theories – but that may lead to omnipotence and an avoidance of the hard edges of disagreement rather than to transcendence. We can be indifferent to the dispute, but that leads to ennui and a subtle form of 'clinical' inflation in which the relevance of theory is denied. Of course we should be pluralistic – but that leads to fragmentation and anxiety (as we shall see). It is hard to act upon, this idea of pluralism!

Political thinkers and philosophers have addressed many of the questions we shall try to answer, and we can learn from that. Later, I will use pluralistic political thinking as a metaphor to further our understanding of psychological processes and of the social organization of psychotherapy.

Let us consider how pluralism conceives of the state. This will be a useful model for a subsequent discussion of the role of national or transnational umbrella psychotherapy organizations. Many people see the state as the container of everything in a society. But it is not. A state may also be regarded as a special interest group within society. Political process in a single society consists of arguments, competitions, bargaining, between the various interest groups in society, and perhaps the state has a regulatory role. But the regulatory role of the state also itself constitutes a special interest. The state may indeed be special when we are talking about regulation. But when we are talking about other things – art, trade, maybe education – then the state does not necessarily have a particularly special place. What I am trying to communicate is a vision of the state in which what we usually think of as the unifying factor, the container, the core, the regulator, is also one of the parts. (In human psychology, the ego, often regarded as fulfilling the functions of 'the state' for an individual, is, as many theorists have pointed out, nothing more than one part of the psyche competing with the other parts.) In modern societies, increasingly, the state has to argue for its place in the sun. The state can be as vulnerable to competitive pressures as any other interest group in a society.

We can move this argument on to cover the question of psychotherapy organizations I referred to earlier. In the case of organizations like United Kingdom Council for Psychotherapy (UKCP), the implication of what I have been saying is that the organization as a whole, with its central committees, is not in fact only a container or regulator of everything going on in it. They (the organization and its central committees) are special interest groups. The centre ('ego') of UKCP is only a special interest group! The Annual General Meeting, supposedly the container of everything, is only a special interest group. There is a paradox here. What looks like the big thing is only in certain respects and at certain moments the big thing. For much of the time the big thing is only one of a number of little things. This is political pluralism applied to or understanding of umbrella psychotherapy organizations.

The manyness – the sections, the organizations, the individual psycho-therapists – and the oneness – the UKCP as a whole – are in a competitive relationship. It will be important in the future to re-imagine and re-vision the centre or the conference as a whole also as parts. The centre, the Governing Board, the Registration Board, are not above the fray. They have their own state-like interests at stake. They, too, are involved in the bargaining process – as parts relating to parts not as a whole relating to parts.

What I want us to do in future is to get beyond either maternal or paternal models for our professional organizations. In the maternal model, the big thing, the UKCP as a whole (to continue with the British example), 'holds' everything else in it. Holding as in Winnicott's idea of maternal function. In the paternal model, the UKCP sets standards and guidelines, makes regulations which everyone has to adhere to. A pluralistic model moves beyond the family altogether to try to find a new way to approach this organizational problem, which everybody is worried about: the relations between the organization as a whole (and its central committee) and the rest. By this simple and yet complex device of reconceiving the whole as a part, we can at least make a psychologically valid beginning in working out new models – pluralistic models – for psychotherapy organizations.

Can diversity be analysed so as to reveal its special requirements and guidelines? And can we develop a vision of diversity which makes a place for unity? For, as I have said, pluralism, as I use the term, does not simply mean diversity or multiplicity, not just the Many.

We know from politics that freedom does not guarantee diversity, for freedom can lead to a part of a system expanding to take a tyrannical hold over the whole. If I am free to do or be what I like, this will produce an unequal state of affairs between you and me. To make sure that does not happen, we may be required by political consensus or law to be more equal in some or all respects. But then an inhibition has been placed on my freedom. Exactly the same conundrum faces the psychotherapist today. If I act on, live out, hold dear, fight for my ideas, what am I to do with the differing points of view of which I am aware? I can't just deny that these points of view exist! My freedom to have a particular point of view may lead to an unhelpful, destructive denigration and abandonment of other people's ideas to the ultimate detriment of my own position.

Equality doesn't guarantee diversity either, for equality may lead to the perils of indifference and boredom stemming from an unreal and infinite tolerance that lacks passion, is flat, bland and mediocre. This ennui can be seen in the attitude some practitioners have towards theoretical differences: that they don't matter when compared with clinical inevitabilities. This myopic, clinical triumphalism overlooks the fact that everything in one's practice is suffused with theory (and, hopefully, vice versa). But if all views are considered to be of equal worth, what is to become of the freedom to feel a special value attaching to one's own view?

So, surprising to psychotherapists, perhaps, but not to political theorists, neither the freedom to think nor an egalitarian approach to thought can be said to guarantee diversity in a way that permits a unified view to co-exist with it. Perhaps there is a problem with the way I have formulated things, and so I want to make a most radical suggestion. Instead of advancing pluralism as a desirable state or goal, let us begin instead to *use* it as a *tool* or *instrument* whose purpose is to make sure that diversity does not lead to schism and that differences between particular points of view are not smoothed over. Pluralism can function as an instrument which monitors the mosaic of the psyche rather than as a governing ideal.

Pluralism, gender and morality

Rather than setting pluralism up as a goal or an ideal, we can employ this tool to explore the psyche, or personality development, or what is happening in psychotherapy generally, and also as a means to bring a psychological dimension to cultural, political and social debates. For example, I am interested in the role of the father in the evolution of psychological pluralism in the daughter – her capacity, or lack of it, on the cultural as well as on the identity level, to be many things (wife, lover, daughter, career woman, spiritual voyager) whilst retaining a sense of being an integrated person. She is One woman and many women at the same time (see Samuels, 1993, pp. 125–75 for a fuller account). Similarly, primal scene imagery, in which parental union and separation alternate, also refers to the individual's capacity to deal creatively with conflict and difference, whether this is internal or met in political strife in the external world. When the parents unite, they are One; when they separate, they are Many. The tension between these two parental positions reflects the emotional experiences of intrapsychic conflict and of political dissensions.

This approach can be extended into other areas such as morality and gender identity. The way I conceive morality is that it incorporates a ceaseless dynamic between a passionately expressed, codified, legally sanctified certitude, which I call original morality, and a more open, tolerant and flexible style of morality, called moral imagination. These two aspects of morality are equally archetypal and inborn; one doesn't develop into the other. Nor are they always in harmony – quite the reverse. A morality based exclusively on original morality or exclusively on moral imagination would be a useless morality. But the two styles of morality go on competing: sometimes one prevails, sometimes the other, sometimes a bargain is concluded between them and, sometimes, less often than Jungian theories of the *conjunctio oppositorum* would predict, there is a synthesis (see Samuels et al., 1986, pp. 35–6 and pp. 101–4 for a fuller account).

As far as gender identity is concerned, I want to make the following suggestion. In each of us, there are areas of gender certainty and gender confusion. It is important not to see gender certainty as good and gender confusion as bad because excessive unconscious gender certainty leads to inauthentic, empty, stereotypical functioning. Similarly, gender confusion has its creative aspects – in artistic activity, for instance, and even in political and social matters. Gender certainty and gender confusion do not merely combine in health to produce an average position. Rather, each of them goes on in the psyche, in competitive opposition to each other but also linked as components in gender identity. Each is part of the whole we call gender identity (perspective of the One); each has its own psychology and psychopathology (perspective of the Many); they cannot ignore each other and so must compete (pluralistic perspective).

Pluralism and dispute in psychotherapy

Now – I hope we are in a position to use pluralism as an instrument or tool to help us look at the topic of dispute and disagreement in psychotherapy. This subject is, I suggest, of the greatest importance to anyone concerned with the training and formation of the psychotherapists of the future, seniors and candidates alike.

A pluralistic approach to psychotherapy, as I have explained it, means that a person interested in any particular area of knowledge should seek out the conflict and, above all, the *competition* between practitioners and ideologues in the discipline. The main implication is that even a so-called beginner should try to discover what the contemporary debate is all about. This approach differs fundamentally and profoundly from the conventional, linear style of training and education in depth psychology. There, one is supposed to start 'at the beginning' and when the 'basics' have been mastered and one is 'grounded', exposure to more grown-up disagreements is permitted. The point I am advancing, backed up by a good deal of teaching experience, is that *starting at the beginning is no guarantee of comprehension*. However, if a person were to focus on the up-to-the-minute ideological conflict then he or she cannot avoid discovering what has gone before; book learning is replaced by a living process. In a way, this is an educational philosophy derived from psychotherapy itself. In therapy, the focus of interest is where the internal 'debate' is at its most virulent; and in therapy the participants do not follow a linear 'course'.

The debates within psychotherapy give it life. They also serve to define the discipline generally, as I suggested in the post-Jungian book, and act as access routes for those who want to learn. What is important is not so much whether people are right or wrong, though it is vital to have views about that, but whether you know what they are talking about. For it is really rather hard to be completely wrong in psychotherapy. Or, as Kafka put it, 'the correct perception of a matter and a complete misunderstanding of the matter do not totally exclude one another'.

I am suggesting that, instead of searching for one guiding theory, we consider several competing theories together and organize our training around such theoretical competition using papers and books written with polemical intent. Actually, if you think about it, that includes a high proportion of the literary output of psychotherapists! What holds these theories together is that the subject – the psyche – holds together; just as for modern sub-atomic physicists, their subject, the universe, holds together. In this viewpoint, passion for one approach is replaced by passion for a plurality of approaches.

Problems of/with pluralism

Let's consider now some of the problems with pluralism. For all manner of psychological reasons, it is very hard to get worked up about being tolerant, to be a radical centrist in psychotherapy, to go in for what has been called 'animated moderation'. Does pluralism condemn us to losing the excitement of breakthrough ideas, which are more likely to be held with a passionate conviction? My view is that such a worry rests on a misunderstanding and an idealization of the cycle of creativity. So-called 'new' ideas emerge from a pluralistic matrix and are re-absorbed into such a matrix. As Donald Winnicott put it, 'there is no such thing as originality except on the basis of a tradition'. Ideas do not come into being outside of a context; nor does the new necessarily destroy the old but often co-exists with it. So, what looks like inspirational conviction arises from a plural *mise en scène* but it is convenient for the debt not to be acknowledged. And before we hail the man or woman of vision, let us not forget Yeats's words: 'the worst are full of passionate intensity'. The well known clinical benefits of having conviction in one's ideas can still be available, but together with open communication and the chance to learn from diversity.

This is not a dry or woolly perspective: passion abides in dialogue and tolerance as much as it does in monologue and fanaticism. The psychotherapist has never been able to work in isolation from others in the same field who have a different viewpoint. That's the conclusion I draw from the history of splits and struggles. People have to fight with one another because they cannot ignore one another. Leaving aside the never settled question of whether any one clinical approach is more 'successful' than the others, the arrogance of isolation was never a viable option. The rows within psychotherapy cannot be ignored in a serene, Olympian fashion.

Even those who feel uncomfortable with pluralism, and seek to render it inaccurately as 'eclecticism', need to recall that their own theories arose from a pluralistic matrix and from a competitive diversity of views. For instance, James Hillman's archetypal psychology was not a single, time-bound, unchallenged, piercing vision of the future of Jungian analysis. This was also something Winnicott noted in relation to Melanie Klein. In November 1952 he wrote her a remarkable, long and agonized letter protesting strongly against 'giving the impression that there is a jigsaw of which all the pieces exist'.

So far, I have been trying to establish that pluralism can be seen as an extremely useful metaphorical approach to the interplay of the One and the Many in the psyche and in depth psychology generally. I have also suggested that pluralism can keep diversity alive in the face of threats from both tyranny and ennui or boredom. I have tried to show that pluralism enables us to harness the competitive and aggressive energy trapped in theoretical dispute and competition. I have given examples of the hidden pluralism in the father–daughter relationship, primal scene imagery, moral process, and gender identity. My overall position is that psychotherapy wants to become, needs to be, and, ironically, already is pluralistic.

This last point – that psychotherapy is, secretly and in spite of itself, already pluralistic – needs some expansion. What looks to us like intellectual discovery or new and original ideas are better understood as *descriptions* of the most progressive contemporary practices, or even as *intuitions* about what is already going on beneath the surface. For example, Machiavelli did not write a handbook for princes, containing smart new ideas. Rather he intuited and described what the most enterprising princes were already doing. Adam Smith's importance is not that he promoted capitalism, but that he described (and hence understood) what the new capitalists were doing. You could say that such writers were bringing something to consciousness and I expect this is true with much of what I write about pluralism and psychotherapy. Originality is a kind of delusion!

Pluralism and its enemies

In spite of all this, pluralism is threatened and under attack from all manner of entrenched interests. I would almost say, thank God that pluralism *is* under attack, for what would pluralism be without its opponents? There are several branches to this attack which it is possible to identify. First, *holism*, which tends to impose a false unity on our thinking, ignoring diversity. Second, *numinosity*, which forms the unavoidable heart of intolerance, for we become overwhelmingly fascinated by our own ideas and correspondingly threatened by other people's. Third, *hierarchy*, which sets up selected categories as prejudged good things or goals. But the enemy of pluralism upon which I want to focus is *consensus*.

Clearly, for there to be any communication at all, some assumptions have to be permitted and agreed, though consensus can become like airline food – just acceptable to everyone but truly pleasurable to none. However, blandness is not what I perceive as problematic with consensus – for consensus is not really cuddly, cosy, friendly and bland at all. In psychotherapy, and perhaps even in science as well, personal allegiance and power dynamics play a part. Orthodoxy, heterodoxy and heresy come into being. I do not see us as being able to get rid of vested interests but I would like us to do something creative with the vested interests we have.

This highly politicized state of affairs can be seen most vividly in relation to training for psychotherapy and therefore lies at the very root of psychotherapy as a social institution. Though the candidate is an adult, a degree of regression seems inherent in the training situation due to the continuing entanglements of the candidate's personal therapy and supervision/control work. It has been claimed that the training posture actually fosters regression in general and persecutory anxiety in particular, and that this is exacerbated by a confusion that often exists in the *trainers'* minds between therapy and training. My concern is different. My concern is that the whole range of careful, thoughtful experiences most therapists have been through in their training might inadvertently have removed the creative sting. I am thinking of syllabi, seminar themes, reading lists, feedback sessions and so forth. *The more integrated and professional the training programme, the greater the denial of pluralism.*

I think that the denial of pluralism has contributed to the formation of cult-like bodies within our little world of psychotherapy. Being in a cult implies obedience. There may be too much obedience in psychotherapy today. There is a serious danger that training programmes will become obedience cults and that this will be rationalized by reference to the advantages of practising on the basis of a system in which one has conviction. It is striking how many of the groups which are active in psychotherapy today either are, or were in the recent past, dominated by leader figures. The leaders may be remarkable people, with a comprehensive vision, which would partially account for the tendency, but I think there is more to it than that. I do not think this pattern results from conscious fostering, but would argue that its effect is to shield the candidate from the stress and anxiety of pluralism. And then the benefits of pluralism are lost as well. The need for strong leader figures has a lot to do with the desire to avoid the anomalous. The leader sorts things out by arranging competing ideas in a hierarchical schema of acceptability, protecting or advancing his own ideas in the process. The desire to avoid anxiety and confusion when confronted with something which feels strange and new strengthens the tendency of groups to select leaders as a combination of leader and safety net.

Now, when I critique consensus like this, I have to answer a difficult question, bound to be posed by the 'eclectics' who depend on consensus: how is our professional world going to be organized and structured at all if we eschew and reject consensus? Surely dialogue between schools is helped along by consensus, not damaged by it?

In answer to this, I say that we should remember that human life is not homogeneous. There are separate spheres of life which are relatively autonomous (perspective of the Many), though also linked (perspective of the One). In the social world, those who rule in one sphere may be ruled in another. By 'rule', I do not mean just the exercise of power but that people enjoy a greater share of whatever is being distributed. For us, what is being distributed is influence, ideological power, and the satisfaction of seeing our own ideas acknowledged and prevailing. Hopefully, everyone has a turn at this some time, though it cannot be guaranteed. My idea is that, from an experiential point of view, the psyche may be seen as containing relatively autonomous spheres of activity and imagery. Over time, and according to context, each sphere has its dominance. Similarly, from an intellectual point of view, each school of psychotherapy (or each theorist) may be seen as relatively autonomous from other schools and its theory as having its own special strengths and weaknesses. We become henotheists: one god at a time but, in time, many gods.

It is a case of taking it in turns to be the dominant theorist, accepting that, in some ways and in some situations, the other person has a more utilizable (more 'correct', from a pragmatic viewpoint) theory. Then we may make bilateral and multilateral agreements to sing each other's song – not the same as agreeing to disagree and different, too, from eclecticism. For eclecticism means singing selected verses only. Eclecticism ignores the contradictions between systems of thought whereas pluralism celebrates their competition. Eclecticism *is* intolerant in that parts of a theory are wrenched from the whole. In a pluralistic approach, the whole theory is used, as faithfully as possible, and together with other theories, until inconsistencies lead to breakdown. Then the breakdown itself becomes the object of study.

To summarize again: I have outlined what I mean by pluralism and suggested that we use it as an instrument. I have suggested what psychotherapy can learn from political theory. An ideology and a methodology for the organization of the profession are beginning to emerge. Some problems with pluralism have been discussed and 'consensus' has been attacked.

Pluralism and the future of psychotherapy

The general impression I have of psychotherapy is that there was a golden age that is now past. The broad outlines of the enterprise are firmly drawn. If that is so, then the fertilizing challenge presented by the arrival on the scene of all-inclusive theories, forcing a person to work out his or her response, has been lost. If our generation's job is not to be restricted to 'professionalization', institutionalization or historical recovery of the happenings of the earlier days, it is necessary to highlight the one thing we can do that the founding parents and brilliant second-generation consolidators cannot. This is to be *reflexive* in relation to psychotherapy, to focus on the psychology of psychology, a deliberate navel-gazing, a healthily narcissistic trip to the fantastic reaches of our discipline; a postmodern psychological outlook, redolent with the assumption that psychology is not 'natural', but made by psychologists and psychotherapists. After that, but only after that, we can turn towards the world.

What would a pluralistic programme for the future of psychotherapy look like? I have already spoken about this in relation to training. What follows is less practical, more a matter of the spirit of pluralism. Can we allow the flowering of pluralism which psychotherapy itself (unconsciously) desires?

We might begin by trying to envision spontaneity as a genre or particular style of psychological life. This means a person's putting trust in the gnostic and revelatory capacity of images and experiences, without stressing any presupposition that these are derivatives of an unknowable absolute. It is the spontaneous and autonomous nature of experience and its images which work to support a pluralistic response to them. As an extension of spontaneity, we may need actively to embrace contradictory positions. Not only because opposites can lead to each other eventually, but because contradiction itself produces novel elements. Spontaneity, as a genre, challenges consensus because of this capacity to generate the novel and the unpredictable; it influences other areas besides those at which it is directed.

It is interesting to consider the influence of gender on spontaneity. When we speak of the 'hard' sciences or facts, we are also dealing with the consequences of gender-based child-rearing practices which have relegated softness, irrationality and spontaneity to an inferior ('feminine') standing. In addition, so-called 'masculinity', supposedly objective in its outlook, is an outcrop of the requirement our culture lays on boys and girls to assert violently their differences from their mother. Hence, the achievement of personal boundaries and optimal separation from the mother may, for some individuals, mostly but not all male, tip over into rigidity and an accent on distance and precision – the objective attitude. Psychotherapists – especially psychoanalysts – who are uncomfortable with transpersonal phenomena (such as mystical experience) because such things cannot be understood from a distance, are, in a sense, 'over-masculinized'. Knowledge that only comes from some kind of merger with what is perceived awakens latent fears of returning to a suffocating symbiosis with the mother.

Coming to the end of this statement of a programme for pluralism, we have to ask ourselves what the moral function of psychological pluralism would be as it struggles to hold the tension between the One and the Many without making them into opposites.

Pluralism is engaged in the discovery of truths as well as in the discovery of Truth. The existence of diverse theories about people complements the psychological diversity within a person and the existence of psychotherapy as a unified field complements psychological unity within a person. My concern has been that pluralism should not follow the logic of competition so fully that an ideological position leading to tyranny results, nor allow its embracing of diversity to degenerate into a farrago of seemingly equal truths leading to ennui as much as chaos. But if all truths are *not* completely equal, what kind of yardstick might we develop?

I will stick my neck out and say that the *telos* or goal of pluralism in relation to psychotherapy, and hence its yardstick, is 'reform'. By reform, I do not mean to make a distinction with revolution, as in 'liberal reform', but reform as a portmanteau ideogram to include renewal, rebirth, resacralization, spontaneous *and* well planned evolutions, and imaginative productivity generally. Reform has a moral connotation as well, and that is deliberate on my part.

Pluralism is an approach to the politics of the psyche. Such a politics resembles sexuality in that it simply must be carried on. We do not create them or decide to join in. We just become aware that we are involved as part of the human condition. The moral factor which attends reformist pluralism also has to do with involvement, with engagement. Involvement and engagement in the experience of psyche lead directly to involvement and engagement in the politics of psychotherapy because, as I have been arguing, they turn out to be largely the same thing. Involvement and engagement in the politics of psychotherapy lead, in turn, to involvement and engagement with contemporary politics in suffering and complicated western societies. We come, then, to questions of social justice with which, as I suggested at the outset, psychotherapy in the future will be concerned.

Psychotherapy and social justice

At its inception, modern psychotherapy assumed the prevailing medical model of one-to-one private practice. Its sibling discipline, counselling, broadly speaking followed suit. However, these professions also established their own institutions, with distinct hierarchies, modes of pedagogy and rites of initiation and passage, usually located outside the medical schools and the universities, which were to become the institutional bases for modern psychiatry and psychology respectively. Consequently, twentieth-century psychotherapy has been both self-regulating as a profession and dominated by an individualist ethos. Psychotherapists have tended to consider the problems individuals face in isolation of the surrounding political, economic, social, cultural and ecological contexts.

Some commentators have critiqued the impact of psychotherapy on society in terms of its being a cult of introspection and self-indulgence, leading to the establishment of a 'culture of narcissism'. This critique would seem to be borne out by the successful cultural penetration of psychotherapy demonstrated by, for example, psychologically oriented chat shows on television and advice ('agony') columns in newspapers and magazines. There has also been adverse comment on the way in which psychotherapy and counselling are deployed in the treatment of offenders. Critics have questioned how a mode of treatment that is predicated on free association can be offered in a compulsory format.

Whether or not such criticisms are totally justified in their negative assessments of the cultural impact of psychotherapy, they do highlight the way in which they have passed largely unaddressed within the profession of psychotherapy itself. Given the rapidly increasing growth of psychotherapy and counselling, and the possibility of its being regulated in the future by statute, reflection on the interface between psychotherapy and society becomes ever more pressing. In particular, if the field is going to develop new forms of social (as opposed to exclusively psychological) intervention, it will need to consider critically its relation to society, its multifaceted roles in social and cultural processes and its attitude to issues of social justice.

This is the background of critical enquiry to what I see as a central issue for psychotherapists in the future: to explore whether or not psychotherapy can be more than a means of understanding or easing personal distress. The aim is to test out the claim that psychotherapy contains within it ways of perceiving the social world of lived experience as well as the inner world of fantasy and emotion, or the domain of personal relationships. If such claims are correct, psychotherapy would provide a basis for reflective commentary and critique on and responsible intervention into that world. Pluralistic ideas, understandings and, in some respects, practices of psychotherapy would offer a means of addressing seemingly intractable social, communal and political problems.

In order to evaluate these claims, it is necessary at the same time to critique the ambitions of psychotherapy and psychotherapists to produce a totalizing discourse in which, via 'psychotherapy reductionism', all social phenomena may be interpreted in exclusively psychological ways. It will be important not to psychologize social issues and to be critical of attempts to do so that have taken up a stance outside society. There has been a long history of work in the psychological field aimed at the transformation of society but the net impact has been slight and, in some instances, oppressive. One reason for this may be that those psychotherapists making their social critiques omitted to locate themselves within the phenomena under discussion. Or they may have offered their services thoughtlessly to the political powers that be. Hence my stress in this chapter on the professional politics *of* psychotherapy as a basis on which to go on building a project linking politics *and* psychotherapy in the future.

One core social and political value of psychotherapy in the future could be the recognition that on-high, experience-distant theorizing is in many ways a betrayal of psychotherapy itself. This is because it is now widely recognized in the clinical community of psychotherapy that the worker is 'in' the therapeutic process as much as the client. The same methodological point is also relevant when the linkage is sought between psychotherapy and society. Hence we need to explore in a spirit of critical enquiry the dialectical interplay between what might be meant by 'psychotherapy' and what might be meant by 'society'.

Some areas of public policy seem more obvious candidates for a psychotherapeutic approach: gender questions, the family (including child sexual abuse and domestic violence), problems of redundancy and unemployment, mental health issues generally. But there are other areas such as foreign policy, war and conflict resolution, economic policy, violence in society, the environment, penology, health and safety at work, and ethnic/racial issues where the potential for a psychotherapeutic contribution has not so far been realized.

In sum, across a wide range of social issues, and attempting always to remain self-reflexive, psychotherapy in the future could aim to open up an interaction or two-way street between an understanding of the construction or production of subjectivity on the one hand and personal narratives of experience of social, communal and political phenomena on the other. The hope is that the imagination – a category with which psychotherapists would claim to be familiar – might be given a larger place in attempts to achieve social justice in modern societies than has been the case up to now.

'Social justice' is, of course, a familiar term from politics and social science. As used here, the reference is not only to a set of abstract principles that might govern the formation of a 'good' or 'just' society. Following current usage in the UK, the idea of social justice also encompasses the organizational and cultural changes necessary to fashion such a society. Thus discussions about measures to alleviate poverty increasingly are not divorced from questions of constitutional change – for example, to a less rigid electoral and parliamentary system incorporating proportional representation, devolved government and a Bill of Rights. The Labour Party set up a Commission on Social Justice to explore these issues and publish a report on them, so this kind of thinking is by no means a fringe phenomenon. But what about the psychological changes that will be necessary?

In my book *The Political Psyche*, I suggest that politics in the west is experiencing a paradigm shift in which old definitions, assumptions and values are being transformed. While politics will always be about struggles for power and the control of resources, a new understanding of all that is political has evolved since feminism introduced the phrase 'the personal is political'. This new kind of politics is often a feeling-level politics, or a politics of subjectivity, that encompasses a key interplay between the public and private dimensions of power. For political power is also manifested in family organization, gender and race relations, connections between wealth and health, control of information, and in religion and art. Hence, to abstract principles of social justice and the organizational changes that are inspired by such principles we can add a frank recognition now and in the future of psychotherapy's role in political analysis – an awareness that there is something like a 'political psyche' at work in political process and discourse.

It is the tragicomic crisis of our *fin de siècle* civilization that incites psychotherapists to challenge some boundaries (between politics and psychology) at the same moment that they reinforce others (concerning professional conduct). Conventional boundaries that might be challenged include those between the public and private, the political and the personal, the external world and the internal world, life and reflection, being and doing, extraversion and introversion, politics and psychology, between the fantasies of the political world and the politics of the fantasy world. If we mount this challenge, then it is easier to accept that subjectivity and intersubjectivity have political roots. Constructed as they are, subjectivity and intersubjectivity are not nearly as private as they seem.

Psychology and the therapies can fill crucial roles in this late modern world we have made. Not only in the rich countries of the west, but also in the former Soviet Union, eastern Europe and developing countries, politics and questions of psychological identity are linked as never before. This is because of other minglings: ethnic, national, socioeconomic, ideological. The whole picture is made more intricate by the rapid course of events in the realms of sexuality and gender.

As I said at the outset, gender is *the* gateway or threshold between the public and the private dimensions of experience. Gender as an exceedingly private story we tell ourselves about ourselves; gender as a set of socioeconomic and cultural realities. I carried out an international survey into what therapists and analysts do when their clients bring overtly political material to the clinical setting (Samuels, 1993). Amongst the questions, I asked some designed to find out which political issues or themes were most commonly introduced by clients. This survey went to 2000 practitioners from 14 organizations of differing theoretical orientations in seven countries. Nearly 700 replied. In a worldwide league table of issues, 'gender issues for women' came top for every group except German Jungian analysts. For their clients, the number one issue was the environment and gender issues for women came second. 'Gender issues for men' came fourth worldwide.

The point here is not that these findings are surprising – they are not, given the liminality of gender referred to above. What is highlighted is that gender issues – which must include desire itself – and sociopolitical issues have become completely intertwined.

Taken overall, the responses to the survey suggest that, in the future, the clinical office can be a bridge between the inner world and the political world as well as being the source of a divorce of the two worlds. This is why I do not support calls for the ending of the project of therapy and analysis. As I noted earlier, clinical practice has been accused of being a bastion of possessive individualism and narcissistic introspection for a hundred years; it is not a new criticism. And it is right to criticize greedy and myopic clinicians who cannot perceive that their work has a political and cultural location and implication. But it is not right to indulge in simplistic, populist rhetoric that would do away with the entire clinical project. Without their connection to a clinical core, why should anyone in the world of politics listen to therapists and analysts at all?

The huff and puff rejection of the clinical forecloses what is, for me, a central issue: the relations between the private/psychological and the public/social realms of life. The funny thing about this foreclosure is that it mimics the attitude of the most conservative, dyed-in-the-wool clinicians and mental health professionals – the keep-politics-out-of-the-office types. As I see it, the high-profile apostates and renegades of therapy and analysis are as terrified and perhaps as incapable of exploring the relations between the personal and the political as are the fanatical adherents of psychotherapy and analysis. Hence, ending the polarization would benefit all involved – clients, psychotherapists and society.

References

Samuels, A. (1985) *Jung and the Post-Jungians*. London and Boston: Routledge and Kegan Paul.

Samuels, A. (1989) *The Plural Psyche: Personality, Morality and the Father*. London and New York: Routledge.

Samuels, A. (1993) *The Political Psyche*. London and New York: Routledge.

Samuels, A., Shorter, B. and Plant, F. (1986) *A Critical Dictionary of Jungian Analysis*. London and New York: Routledge and Kegan Paul.

9

Counselling and Psychotherapy: The Sickness and The Prognosis

Brian Thorne

Mushrooming

In the mid-1960s, there were about 60 models of therapy on the international scene. Nowadays the number exceeds 400 (Miller et al., 1995). This mushrooming could be seen as the sign of a healthy profession where innovation and creativity flourish and improved methods of responding to human suffering emerge as a result of experience and research. Sadly, I cannot embrace such an optimistic interpretation of the developments which have occurred during the period of my own professional life. On the contrary, I tend to regard them with gloom and not a little cynicism. One thing alone is certain: the sum of pain and anguish in our endangered world has in no way diminished over the years and, despite the efforts of increasing numbers of counsellors and psychotherapists across the globe, there is little sign that things are getting any better. Could it be that we therapists have somehow missed the point and that in the history of humankind we shall go down as an irrelevance? There are times, I must confess, when I am haunted by the knowledge that in Hitler's Reich psychotherapy flourished even as distinguished Jewish analysts fled abroad or disappeared mysteriously in the night (Cocks, 1988).

Research

A few years ago I could find comfort in research findings. Hans Eysenck, who claimed in the 1950s that psychotherapy was useless or worse than useless, seemed to have been put in his place (Eysenck, 1952). I remember with pleasure and relief the impressive – and somewhat incomprehensible – meta analyses of statisticians Smith, Glass and Miller who gathered into one volume all the 'respectable' research findings of the past decades and announced authoritatively that psychotherapy was 'beneficial, consistently so and in many different ways' (Smith et al., 1980). As a committed person-centred practitioner I was less enthusiastic about other findings – that, for example, the school of therapy seemed irrelevant to success (no top marks for Carl Rogers and his associates) and that psychotherapy and drug therapy produced greater benefits than either one could produce by itself. Nonetheless Smith, Glass and Miller alleviated my fear – often not far below the surface – that psychotherapists and counsellors were fraudulent, not intentionally duplicitous perhaps, but essentially guilty of misleading their clients into believing that they could bring about healing or, at the very least, the amelioration of distressing symptoms of dysfunction.

Recently my already faltering faith in the persuasiveness of research received a severe blow when I chanced upon an article by Maureen O'Hara (1996) from California which drew my attention to a piece by none other than the eminent behaviourist, Neil Jacobson, entitled 'The overselling of therapy' (Jacobson, 1995). Jacobson delivers a devastating criticism of the therapy industry (note the metaphor) and in particular casts doubt on claims that there is scientific evidence, based on well designed studies, showing either that psychotherapy is an effective treatment for mental illness or that a therapist's training and experience in any particular methodology is correlated with positive outcome. What's more he states that, despite the widespread belief that some therapies (including cognitive-behaviour therapy) are proven effective for certain conditions, when the actual outcomes of these treatments are examined in terms of their clinical significance the results are arbitrary – only a minority of patients (19%–32% compared with 20% placebo) improved (1995, p. 44). To make matters worse, Maureen O'Hara then brings on stage not Smith, Glass and Miller but Miller (a different one), Hubble and Duncan who have recently announced: 'While the number of therapy models has proliferated . . . 30 years of clinical outcome research have not found any one theory, model, method or package of techniques to be reliably better than any other' (Miller et al., 1995).

The vulnerable profession

It is this unwelcome awareness of fragile credibility (concealed for the most part from the would be clientele) which forms the back-drop to much of the current obsession in the UK with professional accreditation and registration for therapists. It is almost as if the lack of ultimately convincing evidence about therapy's effectiveness is driving practitioners to a defensive closed shop mentality so that rigorous criteria for entrance to the 'club' conceal the need for further evaluating the quality of the work undertaken once the club has been joined. That the criteria for entry such as length of training or recognized diplomas may have little proven relevance to the therapist's competence is neither here nor there. Vulnerable people seek to defend themselves especially if livelihoods are at stake and there is not enough work to go round. They also seek to cultivate the image of the expert and nothing does this more effectively than the requirement for lengthy training combined with a hermetic language to describe the mysteries of human development and human interaction.

The British government's decision (in the context of its enthusiasm for National Vocational Qualifications (NVQs)) to set up a 'Lead Body' for advice, guidance, counselling and, belatedly, psychotherapy, has created alarm on another front. A totally skills-based approach to therapeutic practice seems to deny the importance of a knowledge base and to reduce to secondary significance the therapist's personal maturity. There is also the unspoken fear that an entirely skills-based approach to therapy might turn out to be effective and more productive than, for example, a lengthy relationship with an expensively trained analyst or psychotherapist.

The tensions inherent in this complex situation are not difficult to discern. Almost immediately positions are taken up, power bases established and battle joined. For this not to happen, counsellors and psychotherapists would have to accept each other's integrity, celebrate each other's differences and unite in the interests of their clients. Ironically, those whose voices are often loudest in the campaign for statutory registration usually claim to be motivated by a passionate concern for the well-being and protection of clients. The manifest hypocrisy of such claims is breathtaking. It is sadly becoming all too evident that the kind of cooperative and fraternal unity among counsellors and therapists which would assuredly not only benefit clients but provide a strong platform for a radical assault on a dysfunctional political system is now unlikely to occur. The stark truth is that the vulnerable profession is too deeply infected by the sickness which afflicts its clientele and it is to this that we now turn.

The sickness of distrust

In Britain during the past fifteen years a psychological sickness has descended with incalculable consequences for the well-being of millions of people. It is possible that it would have arrived no matter which political party held sway. A new tyranny has been inaugurated in the name of an insatiable god whose baleful influence permeates almost all areas of national life. The god's name is efficiency and his chief archangel is cost-effectiveness. The sickness which this tyranny has brought in its wake relies for its potency on the fear and the guilt which lurk just below the surface of awareness for most people. In the Middle Ages unscrupulous clergy traded on the fear and guilt induced by doctrines of eternal punishment and original sin in order to keep souls in subjection. In our own age an unscrupulous government can trade on the fear and guilt induced by the spectre of unemployment and a sense of personal inadequacy in order to obtain abject acquiescence to policies which are increasingly punitive. In the end, it seems, nothing matters but the balance in the national bank and the sense of financial and material security which accompanies this for those on whom fickle market forces smile for a passing moment.

That people are apparently so easily cowed into submission breeds despair for those counsellors and psychotherapists who aspire to enable clients to find their own way through life confident in their inner resourcefulness. The deep sense of personal inadequacy which characterizes many if not most clients is often allied in the prevailing culture to an almost paralysing fear of failure and rejection. All the therapist can hope to do in many cases is to alleviate the fear, to encourage coping strategies, to put straight some crooked thinking, and to send the client back into the overheated kitchen with marginally improved chances of survival. Many a counsellor working within an industrial or commercial setting will recognize this process all too well and will know that the ubiquitous stress management workshop or relaxation training course may well enable a client to continue functioning without ever having to confront the existential despair which, buttressed by guilt and fear, is always ready to break through into full awareness.

To feel guilty is to walk through the world in permanent fear of adverse judgement. Furthermore it undermines the will to trust. Nobody and nothing can be relied upon and an unutterable loneliness descends upon the guilty, self-negating individual whose only fault may be an inability to be efficient in the way his employer demands. Depression can quickly follow upon such unjust condemnation or, not infrequently, a towering rage which can lead to violence and destructiveness. The housing estates of our land provide evidence enough of both the depression and the rage.

It is no exaggeration, I believe, to see contemporary Britain as a country where there has been an almost complete breakdown of trust at all levels. In 1993 the Catholic historian and theologian, Donald Nichol, went so far as to brand our contemporary culture the 'culture of contempt' and argued powerfully that an obsession with efficiency, accountability, appraisal and performance was producing a society where the invalidation of the person was guaranteed and where attitudes of judgementalism and blame were already endemic. What is more the unholy alliance between efficiency and cost-effectiveness must inevitably produce a world where money, the love of which, ancient wisdom tells us, is the root of all evil, rules supreme and where materialism becomes all pervasive (Nichol, 1993). Nichol's analysis describes for me with alarming accuracy the world in which I live and it would be foolish to imagine that I am myself unaffected by such a culture and therefore immune to the prevailing contempt and its insidious assault upon self-respect.

Infection

In the last few years the joy has all but disappeared from my professional life. At national meetings with colleagues I sense the same absence of joy in them. We are, I believe, infected by the prevailing sickness and are caught up in the fear of judgement and in the need to ward off the contemptuous critics who hover around us. These fears are not the outcome of mere fantasies. Many of us, for example, live in daily terror of litigation at the hands of disturbed clients or even resentful trainees. What is more we have to endure the ill-informed and repeated attacks on therapy in the press and through the media. Motivated by fear and desperate for affirmation it is scarcely surprising that we have fallen victim to the very mentality which has induced our despondency. We have told ourselves that we must improve our efficiency, appraise our performance, render ourselves accountable, seek incontrovertible respectability in the eyes of both government and the public. In short, if we are to ward off the prevailing contempt which surrounds us, we must show ourselves to be the implacable enemies of charlatanism and 'doubtful practice' in all its forms. We must take on the mantle of the stern judge and have no mercy on our weaker brothers and sisters who threaten to bring counselling and psychotherapy into disrepute through their inadequacy or eccentricity. In our fear we mistake our self-interestedness for a concern for clients and our insecurity for a desire for higher standards. The absence of joy is the sign that we have ourselves descended into the very hell from which our clients seek to find release.

Self-betrayal

The irony of this situation for the person-centred practitioner in particular lies in the fact that the prevailing culture constitutes the classical environment for the creation of psychological disturbance. It goes without saying therefore that a person-centred therapist who has capitulated to the 'culture of contempt' will be psychologically disturbed and will, therefore, by definition, be incapable of offering the conditions which Carl Rogers defined long ago as necessary and sufficient for constructive personality change in the client (Rogers, 1957). I am inclined to think, however, that it is not just person-centred therapists who are in danger of being disturbed and therefore unhelpful or even injurious to their clients. Indeed, one of the chief irritants in my professional life has been the repeated boast of therapists from other orientations that they offer the core conditions as a matter of course before they get down to the really serious business of effecting change through the application of more sophisticated knowledge or techniques. If this is anything more than self-delusion, the underlying implication is that therapists in general place considerable importance, at least in theory, on the relationship which they form with their clients. If this relationship is to be characterized, as person-centred therapists would have it, by the therapist's ability to offer acceptance, empathy and genuineness, this places a high premium on the practitioner's own state of being. Of paramount importance will be the establishment of the therapist's own internalized locus of evaluation or, to eschew person-centred jargon, his or her active belief in the trustworthiness of his or her own nature and its resourcefulness as a source of wisdom. Without such a belief it will be difficult if not impossible for the therapist to have that deep respect for the self which makes acceptance of the other possible. True empathy is similarly unlikely unless the therapist experiences a secure sense of his or her own identity and can therefore risk the challenge of deep encounter without the fear of being overwhelmed or sucked into the other's reality. It is also abundantly clear that genuineness or authenticity is by definition impossible if the therapist lacks trust in his or her own inner world and either rejects or blocks off from its promptings.

It will by now be apparent that for the person-centred therapist affirmation of and fidelity to the true self are the cornerstones of practice. Without them the therapeutic relationship is at best a charade and at worst a destructive deception. Self-betrayal on the part of the therapist is not only a tragic squandering of his or her own human potential but it also rules out the possibility of authentic encounter. The harsh truth is that person-centred therapists who fall victim to conditions of worth which alienate them from their own essential wisdom are no longer capable of being therapists. They have succumbed to their overriding need for positive regard and in the process have forfeited their self-respect and their capacity to create an environment in which the other can find safety and healing.

Self-betrayal in practice

In case the preceding reflections have about them the abstract quality of a philosophical discourse I shall illuminate them by anchoring them in my daily experience. Often the first challenge to my integrity will arrive in the morning mail. It may take the form of a moving letter from someone who has read one of my books and is wanting to make contact in a highly personal way. Not infrequently the letter will be from a woman who has clearly suffered at the hands of men and who has intuited in my writings a more tender and compassionate maleness. My instinct is to respond warmly, appreciatively and empathically. I wish my unknown correspondent to know that her letter has moved me and enriched my morning and that I understand something of her world. And then I hesitate. I remember that phoney clients have insinuated themselves into counsellors' consulting rooms with hidden cameras about their person and that these spurious interviews have subsequently been watched by millions of television viewers. I remember that unscrupulous people have faked applications to my professional association and been accepted to the delight of journalists who are bent on ridiculing the therapy profession. Could it be that the beautiful and heartfelt letter in front of me is another example of a cunning trap into which I am about to fall headlong and that next week I shall read my loving response on the front page of the *Sun* with the accusation that I am attempting to seduce my correspondent? The thought – and the anxiety – are clearly absurd. Or are they? I have the choice. I can ignore the letter. I can respond politely in a couple of lines. Or I can write the letter that my true self, my organismic self, my trusting self desires to write. If I take one of the first two courses of action I am guilty of self-betrayal. If I take the third I retain my integrity and I am afraid.

Later on in the day a more weighty challenge confronts me, unexpectedly and without warning. I have been working for some weeks with a young gay man who has only acknowledged his homosexuality to himself a year or so ago and has yet to confront his family with the truth about his sexual orientation. In recent months he has been involved in a number of promiscuous encounters and is confused and troubled about his secretive and deeply unsatisfactory life-style. Today his agitation is more marked than usual and I gently reflect the degree of his inner turmoil. Suddenly he bursts into tears and throws himself into my arms. I respond by doing what instinctively and intuitively I know I must do. I hold him with as much tenderness and compassion as I can muster and I speak gentle words of understanding as he places his head against my chest and sobs compulsively. This continues for many minutes at the end of which he is able to tell me that yesterday he discovered that he is HIV positive. Until almost the end of the session he remains in my arms and only returns to his own chair as I quietly point out that we have less than five minutes to go before we must end. He leaves less agitated but still in deep distress.

After he has gone I am assailed by doubts which contrast strongly with the experience of integrity which only minutes before had informed my feelings and my behaviour. The deep trust which I had both in myself and in my client begins to waver and there flashes into my mind an image of my client's homophobic and alcoholic father and the havoc that he might wreak should he discover what had taken place between his son and his son's counsellor. I begin to tremble at the thought that by holding this young man in my arms for more than half an hour I have colluded with his sexual desire and am now no longer his therapist but the object of his lust. The absurd fears proliferate in my tormented imagination and I am in danger of losing completely my own internal locus of evaluation. This headlong plunge into self-induced anxiety is halted only by the disciplined exercise of self-supervision. I ask myself how I could have behaved otherwise in fulfilling my commitment to offer my client the best possible environment for his development. I find an inner peace once more as I realize that not to have behaved as I have done would, for me, have been a refusal to accept my client in the totality of his being and a failure to offer him the deepest form of empathy of which I am capable. Most significantly of all, however, I regain the assurance that I have acted from the centre of my own being and have at every moment attempted to be true to the flow of experience within me. In short, as a person-centred therapist I have sought to fulfil the costly professional responsibility of being to the utmost of my ability, acceptant, empathic and transparently authentic. It only occurs to me as an afterthought that throughout much of the session I have been praying even as the young man sobbed, and that in my back pocket there remains, as always, the little chaplet of blue beads with its medallion of Julian of Norwich proclaiming: 'All shall be well and all shall be well and all manner of thing shall be well'.

Rogers and spirituality

The international community of person-centred practitioners and scholars is currently much divided on the issue of how much attention should be paid to the last decade or so of Carl Rogers' life. The core of this debate (often contentious) centres around Rogers' identification in his final years of a spiritual dimension in his work. There are those who would certainly prefer that Rogers had never spoken of his discovery. They see it as the aberration of old age and as a betrayal of the lifetime's work of a man who was at all times deeply committed to the essential dignity and value of human beings in and for themselves and to the pursuit of scientific enquiry. For Rogers himself there was no such sense of contradiction. He readily admitted that he had previously underrated and even rejected the importance of a realm which he was now to recognize as the 'spiritual' or 'transcendent' or 'mystical'. His openness to experience compelled him to face what he now perceived to be the 'next great frontier of learning'. This frontier, scarcely mentioned by those whom Rogers described as 'hard-headed researchers', was in his view the gateway to 'the area of the intuitive, the psychic, the vast inner space that looms before us' (Rogers, 1980).

For Rogers, this awesome prospect was signalled by his recurring experiences both in groups and in one-to-one encounters. He described these in terms which leave no doubt that he was profoundly affected and that as a result, he was compelled to reassess the very meaning of relationship:

> I find that when I am closest to my inner, intuitive self, when I am somehow in touch with the unknown in me, when perhaps I am in a slightly altered state of consciousness in the relationship, then whatever I do seems to be full of healing. Then simply my *presence* is releasing and helpful . . . I may behave in strange and impulsive ways in the relationship, ways which I cannot justify rationally, which have nothing to do with my thought processes . . . At these moments it seems that my inner spirit has reached out and touched the inner spirit of the other . . . Profound growth and healing energies are present. (Rogers, 1980)

In the same passage Rogers goes on to suggest that both he and the other are at such times in touch with something larger than themselves and are therefore caught up in a mysterious and unknown stream of being. The 'unknown' within himself and the other are linked to the 'unknown' of which both are but a part.

In my own work I have no doubt that I have experienced the phenomena which Rogers describes and I have attempted to articulate this in a number of publications (Mearns and Thorne, 1988; Thorne, 1985, 1991, 1993, 1994). For me the quality which Rogers describes as 'presence' I have defined as 'tenderness'. I believe, too, that a similar viewpoint is to be discovered in the philosophical writings of Martin Buber and it is not without significance that it was after his momentous 'dialogue' with Buber in 1957 that Rogers was forced to reassess the nature of his therapeutic relationships and to pay increasing attention to the quality of congruence or genuineness in the therapist. For Buber, as William West recalls in a recent paper (West, 1995) there are two types of relationship: the 'I/It' relationship in which the other is treated as different from oneself and is little more than an object, and the 'I/Thou' relationship in which the other is treated as a member of the same family, as kin. In such 'I/Thou' relationships a merging of energy between the two people becomes possible and there takes place a meeting, according to Buber, where God is to be found and experienced (Buber, 1970).

Spirituality and therapy's sickness

When Carl Rogers speaks of a relationship in which he 'behaves in strange and impulsive ways', ways which he 'cannot justify rationally and which have nothing to do with my thought processes', I sense a mounting excitement and the permeating anxiety which temporarily overwhelmed me after the departure of my gay client. The excitement comes from knowing that Rogers is speaking of the cutting edge, not only of therapeutic encounter but of human relating in general. He is speaking of those moments when, as persons, we recognize the essential mystery of our being and our interconnectedness not only with each other but with the whole created order. My permeating anxiety comes, on the other hand, from the recognition that I live in a culture whose manifest structures and prevailing values are not only closed to such insight, but wilfully blind or hostile to its implications. Such knowledge is often too much for me. To act upon it is to run the risk of humiliation at best and professional suicide at worst.

Here, then, I am brought with implacable and inevitable logic, to the root of the sickness which has therapy in thrall or at least the kind of therapy which I profess to practise. As a person-centred practitioner I embody a belief system and I lay claim to a realm of experiencing both of which run counter not only to the prevailing culture of the age but also to the increasingly craven and defensive posturing of the profession of which I am a member.

The dilemma posed by this awareness becomes progressively more intolerable. I find it painful, for example, to recall that it was I who in the mid-1970s helped draft the first individual accreditation scheme for counsellors in the UK. My colleagues and I in the Association for Student

Counselling of those days were fired with an enthusiasm for our work and were keen to raise standards and to develop our knowledge and skills. We saw an accreditation scheme as an encouragement and an incentive to those who, like us, were dedicated to providing a better service for the young people who consulted us. At the same time we wished to give added credibility, principally for the benefit of our academic colleagues, to the value system which inspired us. If this sounds like missionary zeal, I believe that would not be an altogether inappropriate metaphor.

The situation today could not be more different. Accreditation and registration are no longer incentives to excellence and the proclamation of an inspirational value system. They are instead the necessary route to respectability and financial viability. There are times when the cynic in me sees the current obsession with registration as little more than the neurosis of a profession which is desperate for approval and terrified of the dole queue. If this is indeed the case, then we can be sure that we have succumbed to the sickness of the culture and can have no legitimacy as healers of its ills.

I am preserved from almost total pessimism by the fact that the tension which I experience within myself refuses to go away. This openness to inner promptings is, after all, a hallmark of my professional commitment and I find reassurance that, to this extent at least, I remain faithful to my vocation. I find encouragement, too, in the fact that many therapists of my own generation have begun, like Rogers, to take an interest in spirituality as they have grown older (e.g. Rowan, 1989, 1993; Heron, 1992). Such 'conversion' is the more remarkable when it occurs in those who previously ignored such experience or even regarded it in terms of regression or immaturity. Interestingly the recent work of William West points to the findings of public surveys in the USA and the UK which show that up to one third of the adult population have had religious or spiritual experiences at some point in their lives (West, 1995). What is more, correlations have been demonstrated between well-being and the experience of the spiritual dimension (Hay, 1982; Hay and Morisy, 1978). A resurgence of hope which springs up within me as I consider these developments and research findings receives a further boost as I think of clients with whom I have worked in recent years and of trainees who come to study in the Centre which I direct. There can be no doubt that many of these people seek counselling or counsellor training so that they can be strengthened in their determination to resist what they experience as the death-dealing characteristics of the culture from which they feel alienated. Most reassuring but frightening of all, however, is the humbling realization that such clients and trainees have often sought me out to be their companion in their fight for a life worth having. The reassurance comes from being perceived as someone worthy of such companionship but the fear lies in the realization that I cannot for ever ignore the responsibility of such a privileged task. In the concluding section of this chapter I consider what it might mean to come down off the fence.

Coming off the fence

The fundamental belief of the person-centred therapist is that the client knows what his or her own needs and desires are and has the necessary inner resources to move towards their fulfilment if only the right conditions for growth can be provided. As the history of counselling and psychotherapy unfolds little has occurred either to refute this contention or, despite the extensive research studies inspired by the work of Rogers and his associates, to validate the hypothesis convincingly (Watson, 1984). What is becoming clearer, however, is the relatively ineffectual impact of all therapeutic orientations on the generality of human suffering and the failure of any one approach to achieve the primacy in the therapeutic competition. This somewhat disappointing record is not reflected in the burgeoning of the therapy industry in our culture. On the contrary, in recent years there has been an explosion of training courses for counsellors and therapists while counselling agencies up and down the country report an ever-growing clientele and lengthening waiting lists. It is clear that, however ineffective, counselling and psychotherapy have entered the mainstream of our national life and are exposing, even if they are unable to satisfy, a widespread malaise.

It has been the main thesis of this chapter that the malaise which has descended upon the British people in the past decade cannot satisfactorily be explained solely in terms of individual disturbance or pathology. It needs to be viewed in the light of a culture which has increasingly fallen victim to the savage onslaught of an economic philosophy based upon depersonalizing concepts of efficiency and cost-effectiveness. These have brought in their wake a psychological environment characterized by the fear of judgement and failure and by a sense of impotence leading to guilt, depression and violence. In a striking way this prevailing culture constitutes the classical context in person-centred terms for the creation of psychological disturbance and as such poses a massive challenge to the integrity of the person-centred therapist. To capitulate to such a culture and to collude with its depersonalizing and materialistic value system is to become infected by the same pathology that drives increasing numbers of clients to the counsellor's door. And yet there is every sign in the frightened ranks of the therapists that such collusion is taking place and that creativity and integrity are being sacrificed on the altar of self-interest and self-protection. If this process continues the future for the therapy profession is bleak.

I am increasingly convinced that Rogers' discovery towards the end of his life of the healing power of his presence is central not only to the future of person-centred therapy but to the development of counselling and psychotherapy in general in the years ahead. Rogers, it should be remembered, discovered the offering of acceptance, empathy and congruence could lead to an intensity of relationship where great power for healing could be released. The meeting of the essentially unknown inner cores of two human beings could give access to previously untapped resources which could bring about a transformative process. For Rogers and for many person-centred therapists since, this process can only be satisfactorily defined in terms of spiritual or mystical experience. Throughout the centuries it has been frequently acknowledged that human sexual loving can lead men and women into a world of ineffable bliss: it is perhaps psychotherapy's gift to humankind to point the way to an intensity of relating both to the self and to the other which can lead to a trans-figuration not only of individuals but of the whole human family.

Let me finally come off the fence and take upon myself the prophetic mantle which crystal-ball gazing inevitably demands. I believe that the increasing interest in spirituality which is being shown by many clients and some therapists, of whom Carl Rogers was one but by no means the only precursor, could be a sure sign that counselling and psychotherapy are returning to their origins. As the influence of religion has diminished, the spiritual yearnings of western men and women have been denied or distorted as the age of reason led to the imperialism of the scientific method, the technological revolution and the arid deserts of materialism and consumerism in which we currently live. Of all the social inventions of the last two hundred years it is perhaps the psychotherapeutic relationship and the powerful experience of group therapy or group encounter which have done most to nourish and sustain the neglected spiritual yearnings of an increasingly secularized society. This, I would suggest, is their true significance and once this is acknowledged explicitly and authoritatively, counselling and psychotherapy need no longer pretend to be what they are not. The claim to scientific objectivity or to psychological inerrancy can be dropped. The fascinating exploration of human behaviour, cognitive processes and unconscious drives can be placed at the service of the spiritual evolution which may yet preserve us as a species and save our planet. This, I believe, is the true calling of counsellors and psycho-therapists and once accepted it will give us purpose and meaning and ensure for us not a footnote in the history of humankind but a primary position in the unfolding story of our ultimate destiny. It may also wake us up before we have sacrificed the final spark of our *élan vital* to the creation of statutory registers for robotic therapists with NVQs or com-pulsory certification to keep out those who might still have the courage to overturn the tables of the money-changers and to remind us that we are only a little lower than the angels.

A costly vocation

Those therapists who dare to pursue their spiritual vocation in the years immediately ahead will pay a heavy price for their commitment. It is likely that they will be driven to the margins of the therapy world and that they will be ridiculed by those who seek to deploy increasingly sophisticated techniques and to bolster their financial and public status through statutory legislation or professional exclusiveness. It is my belief – and hope – that person-centred therapists will be prominent among those who migrate to the margins. I am persuaded, however, that there are many from other therapeutic orientations who will join them there. Indeed, in my more visionary moments I see this movement as heralding the beginning of the end of psychotherapy and counselling as we know them. If, as I believe, our current culture stands in need of radical and urgent reform if it is not to disintegrate completely, it is self-evident that those therapists who have capitulated to or colluded with the culture cannot convincingly participate in its reformation. In the years ahead the divisions in the ranks of the therapists will become more manifest as our society shows signs of progressive collapse and millions more human beings join the ranks of the invalidated and dispossessed. In the period of chaos which must inevitably follow there will be those therapists who will continue to minister to the human spirit because they have long since acknowledged that men and women are spirit in their essence. They will be the beacons of light in a dark or often terrifying landscape and they will be aided by those other therapists who at the eleventh hour, no matter what their orientation or professional status, will dedicate their skills and their knowledge to the preservation of human dignity in the midst of panic and confusion.

At such a time what will matter is neither the impressiveness of a therapist's credentials nor the eminence of his or her professional standing. It is even possible that the effectiveness of a therapist's methods in treating the crippling symptoms of suffering individuals in a disordered society will have only marginal relevance in the sum total of things. Perhaps there will always be a place for psychological technicians who can render the intolerable somehow survivable. If I am right, however, humankind will increasingly turn to the counsellors and therapists in order to find the hope which lies beyond despair. The yearning for meaning and for faith in human nature will become universal and on its fulfilment the destiny of the world will depend. No vocation could be more onerous and none more awesome.

References

Buber, M. (1970) *I and Thou*. Edinburgh: T and T Clark.

Cocks, G. (1988) *Psychotherapy in the Third Reich*. New York: Oxford University Press.

Eysenck, H.J. (1952) The effects of psychotherapy: An evaluation, *Journal of Consulting Psychology*, 16: 319–24.

Hay, D. (1982) *Exploring Inner Space, Scientists and Religious Experience*. Harmondsworth: Penguin.

Hay, D. and Morisy, A. (1978) Reports of ecstatic, paranormal religious experiences in Great Britain and the United States – A comparison of trends, *Journal for the Scientific Study of Religion*, 17(3): 255–68.

Heron, J. (1992) *Feeling and Personhood*. London: Sage.

Jacobson, N. (1995) The overselling of therapy, *The Family Therapy Networker*, March/April: 41–7.

Mearns, D. and Thorne, B.J. (1988) *Person-centred Counselling in Action*. London: Sage.

Miller, S., Hubble, M. and Duncan, B. (1995) No more bells and whistles, *The Family Therapy Networker*, March/April: 53–63.

Nichol, D. (1993) A culture of contempt, *The Tablet*, 6 November, 1442–4.

O'Hara, M. (1996) Why is this man laughing? *A.H.P. Perspective*, June/July: 19–31.

Rogers, C.R. (1957) The necessary and sufficient conditions of therapeutic personality change, *Journal of Counseling Psychology*, 21(2): 95–103.

Rogers, C.R. (1980) *A Way of Being*. Boston: Houghton Mifflin.

Rowan, J. (1989) A late developer, in W. Dryden and L. Spurling (eds), *On Becoming a Psychotherapist*. London: Tavistock/Routledge.

Rowan, J. (1993) *The Transpersonal, Psychotherapy and Counselling*. London: Routledge.

Smith, M.L., Glass, G.V. and Miller, T.I. (1980) *The Benefits of Psychotherapy*. Baltimore, MD: Johns Hopkins University Press.

Thorne, B.J. (1985) *The Quality of Tenderness*. Norwich: Norwich Centre Publications.

Thorne, B.J. (1991) *Person-centred Counselling: Therapeutic and Spiritual Dimensions*. London: Whurr.

Thorne, B.J. (1993) Spirituality and the counsellor, in W. Dryden (ed.), *Questions and Answers in Counselling in Action*. London: Sage.

Thorne, B.J. (1994) Developing a spiritual discipline, in D. Mearns (ed.), *Developing Person-centred Counselling*. London: Sage.

Watson, N. (1984) The empirical status of Rogers' hypothesis of the necessary and sufficient conditions for effective psychotherapy, in R.F. Levant and J.M. Shlien (eds), *Client-Centered Therapy and the Person-Centered Approach*. New York: Praeger.

West, W. (1995) Counsellors as healers. Unpublished paper.

10

Counselling and Society

Richard L. Wessler and Sheenah Hankin Wessler

Negative thoughts about the future form one third of Beck's (1976) cognitive triad of depressive thoughts (the others are the self and the world). We try, therefore, to maintain positive and optimistic thoughts about the future, and have learned to do so quite consistently and with beneficial results. However, we are not very good at making specific predictions. Neither of us forecast that Windy Dryden would write or edit a hundred books and become a major force in counselling in Britain, when we each met him in the late 1970s. We were no better at forecasting our own future: we had no idea when we met as a result of Windy's inviting us separately to a training programme, that we would eventually wed, work together, and create cognitive appraisal therapy (Wessler and Hankin Wessler, 1986).

We are good psychotherapists but mediocre prophets who like having a chance to review portents of the millennium. Having admitted little talent for seeing the future, we now embark on our vision of counselling and psychotherapy in the twenty-first century. It is mostly about counselling in America; although we are active on the international counselling scene, New York has been home to our practice for over a decade. To be honest, we are not very aware of what is happening in other countries. Our vision is infused with optimism, but the specifics are only speculations, and our reading of the trends is laced with hopes for the way things ought to be.

Looking backward

Counselling and psychotherapy have come a long way in our lifetime. Forty years ago, counselling consisted of nondirective counselling (Rogers, 1951) and its misguided opposite, heavily influenced by psychodynamic concepts. My (Richard) first encounter with counselling occurred when I was a new university student without a clue about most things but especially baffled about a career. After taking the usual ability and interest tests, I sat face-to-face with the first live counsellor I had ever seen. (Actually, I discovered that he was an aspiring counsellor – a graduate student named Mr Smith.) He sat in silence as I examined the test results and tried to make sense of this and that percentile. (I understood what a percentile was but I didn't know what each score meant about me.) I looked at him for guidance and he looked at me, and we looked back and forth a few more times before he asked, 'Would you like some help with these scores?' I uttered a relieved, 'Yes,' and noticed that he looked a bit guilty. He glanced around the room as though searching for a hidden microphone. (For all I know, there may have been one.) I later realized that he had spoken before I had! He had said something directive rather than reflective. I didn't know it then but I soon learned what he was not supposed to do. He had not maintained a nondirective approach, but was actually very helpful.

As a graduate student, I had to study psychoanalytic theory and nondirective methods, but I was more interested in social psychology (an interest I share with Windy Dryden). By the time I concluded my graduate studies, the field of counselling had been enriched by several other therapies that still exist in one form or another. I discovered gestalt therapy (Perls, 1969), transactional analysis (TA) (Berne, 1964), a lot of people's behaviour therapy, and somewhat belatedly, rational emotive therapy (RET) (Ellis, 1977) and even later, cognitive therapy (Beck, 1976). There were others – too many to mention. An explosion of approaches to counselling erupted during the 1960s and 1970s. Many of these were simple variations of something else, and some were genuinely zany. Most of the truly zany ones came from southern California and required me to believe that my birth had been traumatic and had to be done over again (Orr and Ray, 1977), or that I had been victimized in one or more previous incarnations and had to have my past lives analysed (Netherton and Shiffrin, 1978).

By the time I (Sheenah) began graduate studies, innovative approaches to counselling had become standard theories and procedures every new counsellor had to know. There were not many counsellors in England and Ireland (where I later practised) when I studied with Richard Nelson-Jones and Windy Dryden. Richard was thoroughly grounded in nondirective, person-centred counselling, and very knowledgeable about other systems as well. Windy was a tough task-master, due to his own personality at the time (he's since become warmer and fuzzier) and his contacts with Albert Ellis. Sitting in his chair, a pipe in his mouth and a tape recorder attached to his wrist with a small strap, he would glare at and remark unfavourably about anyone who was as much as a minute late. What some regarded as rigidity, I came to understand as dedication – he took counselling seriously (and still does), the way it is supposed to be.

As immersed as he was in rational emotive therapy, he did not sell us on the approach. Basic counselling skills are what he taught, with a little RET and much more of it if we care to consult with him independently. Windy continued to supervise me for the next two years, as I sent him tapes of my work from Dublin and he returned them to me with insightful comments. He did not object to my inclusion of interventions gleaned from the writings of Rogers, Perls, and Berne, nor did he insist that I confine my counselling to pure RET.

That same spirit pervades his writing and editing. Whilst his own writings are overwhelmingly about RET, he has encouraged and published writers with other orientations. It is little wonder to us that counselling in the UK has flourished, and we know that Windy Dryden had a great deal to do with it. The growth and spread of counselling was in many ways inevitable. However, the way in which it developed – professional and sensible as opposed to amateurish and zany – owes a lot to Windy's persistent promotion of well-grounded counselling.

How professional counselling became important

Perhaps we did not look back far enough in the previous section. We believe that some form of counselling has always existed. The people who did it were not necessarily called counsellors; they went by other titles, some religious, some familial: priest, shaman, sage, elder. The emphasis was on wisdom and on having an obligation to use that wisdom to guide others. The meaning of the word counselling historically has included *advising* and *recommending*. A counsellor was one who shared wisdom and experience, and advised and recommended courses of action to others. Counselling, unlike psychotherapy, has always had an implied educational mission. Counsellors have specialized knowledge that the average well-intentioned layperson does not have; for example, they know about addictions, careers, AIDS, finances, etc.

The exception is counselling in which psychotherapy becomes an essential part of the mission. We formerly called this 'psychological coun-selling', but there is a new (to us) term that describes it better – psychotherapeutic counselling. Herein the counsellor has no special *factual* information about drugs, jobs, diseases, or money to give. Instead, using a theoretical frame of reference, the counsellor imparts a special awareness to the person about himself or herself. From such awareness the person has a better idea about how to live, which is the ideal outcome of psychotherapeutic counselling.

No aspect of living is off-limits for the psychotherapeutic counsellor. Counselling now fulfils certain societal functions that in the past were done by others. With a decline of traditional religious influences in the USA and UK people less frequently turn to the clergy for guidance and wisdom, and the clergy have turned to *us* for training in counselling. In a world in which the elderly (and even the middle-aged) are sufficiently out-of-touch with technology, people seek their wisdom less often. Technological changes inevitably bring social changes, and it is a challenge to keep abreast of them and to adapt. The global village has become the mirror opposite of the communal village – the old follow the advice of the young, and the young are guided by each other. It's a pity, because some things about human existence do not change, although our understanding of them changes a great deal; but few people would believe an old man's wisdom about human nature when he finds the Internet perplexing and cannot even get lost in cyberspace. So it falls to the professional counsellor to be a conduit for the wisdom of the ages – it's a tough job but someone has to do it.

Professional counselling, like other professions, has developed many specializations and will probably develop many more. A good example is the specialized area of eating disorders. In working with the dangerously overweight and underweight, a counsellor has to know principles of good nutrition, tactics for managing eating behaviour, and cognitive and affective reasons why people do not stick to what is good for them. Similarly, in the substance abuse field, counsellors must have specialized knowledge of prescription and illicit drugs, but must also know the psychological factors in addiction. These go beyond a simple cliché about an 'addictive personality', as though there were only one type of person (or personality) that becomes addicted. The counsellor must also navigate between a psychological understanding of the addict and allowing that understanding to exempt the addict from personal responsibility.

What you don't know can hurt you

We have just touched on what is both powerful and potentially dangerous in psychotherapeutic counselling. Explanations of why people do what they do involve the operation of something the person is not aware of. Indeed, it is the task of psychotherapeutic counselling to make the person aware of what is operating without his or her knowing it. Once we take seriously the assumption that people's actions are influenced by factors they are not aware of, we open up the possibility of excusing rather than explaining their behaviour. People can easily be portrayed as victims of their own unknown processes rather than as humans who must make responsible and at times very tough choices.

The most obvious example of forces at work beyond our awareness is psychodynamic theory. Freud did not originate the notion of an unconscious, but he developed the concept in ways no one had done before him. He challenged the then popular conception of humans as reasonable creatures and claimed that, without knowing it, they were driven by primitive forces. In its extreme form, this version of human nature made humans into puppets who are blindly guided by drives so animal-like that they were called 'instincts' (in English; Freud's term *das Trieb* simply means 'drive'). These drives led to all sorts of conflicts and complications, and had to be sorted out by the interpretations of the analyst. Once the contents of the unconscious were known to the patient, he or she could make conscious decisions and not be governed by 'instincts'. Aside from theoretical differences you might have with the explanation, focus on its subversive implications. First, one could claim with theoretical justification that he or she was not responsible for his or her own actions, and those actions, therefore, are excusable. Second, some patients use insight into unconscious process as a conscious excuse not to take responsibility rather than to take conscious control over their own actions. They say, in effect, 'I know I have this unconscious need (or conflict, etc.) and therefore I must do what I do'.

To Freud's credit, this is not what he had in mind. To his successors' credit, no one takes drive theory very seriously these days. But the general impression that one can be victimized by one's own unconscious mind remains. One need only watch American television talk shows to confirm this observation. They, of course, present a highly selective slice of American society ('flotsam and jetsam' is how one commentator describes the guests on these shows), but claims that they are either victims or that they 'have to' do something odious or both, are relics of the version of human nature as nonreasoning.

Other approaches to counselling have a similar feature. Rogerian counselling methods have emphasized the warm, empathic, genuine, etc., nature of the counsellor, and with this we have no quarrel. However, the counsellor should be all these things not because authentic people are good guys, but because the client needs such a positive human interaction in order to become aware of certain aspects about himself or herself. These characteristics had been fenced off into unawareness so that the individual could function in the real world, albeit in a restricted way. By becoming aware of these characteristics and having himself or herself accepted by the counsellor, growth becomes an actuality. The important curative feature of gestalt therapy was awareness of needs and of their fulfillment or frustration. In TA, awareness of one's ego states and of scripts allowed new decisions in one's life – and the end of slavishly playing out childhood scripts and games. All of these approaches say, in one way or another, to 'know thyself' is to free thyself.

Behavioural approaches likewise assume some things that are unknown to the person. What reinforces and maintains behaviour, is one example. All forms of self-talk, including irrational commands and demands, that one did not know one had are matters to become aware of, with the help of a counsellor. The distinctive meaning the individual attaches to experiences forms the core of cognitive therapy. These are meanings the person has but has not articulated, and therefore has not been aware of them. The discovery of these meanings is a crucial process in cognitive therapy. Without knowing what meanings one attaches to experiences one cannot consciously change them. In psychoanalytic approaches the counsellor furnishes the meanings of an individual's actions and fantasies by making interpretations. In cognitive therapy, the counsellor merely helps the individual discover his or her *own interpretations*, and questions whether these conform to reality or whether they are adaptive interpretations to make.

Without having some unique, nonconscious aspects of each client to discover, the counsellor would be reduced to giving information – to teaching. While counselling always has some inseparable facet of education about it, what is unique about psychotherapeutic counselling is its focus on what the person does not know about himself or herself. Other forms of counselling can be computerized, i.e. programs can be created that take information from the client, process it and produce new information or a set of recommendations. Psychotherapeutic counselling cannot be handled in this fashion because the counsellor seeks information that the client cannot consciously furnish. That human counsellors are needed to do psychotherapeutic counselling is especially true for the cognitive therapies, where the meanings attached to experiences reside in the individual and not in the theory. Only theory can be programmed. Although practitioner and patient are collaborators in the counselling endeavour, the counsellor is by virtue of training and experience an expert and able to do things that no computer can ever match.

Trends in the USA

We have extensively discussed humans as indispensable to the counselling process because there are some who think otherwise. Some people love to automate everything, getting a high from applying high technology. Tell your troubles to a computer? Not exactly a new idea. Over fifteen years ago someone tried to get me (Richard) involved in such a project, but all we could ever conceive of was psychoeducation, not psychotherapeutic counselling. The principles of mental health can be taught by computer, and the computer can present a systematic, step-by-step programme to, say, control anger, but it cannot get to know you or your idiosyncratic thoughts and feelings – your 'unawarenesses'.

The other people who think that the automation of counselling should happen are those who would derive financial benefits from it. In the USA, these are insurance companies. At the present time, most health insurance policies, which are purchased by individuals or by their employers, pay very little for psychotherapy and rarely if ever pay for any form of counselling. You can insure against illness but you cannot insure against the possibility of having personal problems. Nonetheless, counselling in the USA has reasons to be optimistic about future insurance reimbursement: there are a lot of counsellors, and many of them are mental health counsellors who want reimbursement enough to collectively go for it; insurance companies look for cheap solutions, and mental health counselling services cost less on the whole than other psychological/psychiatric ones. What would please the insurance companies even more than cheap labour is no labour at all. That's where computers come in – the client puts in a problem, the computer puts out a solution.

Here's how it might go. Client feels depressed, seeks mental health counselling. Insurance company authorizes one paid-for visit – to a computer. When prompted client enters 'depressed' and awaits further instructions. In nanotime the computer searches for the appropriate routine, and begins to ask questions about the nature and duration of the depression. Convinced that it does not require medication and a referral to a psychiatrist, the computer prints out basic information about depression.

'It's the common cold of mental health. Afflicts more women than men. Depressed mood is associated with negative thinking. SOLUTION: Check your thinking to determine whether real life events support your negative conclusions. HOMEWORK: Don't worry! Be happy!' (That ubiquitous American icon the cartoon smiley face appears at the end of the print out. In the British version of this vision, it's government that decides to cut costs.)

If counsellors keep their unique mission in sight and remind the various publics they serve of their important function in society, they need not fear replacement by automation. However, for any human to remain indispensable he or she must dispense something no one else or no other thing can. Counsellors are in the awareness business – they are not educators (computers can do that), healers (physicians and charlatans have that locked up), or mere listeners (friends or even strangers will do just fine).

Medication

In all seriousness, we forecast that in the USA counselling (and psycho-therapy) will be offered by insurance providers and health maintenance organizations (HMOs) nearly to the exclusion of independent practice. Their emphasis increasingly will be toward short-term and very low cost services. Because they want to maximize cost-effectiveness (known as 'more bang for the buck') they will move toward increasing use of medication alone to treat problems of mental health. While it may seem that MD physicians and especially psychiatrists would benefit most from a move toward medication, we forecast that non-MD practitioners, including psychotherapeutic counsellors, will become enfranchised with the right to write prescriptions. Physicians will oppose this privilege, of course, but the power rests with the money and the insurance companies will get their way.

We foresee bad things for counsellors who can prescribe psychotropic medication (as well as for their patients). Psychiatry in the USA furnishes an instructive example. With the power to prescribe *and* the exponentially increasing availability of new medications to treat anxiety and, especially, depression, psychiatrists prescribe more and think psychotherapy less than ever before. Counsellors, too, can be expected to rely on tablets rather than awareness in working with distressed people. Prescribing medication does not appear to be all that tricky (at least to us outsiders), but responsible prescribing and monitoring requires considerable training. Counsellors who seek such training will do so at the expense of other important activities, e.g. learning to do first class psychotherapeutic counselling. In other words, what we risk is both inferior medicating and inferior counselling.

Medication will be used more, not less, in the future, and as a consequence everyone in the mental health field needs to know more about it. The reason for the emphasis on medication is not its effectiveness – in some instances it is irreplaceable and in others simply not needed. The push for medication will come from third party players, including insurance companies, self-insured employers who pay employees' medical costs, and various government agencies. Short, cheap solutions might alleviate symptoms but they are not likely to fix problems of living the way counsellors can.

Group therapy

The need to contain costs will also foster the expansion of group therapy. There is plenty to be said about the advantages of psychotherapeutic counselling in groups, and indeed group therapy is one of our specializations. A group setting provides opportunities for feedback about interaction and self-presentation that can be both more perceptive and more awareness-promoting than the individual-and-counsellor pattern. In addition, there are possibilities for social risk-taking and corrective emotional experiences that one-to-one work can only approximate. However, none of these very sound reasons for doing group therapy is what is likely to promote it. The rationale for its growth is cost-effectiveness rather than therapeutic effectiveness.

We forecast, therefore, that counselling in the millennium will feature more group work. It is entirely possible that individual sessions will be limited to gathering intake information and possibly diagnosis and assessment. Therapeutic interventions themselves would take place later in groups.

We suspect that the future will see persons with similar problems funnelled into homogeneous groups. There are already treatment protocols for certain emotional problems, e.g. anger, and for common psychological issues, e.g. eating disorders. We foresee the emergence of even more specific counselling specialities and the delivery of these counselling specialities in group formats. The counsellor–leader will be no mere facilitator, except in certain instances, but will have expert skills anchored on the one hand in counselling theory and tactics, and on the other in specific content about which he or she can give accurate information. Self-help groups will be confined to problems wherein shared common experiences have been helpful; so-called 'survivors' groups get along well with a facilitator or even without a professional leader, and seem to develop into friendship groups in which the members' mutual traumatic experiences are seldom discussed.

Focus on specifics

Much of the older counselling literature is pretty nonspecific. The goals of person-centred counselling, gestalt or TA were hard to pin down. Vague concepts like 'growth' and 'self-actualization' were said so often that they became counselling clichés and eventually entered the language of everyday life as meaningless psychobabble. Counsellors had faith that something good would happen as a result of their efforts, and often they were right. Behavioural counselling was better at saying what results it should get, and could be more explicit when talking about what it was doing.

Partly as a result of the success of behavioural counselling, but mostly because those who pay want to know the results they can expect (i.e. insurance companies, government agencies, and even client–consumers themselves), there has been a trend toward specifying concrete outcomes. We see this trend becoming stronger, particularly in three areas: crisis intervention, symptom-focused treatment, and problem-focused treatment.

Crisis intervention is one of the most important and distinctive purposes of counselling. When in crisis, people want to see and talk to real, live people. No computer can replace the human who is on the scene of a tragedy or speaking face-to-face with someone having a life crisis. No chemical mood-altering substance, whether professionally prescribed or self-administered, can replace the person who is there, who cares, who understands, and who can help resolve the psychological impact of an emergent crisis. The outcomes of crisis counselling are not hard to specify. Somehow, after counselling interventions, the person in crisis can function better and with less distress; the person knows and can report whether or not he or she is better. (Lest the reader find the self-report too nonspecific, we hasten to point out that much medical research measures outcomes by means of a questionnaire on which subjects report their subjective experiences, e.g. 'It doesn't hurt as much'.)

Symptom relief or elimination used to be sneered at. Psychodynamic folks said such goals represented a failure to get at underlying causes, and even today clients often talk about 'getting to the root of the problem'. Further, the elimination of a symptom without uprooting and curing the cause would simply lead to symptom substitution – another symptom would replace the one vanquished by counselling. This prediction is consistent with classic psychoanalytic thinking – unresolved conflicts have to be expressed symbolically; erase one symbol and the unconscious will create another to represent the conflict and partially and temporarily relieve it. There is no empirical basis for this prediction, although it is widely believed. It reminds me (Richard) of when I was learning to pilot an airplane as part of a self-designed programme to overcome a fear of flying; some psychologists told me not to bother, since I'd only develop a new phobia as a substitute for the old one. I didn't.

Reducing or ridding oneself of symptoms may still be the subject of debate – e.g. between so-called constructivists and rationalists (Wessler,

1992) – but let's ask clients. Most of them welcome the departure of anxiety or depression; only a few would say that they would miss it (and we will have more to say about them later). Even fewer say that they desire the experience of anxiety because it promotes growth and insight. The cognitive and behavioural therapies were created to reduce and eliminate distressing emotional experiences and dysfunctional behavioural patterns (or 'symptoms').

We forecast a continuing trend toward more specific interventions designed to treat symptoms. This approach will be ill-suited for some clients who truly do have vague distresses and would truly benefit from aimless but brief self-exploration, and we hope that they will not be lost a world of treatment manuals and procedural protocols. (Maybe they won't, since we think that brief – and therefore cheap – is the goal of those who fund counselling, and later in this chapter we present some ideas about brief counselling.) In general, we applaud the efforts to make interventions more tailored to specific symptoms; at the same time, we recognize that so-called symptoms in some ways have a life and a function of their own.

Problem-focused intervention and its positively stated twin, solution-focused intervention, represent yet another attempt to deal with specific issues rather than global ones, to target particular areas for change rather than taking a shotgun approach with the attitude that everyone needs some counselling and that counselling is good for everyone. One of the venerable forms of problem- or solution-focused counselling is RET. For those of us versed in that approach, we find other ways of helping clients to be terribly amorphous. In RET and its cognate forms of treatment, including our own cognitive appraisal therapy (Wessler and Hankin Wessler, 1986), we start with what the client finds problematic. Feelings the client has are about *something*, behavioural reactions are reactions to *something*. In the real world people confront situations and circumstances that are distressing, and a problem- or solution-focused approach deals with those situations and circumstances – at times to work out plans to alter them, and at times to react differently to them. For us, the question, 'What problem do you want to work on?' is more than just a way to begin a counselling session; it is an orientation to what is important: particulars, not vague self-examination.

It is both economical and sensible to deal with specific problems and seek specific solutions. We hope that the field of counselling is both practical and sensible enough to move in this direction. Of course, there is a place for more global, less specific client concerns, including our specialization, which is personality itself. But even so, our emphasis is not on discovering who the client is (whatever that might mean), but on deciding who the client would like to be.

All three ideas discussed in this section – crisis counselling, symptom treatment, problem- and solution-focused interventions – may include something that is nontraditional in most forms of counselling. We refer to environmental interventions. So much counselling is directed at intrapersonal processes and some at interpersonal processes. Relatively less attention is given to changing the client's environment to produce happier life results. More accurately, we speak of assisting the client in changing his or her environment in order to relieve distress or deal with a crisis. For example, a person can learn to adjust better to a very abusive spouse, but a simpler and more effective solution is to get away from the abuser. Or, perhaps the spouse is merely cranky, not abusive. A client can gain a certain degree of serenity as a result of counselling or get coached by the counsellor in how to deliver an ultimatum to the cranky partner ('lighten up or else!'). The first example illustrates a change for the better in the physical environment, the second a change sought in the behavioural environment.

While we believe that psychotherapeutic counselling should deal with such psychological processes as affect, behaviour (especially interpersonal), and cognition, we also recognize the importance of being both prepared and willing to help the client handle his or her world of events. It is not enough to help people adjust to adversity or even to overcome it psychologically. People need to take a proactive approach to their lives, and this means trying to change what goes on around them. We forecast an important role for counselling in this regard, and although we may be too optimistic, we forecast a trend toward that role. In our own work, we try to influence clients to become more active in their own lives – to take charge by taking action. Passivity underlies so much of psychopathology.

Prevention programmes

We would like to forecast the development of programmes to promote mental health and reduce the need for psychotherapeutic counselling in the millennium. We are not sanguine about the prospects. There is no effective inoculation against psychological problems of which we are aware. So, here are a few ideas that might come to pass.

People need to be better informed about how to handle little problems so that they do not become big ones. The difficulty is, various schools of thought about counselling have various ideas about what might be helpful. None of them have worked particularly well so far, partly because they were misapplied and partly because they were not applied at all.

With respect to the latter point, knowing about something, or even knowing how to do something, does not necessarily lead to actually doing it. Good examples of these are all the self-help books, past and present. A random sampling of these will reveal some good ideas which, if properly applied, would get pretty good results. The difficulty is, people do not use what they know unless there is some payoff for so doing. One might think that mental health would be sufficient incentive to employ self-help ideas, but apparently not. Most people want change but do not want to change (i.e. take an active part in the change process). Countless clients present themselves for counselling expecting the counsellor to change them ('it's not working', they whine). We have heard people say that they read a self-help book but it didn't help. It's like saying, 'I read a book about music but I still can't play the piano'.

Even if people would follow through and actively do what they have learned (and some do), there is still the problem of what they learn. Some ideas start off well and end up poorly. Unconditional positive regard, a sound Rogerian notion, can serve as an example. He proposed it as an antidote for lack of self-regard brought on by parents who selectively loved their children – loved them when they fulfilled parental expectations. So far so good. But then the message got distorted and some parents pushed permissiveness to an extreme, believing that horrible things would happen to their children if the parents uttered a disapproving word. The result are kids without limits, without a sense of regard for others.

Here's another example, one of our favourites, to do with self-esteem. No one knows exactly what self-esteem means, but nearly everyone agrees that it is good for you. Some people believe that without self-esteem all sorts of bad things will befall them. In some circles, it is firmly believed that no one can do anything without self-esteem, and that the main mission of schools is to foster self-esteem. In the USA, the traditional three Rs, reading, writing, and 'rithmetic, have been replaced by one R, relating (to others). American kids may be ignorant and illiterate, but they can relate better than anyone else in the world, and do they ever like themselves! Ironically, a hundred years ago, Americans believed that you should not hold yourself in high esteem unless you had truly achieved as a result of your own efforts. Nowadays, it is believed that you cannot achieve unless you already have high self-esteem. There are books aplenty to tell you how to gain it if you don't have it or increase it if you have too little.

Our limited optimism about psychological prevention programmes stems from listening to people talk about what they think is essential for mental health. They need better ideas about what do, ideas that promote activity rather than passivity, optimism rather than pessimism, and respect for self and others. Possibly, through mass communications, more people can be reached with a sensible and helpful set of ideas. Even then, distortions are likely and failure to enact the message probable. We'll keep trying.

Short term integrative counselling

We have Windy Dryden to thank for urging us to develop our ideas into cognitive appraisal therapy (CAT), and its derivative, short-term integrative counselling (STIC). We have not responded to his prodding us to publish more, although we are grateful that our earliest articles appeared in books he edited. It's a rationalization to say that we have been too busy doing CAT to write about it, but ever optimistic, we believe that one day his tenaciousness will be vindicated and we will produce a full length book about our work. We offer a brief description here to illustrate a future direction in counselling – short-term and integrative.

Cognitive appraisal therapy was developed as an integrated approach to personality modification (or *P-Mod*, as we sometimes call it) (Wessler, 1993a). It assumes that affect, behaviour and cognition are interdependent, mutually influential psychological components, and that a significant source of motivation is a person's seeking psychological security by repeating certain familiar experiences. Its theory draws upon social learning and interpersonal theory, and its procedures include elements of person-centred counselling and gestalt therapy in addition to RET. Theodore Millon's (1996) theory of personality heavily influenced our own conceptualization.

Cognitive appraisal therapy is not a set of specific procedures but rather a unique theoretical understanding of affect that a client can comprehend and be helped to change. An excess of affect brings the histrionic borderline personality disorder into treatment, just as it is a seeming lack of affect that is the complaint of the isolated, passive–aggressive client. To date, psychoanalysis and allied approaches have claimed the distinction of treating affect, though in reality they are curiously cognitive and rationally intellectual.

When therapy stalls, CAT can be the approach of choice. Though practitioners stick to the familiarity of a favoured set of theoretical concepts and clients to familiar affective habits, it is helpful for counsellors to experience the unfamiliar and experiment with CAT's approach, especially for personality disturbances and for the more recalcitrant client for whom this approach was created.

The term cognitive appraisal therapy was adopted to emphasize the fact that the *evaluative cognition* (a synonym for appraisal) is a target for intervention (Wessler and Hankin Wessler, 1986). It became increasingly apparent that people are seldom aware of some of their most significant appraisals; they function as nonconscious algorithms – stored routines for the processing of social information (Wessler and Hankin Wessler, 1989). (Algorithms are specific and separate rules for evaluating experiences, and are not assumed to cluster together as schemas; the concept of schema is no longer used in CAT.) This discovery also signalled a shift in emphasis from consciously held cognitions (or what people can say about their thinking) to nonconscious cognitions that must be inferred from what people say and do.

Like most forms of psychotherapy in the early 1980s, CAT was used mainly to treat such conditions as anxiety and depression. Some clients did not improve, or did not maintain their improvement, or continued with us after they had improved. Why? The answer was found in their pre-disposing personality characteristics. Disorders are the result of psycho-social stressors interacting with personality variables. In response, CAT focused almost exclusively on the treatment of personality vulnerabilities.

Basic assumptions of CAT

Cognitive appraisal therapy takes from general systems theory the assumption of interdependence among components. In CAT the components are the psychological processes affect, behaviour and cognition. The term affect refers mainly to subjective emotional feelings and bodily sensations. (The term emotion refers to physiological changes as well as overt actions, and facial and postural displays.) Behaviour refers to patterns rather than to isolated events, especially those that take place between people – interpersonal behaviours are more significant to understanding personality than are an individual's tics. Cognition refers to the content of mental activity, and can consist of logical and illogical sentences, factual and fantastic information, and images or pictures in the mind, and most importantly, evaluative cognitions or appraisals. Cognitive dissonance theory supports the idea of interdependence of affect, behaviour and cognition. The research it inspired showed that changes in overt behaviour result in internal changes in affect and cognition, contrary to common sense which says that if you change your mind you will act differently.

Many forms of cognitive-behaviour therapy acknowledge the interdependence of these three components but do not employ them extensively in practice. This may be due to their adopting a mediated stimulus–response model in which emotion is seen as a result of the cognitive processing of certain internal or external stimuli. In RET, for example, beliefs are said to mediate between a stimulus and an emotional response, and beneficial results are achieved by changing beliefs in order to have new emotional responses. This is what might be called 'the frightened animal' mode of emotion – an animal reacts with flight and fear to a stimulus it perceives and evaluates as dangerous. This is the emotional episode.

The emotional episode (Wessler and Hankin Wessler, 1990) consists of the following steps: (1) stimulus; (2) detection of stimulus; (3) covert description of observed stimulus; (4) inferences about the perceived stimulus, including attributions, forecasts and other elaborations; (5) appraisals; (6) emotional response determined by appraisals; (7) decisions about how to react and behavioural response; (8) feedback (reinforcement) about behavioural response. In addition to external stimuli, humans react to the internal stimuli of their own thoughts and feelings.

In CAT, inferences and appraisals are based on what are labelled *personal rules of living*. These are personal versions of correlational and cause-and-effect relationships that exist in the natural and social world, and personal versions of moral principles and social values. For example, one may have an inferential rule that all dogs will bite if one gets too close, and an evaluative rule that physical pain is bad and should be avoided. Based on these rules, the logical conclusion is to avoid dogs in order to avoid pain, and the phobic person does exactly that.

This cognitive mediation model of episodic emotion accounts for a person's reactions in specific situations, and is especially applicable and helpful in understanding and relieving emotional distress associated with crises. However, a mediated stimulus–response model of emotion does not apply to clients who are not in crisis. The disordered emotions for which people seek treatment are more habitual than reactive, more chronic than episodic. The emotional episode became less important as CAT focused more exclusively on personality disorders.

The third direction of influence is that of affect on behaviour and cognition. Assume that people have emotional habits, i.e. that they are accustomed to certain emotional feelings. In order to sustain their emotional habits they must bring their thinking and actions into harmony with their feelings. For example, persons give negative interpretations to the statements and actions of themselves and of others, but when they adopt more positive interpretations they feel less depressed. Habitual emotions depend on behaviours and cognitions to sustain and reproduce them.

Not only do people become accustomed to certain emotional feelings, but they need to re-experience those feelings in order to have a sense of psychological security. People feel most comfortable and secure in familiar surroundings, with familiar people, and with their own possessions (familiar objects) present. Too much familiarity can be boring, but too much novelty can be threatening. According to CAT, each person has a nonconscious personal rule of living that prescribes how he or she should feel; this is known as the *emotional setpoint*.

When one's subjective emotional feelings fail to match his or her emotional setpoint, automatic processes are activated to return the person's feelings to the prescribed range around the setpoint. Deviations below the setpoint, i.e. when one feels worse than the setpoint prescribes, are corrected by certain mood-lifting thoughts and actions – these are commonly known as defences. Psychological defences, according to CAT, are simply automatic processes that return a person's emotional state to a familiar point. Conversely, when one's feelings exceed that setpoint, i.e. when one feels too good, automatic processes go to work to return the individual to his or her accustomed (and therefore secure) state.

The emotional setpoint varies among individuals according to their personal developmental history. Familiarity comes from repeated exposure to certain events, usually within the family, but also to certain models of emoting and interacting. In CAT, familiar emotional experiences that provide a sense of security are called *personotypic affects*. When they are positive, no one gives them much attention, because there is a cultural value (at least in the USA) that feeling good is good. We consciously strive to experience good feelings and are motivated to engage in pleasurable activities and satisfying interpersonal relations.

When one's personotypic affects are negative, e.g. anxiety, anger, they motivate people to seek experiences that produce these negative feelings. The person is 'starved' for negative but familiar affects, and seeks them out. At the same time, the person consciously subscribes to the cultural norm that feeling good is good. Such a discrepancy between what one consciously wants and at times nonconsciously seeks can be confusing for the person and prompt him or her to seek help. Treatment, however, will be limited by the client's need to feel contrary to what he or she deems desirable. The conservative tendencies of personotypic affects impede progress toward the goals of therapy, and lead to the retaining of symptoms.

To say that some people, without their awareness, prefer to feel bad rather than good seems to go against a cherished principle in psychological theorizing. Underpinning most psychological accounts of human nature is the principle of hedonism – that living creatures, including humans, seek pleasure and avoid pain. The seeking of negative personotypic affects seems to be an exception to the pleasure–pain principle. How can the experiencing of negative affects be reinforcing? The answer is that familiarity is more reinforcing than pleasure or pain-avoidance under certain conditions. The conditions are the same as those required for hedonistic reinforcement – deprivation.

No reinforcer is absolutely reinforcing. Its potency comes from the organism's state of deprivation or satiation. Food is reinforcing when the organism is deprived and hungry, but it has no reinforcing properties when the organism is satiated. Similarly, when a person is deprived of familiar feelings, he or she will seek them – without awareness and without making a conscious decision to do so. When the person is satiated with familiar feelings the emotional setpoint is matched and the person has a sense of psychological security.

To complete the special vocabulary used in CAT, behaviours that service personotypic affects are called *security-seeking behaviours*. Typically, they are interpersonal behaviours that 'pull' predictable responses from other people, and these responses stimulate predictable feelings in the actor. For example, if anger is a personotypic affect, the actor can engage in provocative actions that will surely result in responses that make the actor feel angry. The cognitions that serve personotypic affects are called *justifying cognitions* because they provide a rationale for feelings. For example, if anxiety is a personotypic affect, a person might believe that something dreadful will happen. When there is no evidence that anything dreadful might happen and the person continues to think that it will, it is a justifying cognition – the thought justifies the feeling.

The plan in conventional cognitive-behavioural counselling is to specify certain behaviours and cognitions as targets of change. These targets are addressed logically: homework is assigned to encourage new patterns of behaviour, and cognitions are challenged with disconfirming evidence of their validity. Everyone has had clients who just will not do what they agree would be more adaptive, or change their mind when they agree their beliefs are false and maladaptive. Why would clients act against their own rational best interests, especially when they acknowledge that neither their actions nor their beliefs are sensible? What is a counsellor to do when the client agrees with cognitive interventions but does not change?

In CAT, we assume that people who act against their own interests are seeking the security of familiarity. What we do *not* do is continue to dispute beliefs or present evidence to disconfirm the client's misconceptions. Instead, we infer the presence of personotypic affects, security-seeking behaviours, and justifying cognitions, and explain them to the client.

The main tactic in CAT is the understanding of one's affective, behavioural and cognitive patterns, so that the client can understand them too. Self-understanding, or insight into one's own personality, is the foundation for change. The client can then consciously work against his or her own very powerful tendencies. The client can be warned about the power of familiarity – the power that works against change. When clients know that they consciously seek the novelty of change and expect to feel psychologically insecure, they are prepared for dissonance and discomfort. They can then work on emotional self-care.

Emotional self-care consists of soothing one's feelings, reducing their intensity, and reassuring oneself. For some people, spirituality and religious faith are legitimate and important factors in the management of affect. Other ways to reduce feelings involve drugs and substances which can have side-effects and be addictive, or the excessive use of distraction, which can produce attention deficits. Some of the best methods for emotional self-care consist of traditional cognitive-behaviour therapy, especially self-talk that creates reassurance. Whether they are called self-instructional statements or stress-inoculations, they are intended to reduce excess affect and keep the person grounded in reality.

Shame, self-pity and self-respect

Two important but easily overlooked feelings that receive close attention in CAT are shame and self-pity. Shame is a feeling of personal deficiency, of personal flaws and defects that are so bad that they must be kept secret. Unlike guilt, which pertains to acts that violate a group's rules, society's norms or a religion's commandments, shame pertains to a feeling of personal inadequacy or unworthiness. It is a form of self-criticism and self-damnation so extensive that one feels like an outcast from the company of friends and family. These feelings may be accompanied by self-imposed alienation and isolation to avoid exposure and further criticism. Anxiety occurs when one fears that one's secret weaknesses will be discovered by others. Shame is usually defended against in a variety of ways, especially withdrawal, anger, denial and humour (Nathanson, 1992). Shame issues must be addressed in treating social anxiety.

However, when shame is a personotypic affect it will be sought rather than avoided even though it makes no rational sense to seek humiliation or mortification. Why would a person act as if he or she seeks shame? Because it is a familiar emotional state, and brings with it a sense of security. (Not surprisingly, these are people who frequently experienced shame in childhood and adolescence; they were often humiliated by their parents and many of them have been sexually abused.) While they consciously abhor shame, their repeatedly acting as if they seek it provides confirming evidence that the feeling is a personotypic affect and that their actions fit a pattern of security-seeking behaviours.

Self-pity is ubiquitous in the USA today and perhaps elsewhere as well. It is the feeling that one is weak and disadvantaged through no fault or one's own – a victim. The pity people feel for the less fortunate may motivate them to help, and a technique used to elicit help from others is to portray oneself as a poor, deserving victim of injustice, of indifference. Pity for oneself, however, does not lead to self-help initiatives, because the feelings confirm that one is powerless. When self-pity is a personotypic affect, people engage in security-seeking behaviours that result in others taking advantage of them, and they justify self-pity by thinking of themselves as victims. Because they imagine themselves as weak but deserving of help, they appear passive, dependent, and reluctant to take responsibility or initiative to satisfy their own wants and desires. Depressed people commonly see themselves as victims, and self-pity must be addressed in treating depression.

Both shame and self-pity are often implicated in rage. When prompted by shame or self-pity the target of rage is usually the people who shamed or victimized the enraged person, or who refuse to help. Because one feels weak whenever one experiences shame or self-pity, the rage is impotent and seldom expressed directly towards the appropriate target due to fear of retaliation. In treating anger problems, it is advisable to look for shame and/or self-pity, and self-perceptions that one is inferior and/or a disadvantaged victim.

Some forms of cognitive-behaviour therapy emphasize the correcting of negative self-evaluations in treating depression and anxiety. Likewise CAT advocates less negative and more positive self-appraisals, and works towards increasing clients' self-respect. Further, CAT proposes that self-respect be based only on the individual's own decisions and actions that are consistent with his or her consciously held personal rules of living. People should respect themselves when they do what is right *as they understand right and wrong at a given time*. Self-respect, then, is entirely under the person's control; he or she needs only to do what is right. The individual, and not other people, has the power over self-appraisal – how you feel about yourself is a matter of making moral choices not gaining others' approval, although a self-respecting person insists that others treat him or her with respect. The counsellor does not decide what is morally right for the client – that is the client's task, according to the client's moral principles and social values.

Self-respect is necessary to combat shame and self-pity. It is difficult to feel guilty or ashamed when you do what is right, nor can you easily feel sorry for yourself. The CAT approach to self-appraisal – self-respect based on moral actions – gives power to the person. A person who feels powerful cannot readily feel shame or pity, because the person feels adequate and worthwhile, not inferior and vulnerable.

Emergence of STIC

Although CAT was developed for individual psychotherapy, its concepts have also been successfully applied to groups, couples (Wessler, 1993b), children and child–parent interactions (Stern, 1996). Because CAT is a theoretical perspective on personality and motivation, it can be adapted to other forms of treatment that deal only with DSM-IV Axis I conditions. Its concepts can be helpful by offering a fresh perspective on factors that resist change and preserve the status quo. Familiarity is a powerful (conservative) force in people's lives.

Short-term integrative counselling (STIC) was developed to address the need for short-term counselling interventions. The procedure is quite simple. The counsellor quickly assesses the aspects of the client's personality that hinder his or her daily living. Listening to the client describe difficulties in relating to others, self-defeating and other patterns of behaviour is usually sufficient. (Psychological tests may be used to accelerate this process.) Then, the counsellor feeds back impressions and shows the client how he or she has trouble. Rapid self-understanding is the goal here. Then counsellor and client develop plans for working against the dysfunctional tendencies in the client's personality patterns; these are plans for short-term personality modification.

Armed with self-understanding, many clients can help themselves without frequent contacts with a professional counsellor. The deliberate concentration on psychological processes of affect, (interpersonal) behaviour, and cognition as the proper foci for counselling eliminates a need to know many time-consuming details about the client's world of events or for so-called multicultural counselling.

Twenty-first century counsellors

We think that there is much for counsellors to do in the twenty-first century. However, the overall success of counselling depends upon well trained and creative counsellors. Therein lies the problem.

If we are correct about the growing influence of third party payers, then a dismal picture emerges. Those who can and are willing to fall into the lockstep of institutional dictates are surely those who lack creativity and desire for independence. Progress or innovation depends upon creativity and the ability to work outside or beyond convention. Will the future see only conforming counsellors who follow the orders of others, and mavericks who are so outstanding or outrageous that no one bothers them? What about the middle where qualified professionals do a yeoman-like job? We foresee the loss of the middle. There will be a few people so outstanding as to attract a following, and a few so outrageous as to do the same. Other counsellors will mindlessly soldier on without much thought for what they do or how they do it. Without an independent counselling profession there is little chance for quality.

If we see these things too darkly it is due in large part to many years spent as trainers of counsellors. So many we encountered, and these included persons already working in the profession, seemed ill-suited for the career they had undertaken. Not that everyone is born to be a counsellor. We are an unusual pair in that one of us (Sheenah) has a natural talent for counselling and the other (Richard) had to acquire skills through practice. We found that many people did not think they had to learn or if they did that they did not have to practise very much to become proficient. They were wrong.

Counselling skills can be acquired, perhaps not by everyone who wants them, through practice and learning from the feedback they get from trainers and supervisors. Where will the counsellors of the future get such opportunity? How can they avoid being poorly trained?

To be very candid, we do not have much confidence in the graduate schools, at least in the USA. Whereas counsellors should be practical and street-wise, academics are theoretical and unworldly. (Yes, we know there are exceptions to this huge generalization.) The problem is, the average academic counsellor simply does not see enough clients to have the practical experience necessary to prepare students to deal with real people in the real world. We once surveyed our colleagues at a conference about how many clients they saw each week. Fewer than five was not unusual, and zero was the norm! It's like a surgeon saying, 'I haven't done any cutting but I read about it in a book'!

The situation for graduate students is worse when there is a research component in their programmes. While it is *de rigueur* to endorse research and its importance, we cannot. Most of the research in counselling is pedestrian and totally unnecessary. I (Richard) serve on the editorial boards of several professional journals, and have been kicked off one for rejecting too many manuscripts. Most of what I read was silly, especially those articles that analysed minute portions of one or more of the 'Gloria' episodes. What Rogers or Perls or Ellis said that day became significant beyond belief, as though what happened during the filming that one day was representative of everything each had ever done. Ellis once told me (Richard) that his interview with Gloria was not good RET because he tried to do too much and get everything into the time allotted him. To draw any conclusions from the utterances made during the filming with Gloria seems highly suspect.

Meaningless research takes time away from graduate student preparation in counselling and from faculty members becoming proficient counsellors themselves. Both students and teachers should realize that they have much to learn from clients and from people who have helped themselves without professional interventions. New developments in psychotherapeutic counselling come not from empirical research but from failures in the counselling process. Every new approach to counselling and psychotherapy was inspired by a counsellor or therapist being unable to make what he or she learned work in a way that helped a certain person. That is the way we developed cognitive appraisal therapy – by discovering the limitations of what we knew and then trying something new to expand the limits.

Having too many counsellors in the millennium risks having poorly trained practitioners. Too many risks the watering down of the proiession. Too many will see the eroding of standards.

It all depends

The future of counselling does not depend upon research or new discoveries as much as it depends upon developments in the societies where it operates. We have already opined that the growth of counselling is largely due to the decline of other social institutions that formerly provided such services. When people think they can no longer turn to traditional sources of counselling such as family, church or community, they must look elsewhere. The cultural message to the troubled has become, 'seek professional help; seek counselling'. We do not see a revival of importance amongst the traditional social institutions, and as societies become more complex traditional, simple messages delivered by well intended but not especially informed persons are easier to disregard. If society is complex then life is complex and we expect informed answers to our questions and guidance for our actions. We continue to prefer simple messages, but we want to view the messengers not as simple people but as special people.

When counselling does its job in and for society it creates a problem for itself: who is its client? Psychotherapeutic counselling addresses human concerns, principally human emotions and behaviours. Disrupted emotion is subjectively distressing, and at times interpersonally distressing as well. Disordered behaviours are primarily distressing to others, although they may also perturb oneself. When subjective distress is the problem, the individual who is suffering is clearly the client.

However, many counselling efforts are directed toward populations that do not seek counselling; rather, someone decides that counselling should seek them, usually due to troublesome behaviours, e.g. crime, drug abuse, etc. In these instances, counselling functions as an instrument of society, and its mission is to reduce deviant or unconventional behaviours. Such counselling is unlikely to be effective unless the putative client can be persuaded to want to change. Society's continuing support of counselling depends upon how well society perceives counselling as an effective agent of society's desire to bring about the reformation of certain of its members. Counselling has to appear to further the aims of the society that maintains it financially – financial support is merely a tangible way to express society's approval of counselling. The future of counselling very much depends on the availability of moneys to support the delivery of services.

To ensure society's goodwill, the field of counselling must show that it is cost-effective and that its activities are sensible. The former is difficult to demonstrate because outcomes can be so hazy; however, the latter is easy. Counselling has to present itself as scientific – as something to be studied and researched in universities. By cloaking itself in science counselling shows the world that it should be taken seriously.

The problem is, the scientific underpinnings of counselling are spurious. A generation ago this was less important. Rogers and Perls did their thing, their followers proclaimed it to be good and effective, and no one much cared that the scientific foundations were not there to rest upon. Ellis, on the other hand, claimed that his work was itself an application of the scientific method and that he was all for good research; of course, his claim was false in that the basic psychological findings on which his claims rested did not exist (Wessler, 1996). The forwarding of untestable hypotheses had been the rule rather than the exception in counselling and psychotherapy, beginning with Freud and continuing until the present. Why don't we admit it? We cannot afford to.

Science gives legitimacy to the counselling enterprise. However, the various theoretical approaches to counselling are not themselves scientific. What they are is a set of working assumptions and operational hypotheses that allow us to get on with the art and craft of counselling. (These observations should not fall into the wrong hands, therefore, this section of the chapter will self-destruct in five seconds.)

There is a serious implication that follows from the candid admission that counselling and psychotherapy lack scientific bases. It opens the door to both rational and mystical forms of counselling, and gives them equal standing. A serious approach, e.g. Beck's cognitive therapy whose results have been repeatedly documented, gets taken no more seriously than a zany one, e.g. rebirthing (Orr and Ray, 1977). Will society, either through insurance companies or governmental agencies, pay for people to relive the birth trauma by sitting in a hot tub? We think not. We wonder, though, will Beck's cognitive therapy also be denied payment and get thrown out with the bath water? We hope not.

To influence the public's views about counselling is an important task of the field. We need to increase public awareness and explain what coun-selling can and cannot do. Disappointment and disillusionment follow when we imply we can do more than we know how. What we can do is to describe the disorders and dysfunctions counselling can help. We can delineate what should be handled by others, e.g. long-term psychotherapy for the severely impaired. We can educate ourselves about psychopharma-cology and increase our knowledge of medications, even if we never can legally prescribe them. We can combat a certain smug and unscientific attitude amongst certain colleagues who say, 'I don't believe in medication'.

We can work toward an integrated psychotherapeutic counselling without distinctive and competing schools of thought. True breakthroughs that will revolutionize the field of counselling and create a paradigm shift do not seem likely. The refinement of extant approaches leads to the fragmentation of the field. A strong movement toward integration can also result in fragmentation as competing models of integration emerge, but such a state of affairs may be a necessary intermediate step.

Further, we can quietly (because the public thinks this has already been done) develop a scientific basis for counselling and thereby legitimize its standing in society. In the interim, we can adopt sensible assumptions, portray counselling as a rational enterprise, and purge all of the vague and mysterious concepts from our work, and all of the counselling clichés and psychobabble from our vocabulary so we don't sound like blithering idiots who don't know what we are talking about. Let's avoid the temptation to embrace colourful language and practices, and reject guru-driven counselling.

Finally, we can follow the example of Windy Dryden and be open-minded, enthusiastic and advocate for our colleagues and for the field of counselling. His contributions are significant because he has encouraged and developed the talents of others without insisting that they agree with him. He is the model counsellor, bringing out the best in others, working persistently, and promoting the field of counselling rather than himself. He has been as much a change agent in our lives individually as he has to the whole field of counselling. We have much to thank him for.

References

Beck, A.T. (1976) *Cognitive Therapy and the Emotional Disorders*. Madison, CT: International Universities Press.

Berne, E. (1964) *Games People Play*. New York: Grove Press.

Ellis, A. (1977) The basic clinical theory of rational-emotive therapy, in A. Ellis and R. Grieger (eds), *Handbook of Rational-emotive Therapy*, vol. 1. New York: Springer. pp. 3–24.

Millon, T. (1996) *Disorders of Personality: DSM-IV and Beyond*, 2nd edn. New York: Wiley.

Nathanson, D.L. (1992) *Shame and Pride: Affect, Sex, and the Birth of the Self*. New York: Norton.

Netherton, M. and Shiffrin, N. (1978) *Past Lives Therapy*. New York: William Morrow.

Orr, L. and Ray, S. (1977) *Rebirthing in the New Age*. Millbrae, CA: Celestial Arts Press.

Perls, F.S. (1969) *Gestalt Therapy Verbatim*. Moab, UT: Real People Press.

Rogers, C.R. (1951) *Client-centered Therapy*. Boston: Houghton Mifflin.

Stern, J. (1996) A Cognitive appraisal therapy approach to parent training with affect-driven parents, *Psychotherapy*, 33: 77–84.

Wessler, R.L. (1992) Constructivism and rational-emotive therapy: A critique, *Psychotherapy*, 29: 620–5.

Wessler, R.L. (1993a) Cognitive appraisal therapy and disorders of personality, in K.T. Kuehlwein and H. Rosen (eds), *Cognitive Therapies in Action: Evolving Innovative Practice*. San Francisco: Jossey-Bass. pp. 240–67.

Wessler, R.L. (1993b) Groups, in G. Stricker and J.R. Gold (eds), *Comprehensive Handbook of Psychotherapy Integration*. New York: Plenum. pp. 453–64.

Wessler, R.L. (1996) Idiosyncratic definitions and unsupported hypotheses: Rational emotive behavior therapy as pseudoscience, *Journal of Rational-Emotive and Cognitive-Behavior Therapy*, 10: 30–50.

Wessler, R.L. and Hankin Wessler, S.W.R. (1986) Cognitive appraisal therapy (CAT), in W. Dryden and W. Golden (eds), *Cognitive-behavioural Approaches to Psychotherapy*. London: Harper and Row. pp. 196–223.

Wessler, R.L. and Hankin Wessler, S.W.R. (1989) Nonconscious algorithms in cognitive and affective processes, *Journal of Cognitive Psychotherapy: An International Quarterly*, 3: 243–54.

Wessler, R.L. and Hankin Wessler, S.W.R. (1990) Emotion and rules of living, in R. Plutchik and H. Kellerman (eds), *Emotion: Theory, Research, and Experience*, vol. 5. New York: Academic Press. pp. 488–523.

Index